*Inquiry

A Jack Doyle Novel

by
John McEvoy

John McEvoy © 2018

ALL RIGHTS RESERVED

All names, characters and incidents, depicted in this book are totally the products of the author's imagination. Any resemblance to actual events, locales, organizations, or persons, living or dead, is entirely coincidental.

No part of this book may be produced in any form, by photocopying or by any electronic or mechanical means, including information storage or retrieval systems, without permission in writing from both the copyright owner and the publisher of this book, except for the minimum words needed for review.

ISBN: 978-0-9861109-4-8
Library of Congress Control Number: 2018958664
Published by Global Authors Publications

Filling the GAP in publishing

Edited by Kathy Barnett
Interior Design by KathleenWalls
Cover Design by Ron Ruble

Printed in USA for Global Authors Publications

DEDICATION

To my wife Judy, our three children, 10 grandchildren, and to the fond memories of Les Garcons Kenosha.

ACKNOWLEDEMENT

Thanks to Julia McEvoy and Sarah Sehitoglu for their invaluable advice.
To old friend Ron Ruble, ace artist and illustrator, for the cover design.
To Jeff Kubina for the cover photo.
To Bill and Carolynn Sheridan for their continued support.

INQUIRY

CHAPTER ONE

PROMINENT OWNER
BARRED FROM TRACKS

By Matt O'Connor

CHICAGO, IL—Ted Tilley, one of America's leading thoroughbred owners for the last four years, has been refused stalls at five Midwest tracks: Madison Park, Pleasant Prairie, Cahokia Downs, Oakbrook and Monee Park.

A joint press release stated, "Mr. Tilley's horses will no longer be allowed to compete at these tracks. The ban is effective immediately."

Tilley's stable has had some 250 horses competing at these tracks. He has been the perennial leading owner in wins and purses at each of them, on his way to leading the nation in total victories the last two years.

No reason was given for the ban. Attempts to seek clarification from all five tracks were unsuccessful. Only one of Tilley's runners tested medication positive in the last three years, a minor violation involving a Class 3 steroid that resulted in a $250 fine. He has accrued no other penalties.

Tilley's response when questioned by a reporter was: "I wonder what the hell is going on? I've never violated any major racing rule," he told Racing Daily. "All I've done is buy a lot of horses, treat them well, put them in the hands of excellent trainers, and run them where they belong. A program evidently unfamiliar to many of my jealous competitors who are obviously out to destroy me. I say, good luck to them!"

One racing insider, who asked not to be identified, told Racing Daily, "I think what happened here is that Mr. Tilley has just been way, way too successful for his competition to accept. His horses are often so dominant that they result in small fields and less betting. I think the people he's been beating have combined to freeze him out."

Ted vows to fight this ban, first to the state racing commissions involved. Then, if necessary, in civil court. A prominent legal expert predicted Ted would face tough going. He said, "Numerous racing states have ruled that tracks, being private enterprises, have a common law right to bar anyone they want to — owners, jockeys, trainers — as long as the ejection is not for discriminatory reasons. The only exceptions would be cases involving racial, religious, or sexual discrimination. I don't believe Mr. Tilley would qualify for inclusion in any of those categories."

What is the legality of other tracks emulating the suspensions by these five? the expert was asked.

"Well, while there is standard reciprocity among states in honoring the license suspension or revocation of a racing participant in another jurisdiction, it is up to the individual racetracks to decide if they want to honor another track's rejection of an individual."

A spokesman for the Association of American Tracks, asked if other members would accept the Tilley horses, indicated they would not. "Our members will stand in support of these five tracks."

Told of this, an embittered Ted said, "I think the powerful blue bloods in this game have turned on me, who is definitely not one of them. They couldn't stand the fact that I was beating their brains out by going against tradition."

***

Ted Tilley balled up the paper, got up from behind his mahogany desk, and hurled it across the room with the same motion he had used 20 years earlier during his brief career as a minor league baseball pitcher. Now at age 39, carrying his playing weight of 185 on his six-foot frame, he was still accurate. The *Racing Daily* hit the wall with a thump and dropped into the wastebasket.

"That bad, eh Ted?" asked Gary Grunwald, manager of Ted's extensive racing operation. He had been a close friend since they were baseball teammates at Class A. Kenosha in the South Midwest League two decades earlier. Gary had bonded with Ted, not only as a batter mate, but as the only member of the team he could play chess with.

"As bad as it could be, Gary. Here, read it yourself." Ted strode across the black and red-striped carpet in his large office, retrieved the paper and handed it to Gary. Wall photos showed jockeys who rode Tilley's horses - all wearing the brightly colored silks that bore a circled TT logo representing his only child Timothy Tilley. Timothy had died at age 14 in a skiing accident at a nearby resort. It was a tragedy from which neither Ted nor his wife, Sheila, would ever completely recover.

Ted walked to the large west window of his office at Freedom Farm. It overlooked the north pasture of his 300 acre spread located 24 miles north of Saratoga Springs, the site of one of America's oldest and most famous racetracks. It was the track Ted had patronized as a boy, courtesy of his late father, George. First, he was a fan and novice bettor and years later, the owner of a sizeable string of thoroughbreds. Many were now retired on his state-of-the-art, meticulously-maintained farm.

Ted's grandfather, Ethan, had made his living following after his quartermaster service in the Army in World War II as the owner of, first one, then three busy hardware stores in the Adirondack area. Ethan's son, Edward, succeeded his father and expanded the business to nine stores in towns all over the state. After Edward retired and turned control over to his only heir, a huge expansion ensued. Under Ted Tilley's hard-driving and imaginative guidance, Tilley's for Tools and More escalated into a chain of stores dotting the Northeast states. Ted became a multi-millionaire and, tiring of the business side of his life, turned to horse racing after leaving his conglomerate in charge of trusted executives he paid very well.

The early morning May sun highlighted the dappled coats of Ted's two prized broodmares. Doubtless Donna and Delightful Di were half-sisters which had each won major stakes before heading to the breeding shed. Each had a foal nearby, products of their matings with Ted's prominent stallion Chancellor Mac.

Looking at his prized mares, especially in early evening when he and Sheila sat on the veranda sipping cocktails, Ted could watch his lead groom and assistant walk up the slight rise to the far end of the meadow to check the mares and their offspring. He always thought of a poem on that subject titled "At Grass" by Phillip Larkin. Ted's sister, Susie, had given him a framed copy of it that now hung on his office wall.

Ted nodded toward the young horses that were staying close to their mothers' sides as they nibbled the grass. "Great looking little guys," he muttered, "but I may never get to see them race in my colors. Not with this ban, or vendetta, or attack on me." He kicked his desk so hard that the normally imperturbable Grunwald jumped in his chair.

All the years he had known Ted, he'd rarely seen his friend show his feelings so obviously. Oh, sure, there was that time in Oshkosh, WI, when Ted broke a team mate's nose in a post-game locker-room fight. Ted was infuriated because he thought the shortstop had carelessly blown an easy out that ended Ted's bid for a no-hitter. When the errant infielder shrugged it off like it was nothing important to him, he got pummeled. And, of course, several years later, Grunwald had paid for damages after his boss hurled a loud Tea Party advocate through the front window of a popular Saratoga Springs restaurant after the Saturday night races. He remembered Tilley telling him, "Glen, pay for the glass, but don't give a dime to that ass."

But that incident was ten years ago. At Sheila's urging, Ted had entered a course in anger management run by a retired Skidmore College psychology professor named Harman Goetz. Ted emerged as a much more calm and controlled individual and had remained so. Until now.

A squadron of dark gray clouds threw shadows toward the wide window and the pastures Ted overlooked. He shook his head and turned back to face his friend.

"Gary, we've never done anything wrong except succeed in the racing business. Winning races in bunches. Often embarrassing some of the Jockey Organizations mucky-mucks by kicking dust in the snoots of their pampered horses. I guarantee you, my friend, I am not taking this lying down."

Ted's most quoted comment on his success as a horse owner in an extremely competitive business was, "I claim horses wholesale and win with them." This business model was deemed offensive by many members of racing's traditional upper echelon.

As one of them charged, "This guy, Ted, is assaulting the claiming box. He claims a horse, drops the horse down in class, and wins a couple of races before somebody claims the horse back. He's ruining the competitive balance with his tremendously aggressive tactics that lead to huge win totals and pretty big purses, to boot."

Grunwald well remembered another Tilley interview in Racing Daily in which he had declared, "There are people in this business who resent me because my team outhustles and outthinks a lot of the stick-in-the-mud members of the Old Guard. Yes, I've shaken up the game. And they hate me for that.

"I never gave a damn what they thought about. In this sport or business, it's a matter of every man's hand against that of every other man. That's what makes it so exciting. I'm not sure my rivals or critics understand that I value each and every horse I own, from my stakes horses down to my claimers. Every trainer I employ knows that or they wouldn't be working for me.

"You know, we all know racing is a tough game. I've done very well at it thanks to planning, precision, and, of course, luck." Ted laughed before continuing, "I remember the famous quote from the actor Mickey Rooney, an avid horse bettor. He said, 'You want to be a millionaire in the horse business? It's easy. Just start with five million.'"

Ted sat down behind his desk. "Maybe it's the fact that I've been beating this game that drives these people to beat up on me."

As he listened to his revved up friend, Grunwald thought of suggesting that Ted should perhaps turn his immense energy to other pastimes. But Ted was already heavily involved in several major charities, both as an active contributor and fund raiser. Politics? Grunwald had once suggested that field, pointing out more than 100 members of the U. S. Congress were millionaires and that Ted certainly had the wherewithal to qualify for member-

INQUIRY

ship in this wealthy club. "If I want to get into something dysfunctional, I don't need to go to D. C.," Ted had responded.

Grunwald waited, as patiently as the catcher he had been when his signs from behind the plate to pitcher Ted were being processed to be accepted or rejected. He was quite certain his suggestion, for Ted to put this racetrack stuff behind him and move on, would be similarly shaken off.

Ted turned from the window to face his great friend. He lifted an eyebrow, smiled, and said, "You know me, Gary. You think I'll take this, what I guess you could call an embargo against me, lying down? Fat chance, my man. I've never taken anything in my life lying down. I sure as hell am not going to start now."

He stood at the office door. "C'mon, we'll rouse the family, fire up the grill, and have a nice dinner. Maybe watch the Mets game when the kids are off to bed."

Ted took Grunwald by the arm. "You know Samuel Beckett? Who he was?"

"Ted, I was a business major. We read corporate reports and concentrated on Warren Buffett's advice. Wasn't Beckett some kind of writer?"

Ted smiled for the first time that afternoon. "Yeah, you could say so. Sheila was an English major. She loved Beckett's plays. 'Waiting for Godot,' others I can't remember. I went to a couple with her and dozed off early. In one, I think there were people talking to each other out of garbage cans they were in. But she showed me a quote from Beckett after he died. He was making a speech someplace and he started by saying, 'I'll be clear at the start. I forgive nobody.'"

Ted ushered his friend forward. "And that, Gary, is exactly how I feel about the people that have done this to me and my life in horse racing."

An hour later after their dinner, Grunwald said goodbye. For a few moments, he sat in Ted's driveway behind the wheel of his Porshe thinking about his friend's quandary. He laughed as he said to himself, "I'm a practicing realist; Ted is in what he sees as God's choir of good people. There are damn few of those voices I've ever heard."

Grunwald accelerated rapidly out of the parking lot. "Prayer isn't going to carry this day," he said to himself. "No way. Neither are the courts."

Heading toward his townhouse, Grunwald speed dialed on his cell phone. "Hey, Rudy, it's me Gary."

"Well, that's an upset," came the rasping voice of Rudy Ozinga.

"There must be something you want, right?"

Grunwald slowed at an intersection, then pulled off the highway to a rest stop. "Rudy, I understand your construction firm business is booming. Right? But I'm wondering if you still, like, carry out assignments on the side? Straighten out people who need it?"

He heard Rudy shout a stern warning to a couple of his noisy children.

"Kids are driving me nuts, Glen. Wife's on a girls' weekend retreat. These two are something else to handle."

Grunwald said, "I'm not calling for an update on your family life, Rudy."

"Do I still do a little freelancing, Glen? Bet on it. There's only so much fun you can have tearing down and putting up houses."

Grunwald said, "I haven't seen you in awhile. You still in game shape?"

Rudy's laugh blasted over the phone. "Are you joking? I'm strong as dawn, man. Had that damn accident, the concussion; I think you know about that. Kind of screwed me up. But you need some help? I'm in. How about you fly into Chicago and we meet at the Dunkin Donuts, just off Willow by Harms? Tomorrow morning, make it seven." Rudy paused before adding, "And, Gary, bring money."

Grunwald smiled as he drove out of the rest stop parking lot. "Same old Rudy," he said to himself.

"Got it." Grunwald smiled as he drove out of the rest stop parking lot.

CHAPTER TWO

Jack Doyle had just begun a rhythmic tattooing of the Fit City speed bag that Monday morning when he heard, "Jack, your cell phone is buzzing."

He stepped away from the spinning bag, wiped sweat off his sandy haired head, and said, "Thanks, Moe," to his friend who resumed jump-roping with amazing alacrity for a man in his 70s.

Moe Kellman, reputed furrier to the Chicago Mob, a man referred to as that, but never having come close to being convicted of same, and Jack were longtime friends. They were also co-owners of the popular thoroughbred stallion Plotkin, a fairly obscure breed of runner they had raced in partnership through a two-year career that brought in more than a half-million dollars. Now serving as a stud for a $10,000 per mare fee, Plotkin was a gift that kept on giving.

Moe toweled his head of white Don King-like hair, put the jump rope on a wall hook, and dropped down to begin his sit-up regimen.

"Somebody left a message," Jack said. "I'll check it later." He put the phone back in his sport coat pocket and walked across the room to the heavy bag to begin a ferocious ten-minute, non-stop workout that left him breathing and sweating heavily before he said, "Moe, did you hear the latest racing news? About Ted Tilley?"

"No. Fill me in."

When Jack finished, he said, "Matt O'Connor broke the story in Racing Daily. You know him, right?"

"Yeah. I had some dealings with him a few years back when he was on the trail of that mad man who was killing jockeys. He was a major player in cleaning up that mess."

****

Twenty minutes later, out of the shower, Jack dressed quickly in a black, short-sleeved shirt, beige Dockers, and black walking shoes. He sat down on the wooden bench and finished a bottle of water as Moe carefully tied his tie before the long mirror on the far wall. As usual, the little man was impeccably dressed for the start of his day in his impressive Michigan AV office a mile away.

All these years after his U. S. Marine Corps service in what he always referred to as the "Korean Fucking Conflict, during which I spent too much time crawling forward through mud," Moe had devoted himself to both dressing and living well. As he had said to Jack not long after they became friends, "After that Korean misery, watching young guys on both sides get shot up and killed or maimed, I figured anything that happened afterwards to me was gravy."

The men paused as they saw a breaking news report on the television. They listened as WGN-TV anchorman Mark Suppelsa announced, "There has been another in the long recent succession of Chicago shooting deaths. This one at a playground in West Lawndale. Killed was a six-year-old girl playing on a swing set. She was not evidently the intended target. No suspect has been arrested yet."

"Goddamn," Jack said. "Can you believe this shit? Happens all the time, it seems. These knucklehead gang bangers blazing away in the streets of the city and missing each other, but hitting bystanders. Incredible."

Moe, eyes still on the television screen, nodded in agreement. He said, "I have a possible solution to this terrible problem. In fact, I even sent it to my Chicago alderman, Artie Olberman."

"Yeah? What is it? I hope it's about jobs and other opportunities being introduced into these desperately poor neighborhoods. Broken families. Absent fathers. Drugs all over the place. What the hell do you have in mind, Moe?"

Moe sighed. "At this point I am only concerning myself with a program that could cut down on slaughter in the Chicago streets. Okay? I'm not talking about sociology or economic practically or some kind of panacea, okay?"

Jack said, "Lay it on me."

"My idea," Moe said, "is that the Chicago Public School system introduce mandatory marksmanship courses for all male students starting in junior high."

"You've got to be kidding."

Moe grabbed Jack's forearm. "Jack, I am not fucking kidding. I'm talking about courses with hand guns and AK-47s which have recently become popular. Teach them to shoot straight! What we've got down is guys blazing away day and night, mainly not hitting each other. If they're going to be shooting, which I am sure they will be, at least train the bastards so they at least hit each other, not innocent bystanders!"

"Well," Jack said, "good luck with that good idea. Hold it. I'm getting a call."

Jack listened to his phone message and said, "I'll be damned."

"Who called that surprised you? The IRS with a massive refund? Or did Jennifer Lopez finally respond to your entreaties?"

Jack said, "Very funny, Moe. Actually, it was Celia McCann's secretary, Shontanette Hunter. Said Celia badly needed to see me about a matter Shontanette would not describe over the phone, some problem Celia's track was having. You know, Monee Park. Where I worked that year as the public relations director."

"Who could forget?" Moe said. "You almost got pitch-forked to death before that Irish bookmaker friend of yours and his muscle man helped save your ass."

Jack laughed. "Actually, those two saved all of me, bless them. You want to go upstairs and have a coffee before you start your day downtown hustling hides?"

"Such a way with words you have, you smart ass Irisher. Actually, I am having a breakfast meeting with none other than my boyhood buddy Fifi Bonadio. He's gotten himself into some kind of jam with his wife, his current punch, and the two that preceded the latter. It could be a big day for Kellman Enterprises. In my experience, there's nothing like guilt that drives business."

Jack knew that Moe and Fifi went back to their boyhood days on Chicago's Taylor Street, a strip populated primarily by Italian-Americans and a few Jewish families. Friends for life, starting in third grade, Fifi continued on to eventually rule the Chicago Outfit.

Moe reached into his pocket and extracted the rubber band-bound bankroll he always carried. "I am hereby wagering that you will find yourself in another jackpot of some sort after talking to Ms. McCann. You want to go for 100?"

"I don't want to start your day off with a setback. No bet, Moe."

Moe grinned. "As I recall, you had a brief, but memorable, quote association unquote with the beauteous Ms. McCann during your days at Monee Park. Maybe she wants to re-ignite the flame?" He backed up to the door and reached for the handle.

Jack threw his gym bag into his locker and slammed the door shut. "I don't know why I confide in you, you rabble rouser. Yeah, I made a mistake with Celia before her poor husband went down from ALS. We both regretted it. After that, the only thing we shared was embarrassment. Get it?

"Anyway," he muttered, "Celia knows I've become kind of a go-to-guy for racing people with problems."

"Some of those problems were of your own making," Moe shot back. He opened the door. "And you know it, Jack. Good luck."

Jack laughed at his friend's parting shot. He waved goodbye to the Fat City club entrance supervisor. Behind the wheel of his gray Accord, he turned on the radio and heard a sports talk show report on "horse racing's historic banning of prominent owner Ted Tilley."

***

Eleven miles west that spring morning Donald "Skip" Dumke was listening to the same radio program in his favorite hangout, the Last Watering

Hole. He interrupted his usual breakfast, a microwaved piece of pepperoni pizza accompanied by a double shot Bloody Mary, and slapped the bar in approval.

Owner-morning bartender Pete Zocchi looked up from the sink where he was rinsing beer glasses. "What's that show of enthusiasm about so early this morning?"

Skip grinned. "I'm just damn glad this Tilley has been shown to the door."

"Why? What've you got against him?"

"Pete, the guy's been killing me and my bankroll when I bet races where he's got runners. They're winning all the time."

Zocchi said, "So what? What's the problem with that?"

"Obviously, my host, you have no feel for the intricacies of betting horse races."

"Like?"

"Like," Skip said, "you can't bet on Tilley's horses because they're usually very short odds, small payoffs. And you can't bet against them because they win so often. Tilley's stable is a pari-mutuel pestilence as far as I'm concerned. I'm glad to see the bastard thrown out."

INQUIRY

CHAPTER THREE

"What a lousy turnout! After all the great outings we had in the past?" Ted Tilley added bitterly, "When I was allowed to play in the racing game."

Ted and Gary Grunwald sat protected from the sun in a canopied golf cart adjacent to the first of 18 holes at Petrifying Springs Country Club, a championship layout advertised as the "Golf Course Jewel of the Adirondacks."

It was a brutally hot afternoon. In each of the preceding years of this invitation-only event, when host Ted paid all green fees, cart rental fees, the three beer cart girls patrolling the course with stocked coolers, a lavish dinner at day's end, 100 invitees showed up. Gary fended off the dozens of wannabees who tried to wangle an invitation each year. Not this year.

Ted finished his Pilsener Urquell and crushed the can. He said, "Well, Gary, at least this day won't take too long. That group on the tee is the last of the dozen that showed up today. Loyalists, I guess."

"Or dedicated free loaders," Gary said.

Ted opened another beer. "Well, at least they didn't knee-jerk respond and drop me off the social map after those tracks barred my horses. I guess I should by glad they came today. Show of loyalty, support, whatever."

Gary answered his cell phone, grimaced, put it back in his pocket. Ted waited. "Ah, Ted, just another old regular here, Max Bowers, bowing out with some bullshit excuse."

Ted turned to look at the first tee. "Hey, Buck Norman, you've still got that too fast backswing. Slow it down, man. Hit a good one."

Trainer Norman, one of the Tilley Outing regulars, waved back, grinning, wielding a driver with a face like a dinner plate. He launched a mighty swing. The ball dribbled off the tee some fifty yards down the fairway.

"Buck, when will you ever learn?" Ted shouted. "Slow and easy gets it done."

"Not with my wife," Norman answered, picking up his shattered tee and jumping into his golf cart. Speeding down the fairway, driving his cart with his right hand, he extended his left with the middle finger pointing up.

Laughing, Ted said, "Love that guy. Good trainer, terrible golfer. But, a friend. C'mon, we can tee off. That was the last group."

Gary went first. He carefully placed his tee midway between the ball markers once, then repositioned it two feet to the left. The sun beat down as he squinted, looking down the fairway for a hoped for target area.

"While we're young, man," Ted shouted. "Hit the damn thing."

Gary ignored that advice and took several more seconds envisioning the shot he was about to make. When he finally let his driver go, the ball curved majestically high through the summer air, a parabola of failure as it disappeared far beyond the hole's right side out of bounds tree line.

Ted struggled to restrain laughter. "Want a mulligan? It's the only one you get all day. I think you might have knocked some birds out of those tree tops. Hope to God they weren't from an endangered species." Gary, jaw clenched, just walked to the golf cart and took the driver's seat without responding. Ted quickly addressed his ball and, just as he began his backswing, Gary started and revved the golf cart motor. He watched as Ted, unfazed, he unfurled his usual, long, powerful swing that sent his ball some 280 yards down the middle of the lush, green fairway.

Ted picked up his tee without even watching his tee shot land, jumped into the cart, patted Gary's knee, and said, "Let's go." He took a swig of his beer as Gart gunned the cart away from the tee.

"Did you see where my drive went so we can go there after you locate your ball in that forest?" Ted asked.

"Very fucking funny." Gary increased the cart speed. Ted paid no attention.

"When you eventually emerge from the trees, meet me, you know, 'smack dab in the middle.' Like that great song Joe Williams sang with the Basie Band," Ted said. "You know where I'll be, right? In the center of the fairway. Do you have a compass in case you get lost in those woods?"

Gary eased off the accelerator. He had to laugh at his friend's joshing today, this otherwise disappointing afternoon with its absence of former attendees. Gary got out of the cart and stopped at the far end of the rough.

"Don't worry about me. I read *The Pathfinder* in high school."

***

Two and a half hours later, Ted and Gary walked off the eighteenth green toward the clubhouse. Gary added up the scores. "Nice round, Ted. Four over par 76. You owe me 30 bucks."

Ted stopped. "What? I shoot my best round of the year and lose money?"

Gary shrugged. "When I parred 18 after the Calcutta bingo-bango-bungo tripled roll - over connected to my handicap, it cost you."

Forty minutes later, showered and dressed in casual clothes, they joined the dozen or so golf outing participants in the dining room overlooking the first tee. A couple of youngsters, probably caddies now off duty, were evidently readying for a few quick holes before dark. The first to tee off, after

INQUIRY

several seconds of wiggling his driver back and forth, finally swung. His ball shanked into the crash-proof window from where Tilley and his friends watching. They laughed as, in pantomime, they saw the errant driver being made fun of by his friend.

When the kids had left the tee, Ted waved to their waiter to bring another round. "And the menus, too. As always, fellas, order whatever you want for dinner. There's so few of us today I guess we don't have to go into the main dining room. We can eat here."

Buck Norman, one of several trainers Ted had employed in his charge to the top of the national owner standings, leaned forward. "Ted, you don't have to pick up this tab tonight." He motioned to the others at the table. "You've always been very hospitable…generous…I mean good to us in the past giving us a great day of golf plus dinner and drinks, music sometimes, too. Let us pay our way today. We'd all like to do that."

Ted reached across the table and patted Buck's shoulder. "No way, Buck. Look, I may not be in the racing game we all love now. But don't count me out. I've got a couple of court challenges planned against people excluding me. I'm not taking these lying down, my friend. And," he smiled, "I'm a long way from being broke. And miles away from ever forgetting and treasuring the kind of friends like you that showed up here today."

Gary leaned forward, looked around the table, and said forcefully, "Ted is by no means done with this racing industry black ball, or embargo, or bullshit toss-out he's been hit with. This story ain't over. Bet on that, brothers."

"Drink up, men," ordered Ted. "Here come the salad and soup orders. We'll have another round so we can start telling lies about all our golf games here today." Laughter ensued.

Just after ten p.m. their party broke up, well fed, and liquor lubricated. Ted and Gary stood at the main entrance to the Petrifying Springs Clubhouse saying good night to their loyal friends as they waited for their autos to be delivered by the car parking team.

Ted laughed as the last car to leave, his old friend Owen Desmond's, stopped at the end of the small garden circle near the exit. He heard Desmond's not so unfamiliar shout, "Keep the faith, Ted."

Gary said, "I'm going in for a nightcap. I want to catch the ESPN baseball wrap up. You coming?"

"No thanks, Gary. Long day, I'm ready for home. I'll see you in the morning at the office." He patted Gary's shoulder and began moving toward his black BMW. Then he stopped, turned, and said, "Remember, we've got to take the wives to that movie tomorrow night. We signed up for it."

Gary groaned. He had been best man in Ted's wedding, Ted the same for him. They were still married to their originals, so he knew what was coming after all their years as friends.

"Yes, we promised. Your Sheila brought it up, my Sandra said 'great.'"

Ted asked, "Why the long face? What movie is it?"

"It's a blockbuster about some neurotic broad enjoying life with a sadomasochistic rich lunatic."

Ted opened the door to his car. "I hope it's a musical," he said, then drove away.

Gary remained on the top step of the entrance. He heard Ted give a shave-and-a-haircut tap on his horn, something Ted said his grandfather had taught him. Gary smiled briefly. He walked back toward the Petrifying Springs Clubhouse doorway, stopped, and sat down on one of the long benches facing the curling driveway.

He thought about the day they'd had. Ted, as always, was generous and good-humored, the attributes that had led Gary to admire him for so many years. The fact that Ted was under attack by some elements of the thoroughbred racing industry had, for Gary, escalated from rankling status to major pissed off. He sat for a few more minutes, breathing in the pine-scented late night summer air.

Finally, he got to his feet, saying to himself, "I'm not taking this lying down for Ted. I'm going to get an alternative approach." Walking toward his car, he smiled at the thought of meeting tomorrow with another old friend of his, Rudy Ozinga. He was known back in their Kenosha home town as "The Famous O." Help could be on the way.

INQUIRY

CHAPTER FOUR

Big Rudy Ozinga emerged from the steam room of the Arlington Heights, IL YMCA with his impressive muscles attuned, skin aglow. He strode through the crowded locker room bumping fists with two other members of his pick-up, three-on-three basketball team that had just held the "win and you keep playing" court for a busy hour.

Rudy played hoops there twice a week starting at seven a.m. These workouts served to energize the players for the day ahead. And, especially for Rudy, the old, familiar, and very welcome surge of adrenaline.

A few of the other men nodded to Rudy as he strolled to his locker at the end of the row. Toweling off, he heard one of them shout, "Beware, boys, the Bear is here." Everyone laughed, or at least pretended to, at this reference to Rudy's hirsuteness. "You'd need a lawn mower to shave that body," somebody muttered. Rudy heard it. He leaned forward, growled, hands on his knees, jaw thrust out. There was an eruption of locker room laughter.

Rudy had been a local legend since his days as a domineering high school wrestler in the heavyweight division. Three state championships, undefeated in his final two years, preceded his sadly interrupted career at Eastern Iowa University where a terrible shoulder injury ended his wrestling career, the promising athletic life that had defined him.

Three surgeries, paid for by the reluctant Eastern Iowa Athletic Department, enabled him to regain most of the use of his right arm. But those procedures could not restore him to wrestling condition. When the university, realizing that, decided not to honor his four-year scholarship, Rudy packed up and went home to Arlington Heights.

"Why go to college if you can't fucking wrestle?" he said to his widowed mother. "Fuck college."

Marlene Ozinga, retorted, "Why stay in college? And maybe get a fucking diploma? And then maybe a nice fucking job, where you start out clean every morning and not come home dirty every night? Like your old man?"

Marlene's predilection for rude talk had developed after, eight months pregnant, she married Rudy's late father Ignatz, a big, strong, construction crew foreman who had used profanity not only to lace his language, but to embrace it. Ignatz's tragic fall from the slippery, rain-drenched roof of a three-story town house had left Marlene with a decent life insurance payment and a habit of perpetuating his practice of foul repartee.

College career kaput, Rudy accepted a job offer from Guz Perkowitz, owner of the company that had employed his father for many years. Mr. Perkowitz told him, "Kid, you'll never be as good at this as your old man, God bless his soul. But I got an idea you might be pretty good. Genes, and all."

As a construction supervisor and fill-in man, Rudy was as energetic and efficient as he had been when his hometown newspaper referred to him as being "a great grappler."

To him, it was a "so what?" kind of deal. The money was fine. Guys he oversaw were, for the most part, okay. The occasional exception was when he rapidly straightened out a vicious take down. But there was a gap in his life.

The YMCA morning basketball games at least provided him with some competition, the opportunity to impose his will and subtly express his anger as he had so famously done on wrestling mats. The occasional outburst scared the crap out of both teammates and opponents, especially those who saw him engage in one brief encounter with a young black kid who had been invited to play when there was an opening on an otherwise white team.

LaWain Robinson, age 19, a slick hoopster, had taken over the first six minutes of his game against Rudy's team, scoring at will, dunking the ball on breakaways, forcing turnovers. Then, in mid-leap for his attempted third dunk, LuWain was leveled by a brutal shoulder bump from Rudy. His crash to the floor silenced the entire gym. LuWain's teammates dragged the dazed youngster to the bench, glaring at Rudy, who stood still, grinning, hands apart in a "What did I do?" gesture.

LuWain, struggling for breath, muttered, "Fuck you, Whitey."

"Aw, kid, watch your language. And don't ever bring that showboat shit in my gym again," Rudy said.

Driving home late that afternoon, Rudy gave several raps to his head, trying to drive away the increasingly frequent and painful neurological headaches he'd experienced ever since his work site accident two weeks ago. One of his careless workmen accidentally dislodging a concrete block from the second floor of their current project. Even with his yellow hard hat on and having ducked to the side, Rudy had been severely damaged by this glancing blow. Hospital tests confirmed the paramedic's prediction of a concussion. The attending emergency room physician, Dr. Larry Jaffee, advised Rudy should be carefully monitored for the next few months. He also warned there might be Post-Traumatic Stress Disorder like that suffered by "too many of our soldiers in Iraq." Rudy was kept overnight.

In the days following his release, frequent headaches continued. His moods were dark fueled by sleepless nights. They made him uncomfortable, surly, and angry. How could he, a champion wrestler who had experienced years of violent action on the mat, be so affected by a goddam work-place screw-up? He was amazed at how rapidly he'd become short-tempered and often mean. It both scared and thrilled him.

Thinking of the frightened, then defiant, look on young LuWain's face after he'd thrown him to the floor, Rudy said to himself, "Damn, I'm sorry I did that to that kid. That's not like me." Turning into his driveway, he added, "Damn, maybe it is the new me. A bad s.o.b." he grinned.

CHAPTER FIVE

Jack headed his gray 2006 Accord south on the Kennedy to the Dan Ryan. Already 80 degrees on a rainy Wednesday morning, all the lanes were stuck in creeping mode. He relaxed, tuned his radio to WDCB, the Glen Ellyn jazz station he listened to whenever he had the chance.

Suddenly, he felt a jolt. Then a blaring horn from behind him. Glowering through a hulky gray Hummer's windshield was a red faced white guy wearing a Chicago White Sox ball cap over his low brow. Traffic was at a halt, so Jack got out of his car and examined his rear bumper, which appeared undamaged. He walked to the side of the Hummer and motioned the driver to lower his window.

"Who are you blasting your horn at buddy? Lucky for you, Old Reliable there has survived even harder knocks from nitwits like you. Try to stay awake at the wheel, okay?"

Ballcap guy snarled, "I'm late for a job in Kankakee. Stuck in this fucking city traffic mess for miles. You didn't move up fast enough to suit me.

So," he said with a smirk, "I gave you a little, well, horn encouragement. Plus a bumper touch. You want to make something of it?"

The traffic on each side of them started to slowly advance. Impatient drivers behind them were in Chicago Driver Rage Mode. Jack moved closer to the Hummer. He reached up through the open window and grabbed the big driver's left wrist and squeezed. Big Guy yelped. Jack smiled, looking up at the now sweating face beneath the black ChiSox ballcap.

"Yes indeed, I'd like to make something of it. Wanna step outside of that motorized monstrosity you're hiding in?" Jack gave the wrist another hearty squeeze.

The Hummer guy jerked his arm away. Rolled up the window. Sat still, looking straight ahead. The lanes in front of each of their vehicles were now wide open. Jack grinned down at Ballcap, gave his window a little tap, said, "Stay well. And stay well behind me, Asshole."

Back at the wheel, traffic now moving fairly well, Jack laughed at himself having described his Accord as Old Reliable. From the time he was a kid, he and his pals had named their cars. One guy, Bill Mitchell, called his car "The Faithful Elaine," after a woman he eventually married. Moose Miller dubbed his car "Peter." He never said why. Five years later,

INQUIRY

the married Moose fathered a son he named Peter. Then there was Jack's friend, Jerry Pfarr, owner of a battered, but still usable, Plymouth coupe he referred to as "Pfearless."

Nearing his turnoff for Monee Park, Jack wondered if young guys still named their cars in such whimsical ways. He hoped so.

***

Jack parked in the same employee slot he'd used that summer three years before when he worked as Monee Park's publicity director. The old place looked the same, original 1928 red brick stands, crowded parking lot as owners and trainers were on hand for the morning workouts, the sound of pounding hooves and exhalations from equines galloping over the dark loam racing surface. He sat there for a minute or two remembering his first visit to Monee Park when he'd met Shontanette Hunter, secretary to the track's CEO, Celia McCann. She was a super cool African-American woman in her early thirties, devoted to Celia with whom she'd been friends since childhood. For perhaps the 100th time he recalled his one passionate night with Celia, wife of Bob Zaslow, a longtime ALS victim who succumbed to his dreadful illness later that year. It was a night Jack would never forget, both for the pleasure it gave him and, afterwards, the blight of guilt that he knew Celia also felt. He shook his head as if shrugging off a punch as he used to do during his Golden Gloves boxing career and walked briskly to the Monee Park Employee Entrance.

***

Shontanette came out from behind her desk to give the grinning Jack a hug. He stepped back and looked at her. "How the hell do you do it? Every damn time I see you, you look more beautiful than the last."

"Ah, yes, Jack," she laughed. "You could give the Blarney Stone lessons. Come, let's sit down. Would you like coffee?"

He declined, then reclined on the couch and said, "So, what's on Ms. McCann's mind now? What's her problem?"

Her answer made him sit up straight. "To begin with, she is no longer Celia McCann. She is now Celia McCann-Douglass. Since last November. You look surprised."

Jack felt as if a very stiff left jab had landed on his chest, right below the heart. Another few seconds passed that found him uncharacteristically speechless. He gazed around the photo-packed walls of famous thoroughbreds that had competed at Monee Park, then briefly focusing on the pictures of Celia presenting winner's circle trophies.

Shontonette said, "What are you looking for Jack? Looks like you're searching the room."

"I'm looking for my lost aplomb." He stood up. "Yeah, Shontonette, you could say I'm surprised. Kind of blindsided. I never got news of this. Who'd Celia marry?"

"Man named Calvin Douglas. You remember him?"

Jack riffled his mental Roladex. "Was he one of the pallbearers at Bob's funeral. Tall, good-looking black guy?"

"You got it. Calvin and Bob were teammates on Northwestern's basketball team. And great friends. Calvin's wife died of breast cancer about three years ago. After Bob passed, Calvin and Celia started seeing each other. One thing led…"

"To another. Say no more," Jack said. He stood up, walked to the window overlooking the track, and stared out at the last few horses that were being put through the workout drills that morning. He heard the loud blare of the horn that signaled end of training. The final pair of workmates charged through the stretch toward the finish line.

Turning to face Shontanette, he said, "I assume it's all gone well." He shrugged as he said, "Celia, in the old racetrack phrase, 'don't chase no empty wagons.'"

"You seem to be making light of this situation, Jack," Shontannete said sharply. "Or do I detect a bit of bitterness?"

"By no means. I'm just surprised. I'm very glad Celia found a good successor…I mean a good man…to follow Bob. He was a great guy. If Mr. Douglass was a friend of Bob's, I'm sure he'll be fine for Celia."

"He is," Shontanette said. "You'll see." She went on to say, "Douglas is a very successful sales rep for a big sporting goods company, sold his Chicago condo and moved in with Celia shortly after they got engaged. They were married a few weeks later."

Doyle well remembered the five room apartment on the top floor of the Monee Park grandstand. Also on the track grounds was a neat little cottage just yards away from the racing strip backstretch. It was there, she had told Jack, that she spent many happy times when visiting the Monee Park owner, her uncle, Jim Joyce, who left Celia control of the track in his will. "Right around six in the morning, I would make coffee and Uncle Jim and I would sit on the small balcony overlooking the racing strip, watch horses working out through the dawn air. Beautiful times."

Jack's reverie was interrupted when Shontanette said, "Celia wanted me to show you this." She picked up a piece of paper and reached across the desk to hand it to him.

He glanced at the title of the page, "Singles Social," an event scheduled two weeks from Saturday. The first paragraph stated that Monee Park was hosting its first such event. "If you are single and social, sign up," it advised.

"Meet local racing fans for adult beverages, a lavish buffet, the chance to make new friends, and share the excitement of thoroughbred racing in our Park Pavilion. The $50 fee includes admission to the track, a track program, a four- hour beer and wine package, two-hour menu at Appetizer Stations offering antipasti flatbreads, Seasonal Crudite and Bruschetta, Specialty Cocktails, Artisan Grilled Sausages, and a Sweet Station featuring freshly baked cookies, brownies, and other assorted treats."

Jack returned the promotional item. "Singles Social, eh? Celia shows again she has a strong sense of humor. Or needling. Or both."

"Celia thinks you might be interested in this event," Shontanette said. "She has great regard for you."

"Well," Jack said, "I appreciate Celia's interest in my love life. Evidently she's forgotten that I have already screwed up and suffered through two mainly tortuous marriages. I don't plan to make it a trifecta."

Shontanette shrugged. "Okay, Jack."

"Plus," Jack added, "I have a very fine, adult, mutually-shared interests relationship with Nora Sheehan. Unfortunately, she lives in Ireland. But, maybe not unfortunately. Maybe that's the best deal each of us could want. We shall see."

Shontonette's's intercom buzzed. She walked around her desk and took Jack's hand. "C'mon, darling, I'll take you in to see the boss."

CHAPTER SIX

"Mary, I'll get back to you on that problem later," Celia said and put down her phone. Smiling, she stood up and moved gracefully from behind her paper-laden desk to approach Jack, who said, "By God, woman, you are a picture of beautiful happiness. Great to see you."

They embraced and Jack continued to look admiringly at this tall, slender, extremely striking woman. "I don't know about beauty, Jack, but happiness I can attest to. I've been so fortunate, marrying a second truly wonderful man. Come on, sit down. We'll have coffee. And you can tell me what you've been up to since, well, when you were working here…" She paused. Jack leapt right in. "Yes, my ensuing years.

"But first, who were you on the phone with about a problem? Mary who?"

Celia said, "Mary Morton is Monee Park's director of food services. She's losing her two main chefs. They're getting married and moving away."

"Moving after marriage? How come?"

She sighed, "Maurice is marrying Gerald. These are two gay gentleman who have taken too much verbal haranguing from the kitchen crews they supervise. No matter how hard I've tried to protect them. I fired two dishwashers and a janitor, bigoted bastards who gave them guff. But I guess they just had had enough. They're moving out of state. Hate to see them go."

"Not to Alabama, I hope."

"They're smarter than that, Jack. More coffee?"

Jack responded, "No, thanks."

Celia said, "What about your ensuing years?" She leaned forward, green eyes intent, the morning sun flowing in from the picture window behind her as she burnished her long red hair. It made his heart take a jump, much as it had a few years earlier when he worked for her and believed he might very well be in love with her. He had come to think of those chest thumps as emotional tachycardia.

Jack presented a truncated version of his career as a jockey's agent and FBI aide, and, more recently his work leading to the discovery and arrest of an "animal activist" killer of retired racehorses.

"Wow, you've been busy, Jack. Good for you. A man of many tal-

INQUIRY

ents."

Jack grinned. "Do you spell that with a y or an i at the end?"

"I'll always spell it 'many' when I think about you, Jack." She briefly glanced toward the window overlooking the Monee Park racing strip. Jack hardly blinked as he enjoyed his view of Celia's face in profile. He stifled another heart skip.

Jack shook his head. "Celia, let's get down, or up, to business. Why have you asked me here?"

"Ah, Mr. Cut-to-the-Chase in action again. Okay, Jack, we have faced two pari-mutuel problems. One, regarding Ted Tilley's dominant stable, we dealt with by banning him from racing here. He was just so successful that he was discouraging people to bet on other horses in his races. That hurt our business tremendously. So, we tossed him."

Doyle sighed, "I'm not sure I understand the legality of that. Or the morality. It's like when in Vegas a successful card counter who is winning is identified and tossed out. They are happy to take his money when he's losing. Not happy to pay him when he's not. American business ethics at their best. Anyway, with Tilley out of the way what's your other problem?"

"It has to do with the pari-mutuel odds. Every so often, not on a regular basis but still worrisome," she said, "these odds are being manipulated by robo or rebate bettors."

She reached across the desk and handed him a computer printout. "This concerns our fifth race here at Monee last Thursday. On the left side you'll see the morning line odds. Which, as I'm sure you know, are the odds our linemaker, Scott Kristofek, predicts will reflect the public's betting. It's just a seven-horse field. The number two horse, Read Them, on paper at least appears to be a standout. So, Kristofek makes him two-to-one in our track program. Here, take a look at the *Racing Daily* past performances for that race." She reached across the desk to hand him the tabloid paper. "You can surely see why Read Them looked like the logical favorite."

That was apparent to Jack. Read Them, a five-year-old chestnut horse, had won three of his six races this season. "Good speed figures, too,"

Jack commented. "Looks like his owner has found a pretty soft spot for this nice horse. He should win by daylight over this bunch."

Celia said, "That's exactly what happened."

"So? What's the problem? Form held, as the saying goes."

"Jack, after Read Them won, as most expected he would, he paid more than 4-to-1 to win. To be exact, $10.80."

Jack said, "Wow. What the hell? How did this horse go off at odds of 4-to-1 instead of what looked to be a likely 2-to-1 or even 9-to-5? Did he limp along during the post parade?"

"No. This is what happened. With about seven minutes to go to the start of this race, a bunch of money poured in on the other horses in the field! We later established how much, and it was a lot. Way out of line for these supposedly outclassed horses. Some of it, not much, was bet here. The majority of the bets against Read Them were placed at inter-track wagering outlets, or off-track betting parlors, or over the Internet through the Advance Deposit Wagering services that all feed into our mutual pools.

"As a result, Read Them, instead of going off as the strong favorite, has his odds go up to four-to-one. In other words, double what he should have. All because of the money that poured in on his rivals, lowering their odds and, as a result, raising his. I was in the clubhouse dining room that afternoon and I could see people looking around, bewildered, wondering what happened here? Many of them, seeing the odds go up on Read Them, hurried to change their bets, evidently figuring there was something wrong with him. And that is what allowed his real backers, whoever they are, to collect a much bigger payoff than you would expect."

Jack frowned. "I've been involved with racing for a few years now and I've seen some amazing things, most of them heartening, some of them horrifying. But what are you saying is the deal here? What's illegal about this?"

"That's the problem," Celia said angrily. "It is not illegal, at least not yet. What it is, Jack, is very smart and very destructive. People who you would presume would bet on Read Them wound up getting off him. Betting against him when they saw his odds go up. Thought something was off about him, and came out of the experience feeling like fools. They were angry. They believed that they had been suckered in some way. That is not what we racetrack owners want to have our customers feel about what goes on. It's terrible! Image-wise, reputation-wise. We just can't have this sort of thing continuing. It's demoralizing, destructive, disastrous…"

Jack interrupted her to say, "Don't go all Cole Porter on me."

"What?"

He said, "I was afraid you were leading up to not delovely."

"You think this is funny?"

"Celia, calm down. I just think you may be overreacting. What are you so worried about 'image-wise,' as you put it, if it hasn't become a story in the racing press?"

She said, "The so-called racing press hasn't printed a word about this situation. Despite the fact that Monee Park is the third track effected so far. It happened three weeks ago in a race at Pleasant Prairie, the next week over at Cahokia Park. Then, us. Same format. All three tracks with a solid favorite getting his odds escalated by money pouring in on the rest of the field, then winning and paying more than he should have.

"I finally got a call yesterday from Racing Daily's top reporter, Matt O'Connor. Bright guy. He had good questions. Said he'd run it past his edi-

INQUIRY

tors and try to get the story into the weekend editions. I'd just as soon this be publicized as quickly as possible because I know it will eventually get on the Internet and go viral among U. S. horse players. Better we should make clear what is happening."

Jack said, "I shouldn't be laughing, but I am. Another new wrinkle for racing that I've never heard of. Look, I understand how you would see this caper as being, quote, 'devastating' unquote, to your image. Worrisome for your patrons. And, of course, those at the other tracks you mentioned. But let me ask you this. If this unknown evil force is bumping up the odds on the likely winner, why can't alert bettors follow along. Join the party?"

"Because, Jack, that so-called party is over in the last 80 or 90 seconds before the race starts. That's when the final money comes in on the good horse. The people doing this are shrewd. They don't overbet; they don't bet too early. Just in time to get their money down on the Good Horse before any other bettors watching the odds can react. It's like they're trying to embarrass us!"

"Very clever stuff. Is there any way to stop or refuse these late bets that come in and take advantage of the odds?"

Celia sat back in her chair, arms crossed, eyes boring into his. "I wish. We wish, the other track operators that have been hit like this. But Monee Park or any other track can't refuse bets that have poured in at the last minute or so before the race begins. Are you serious? We do that, well, you can start oiling the doors for closing at all of our tracks."

Jack said, "Pardon me, but I have to kind of admire whoever is running this caper. I'm sure you've had your security people look into this. Do you still have that nitwit retired sheriff's deputy in charge of security here?"

"No. I remember you never got along with Laurence Landgren. But he retired. I've got a sharp young guy named Chuck Tilton replacing him. He's on the ball, Jack. But he's got no idea who is making this happen." She walked over to the sideboard, saying, "Any coffee?"

"No thanks. Let me ask you this. Isn't the state racing commission concerned about this?"

She waited until she was seated. "Sure, they're concerned. But Jack, most of the political appointees on that panel couldn't tell American Pharoah from a mule, or understand the difference between a three-horse parlay and a game of three-card Monte. I don't anticipate much help from that sector of government."

"Let me look at those printouts again," Jack said. He went through them as Celia answered a series of emails on her computer.

"I'm thinking," Jack finally said, "that this is no Mob or Outfit exercise. There's not that much money involved. Neither would any 'Goldfinger' or his ilk be a suspect. Could it be some young adult hacker geniuses who have targeted horse racing? Probably not. They don't know or care about racing any more than I care about twitter or twatter or tweet or twinkle, whatever it's called."

Celia said, "That's the problem, Jack. We don't know who, or what, is attacking our tracks like this. We're desperate to find out who, and why."

She came around from behind her desk to sit next to him on the long brown coach. "Here comes the Big Heat," he laughed. He looked on admiringly as the morning and felt another small heart leap. This was rare for Jack.

"All I'm asking is for you to try and help us. All your racing contacts, your friending of the FBI…"

Jack grimaced. " 'Friending', you call it? It started with me being coerced. But you know that story."

"That and a few others, like when you voluntarily helped them out. How about now? How about you using your contacts to try and identify what evil genius is screwing us up out betting pools and our image? Are you so busy?"

Jack said, "Celia, I've got no more chance of identifying what you call this pari-mutuel villain as the Bears have to win the Super Bowl in my lifetime. Wait. I take that back. I probably do have somewhat of a better chance slim as it might be. I'll do what I can. Ask around, the FBI agents I know, my pal Moe Goldin, a few other possibilities. I'll try to help you."

Celia walked him to the door. "Dear Jack, I appreciate any help you can give us." She hugged him. For a moment he held her tight, buried his face in her long red hair which, as in their brief past encounter, always reminded him of a combination of vanilla and lilac. Whew.

"See what I can do, my dear. I'll be in touch."

Celia stopped him, saying "There's something else I forgot to mention. I don't think it means anything, but…"

Jack said, "But what?"

"I received a somewhat alarming phone call yesterday from Nancy Roth. You know, the vice president of Cahokia Park. That's another track that barred Ted Tilley's horses. She said she'd received a threatening email. From an anonymous sender, of course."

"Saying what?"

Celia said, "I quote, 'Change your ways or count your days.' I asked Nancy if she had any idea who could have sent that. She said, 'Not really. Stan Rogin, the guy I just broke up with, is pissed at me. But he's not smart enough to rhyme a threat.'"

Jack said, "It's probably just more Internet, social media, spewing. Let's hope so, anyway. Celia, let me know if Nancy Roth calls you again about that. Okay?"

He slowly walked to the elevator, thinking what a very lucky man Calvin Douglas was. The first race had just concluded as Jack entered the

INQUIRY

clubhouse box seat section. Just 90 seconds earlier, as the horses flashed across the Monee Park finish, Skip Dumke jumped out of his clubhouse box seat and hurled his now crumpled copy of *Racing Daily* to the floor. A torrent of obscene descriptions of his losing horse, its rider, trainer, owner, breeder and parents made a loud dent in the afternoon air.

"Hey, buddy, watch your language," said box holder Steve Holland who was seated with his family directly behind Skip. That request did not register. Shaking with anger and disappointment, Skip staggered down the steps toward the aptly named Woulda-Coulda-Shoulda Bar, a renowned haven for thirsty losers. It was two floors above the My Original Pick, a larger bar named by discerning management to accommodate numerous disappointed bettors. The first time Skip went into that, he asked the bartender, "Why the name for this place?"

The bartender responded, "Just listen." Within five minutes, Skip heard the first of several glum, beaten down horseplayers declaiming "That winner was my original pick. But I got off him."

"Get it?" said the bartender to Skip.

"Oh, yeah."

Continuing down the ramp, with his head down, muttering, he accidentally bumped shoulders with Jack Doyle. Offering no apology, Skip was jarred by the strong hand gripping his forearm and turning him around. "Hey, what the fuck you doing?" he yelped.

"Hey yourself," Jack snarled. "Watch where the hell you're going. And watch your language. I could hear you cussing from yards away."

Skip sneered. "Who the hell are you? In charge of manners here?"

"If I was," Jack grinned, "I'd throw your ass over the sixteenth pole. Get out of here."

Out in the parking lot, Jack opened his car door and looked back up at the Monee Park top floor office level windows. He thought he might see Celia waving at him. Not so.

CHAPTER SEVEN

The year the real estate market plunged off the precipice, Donald "Skip" Dumke barely blinked. His previous short-lived careers as a purveyor at various times of cheap term life insurance, aluminum pots and pans, penny stocks, and pre-driven autos, had produced similarly depressing results.

Before the housing market tumbled, Skip had managed to ring down a mere $285,000 in total sales for Proper Properties in Morton Grove, IL, a sum that after commissions provided him with an income solidly at the neo-poverty level. He realized his current, sorry gig was over when he sauntered into the PP office late one Monday morning, slightly hungover and late as usual, smiling his usual bullshit smile, and found that his desk had been cleaned out. Even his nameplate, for which he'd had to lay out $35, was upside down in the nearby waste basket.

He got the picture. Skip ripped off his slightly food-spotted tie, threw it down on the carpet, and charged into the office of PP manager Brice Bretland. "You think this is a classy way to operate, Bretland? Just mail me my last check. I'm outta here."

Bretland snorted, "What last check? You haven't brought in a farthing since February."

"A farthing is it, you half-educated asshole? Audrey revoir."

***

Skip, alternating between sizzling and sulking, hit the drive-through at a nearby Dunkin Donuts, thinking how he would love to have available right now the kind of drive-throughs he'd read they had in Louisiana, where you could purchase a pitcher of margaritas-to-go through your open car window.

He was close to broke; his rent was overdue. Once again, as he was forced to do several depressing and embarrassing times in the past, Skip would have to put a call in to his twin brother, Dennis.

***

The Dumke boys had been well known in their hometown of Woodstock, IL, since youth. The unplanned arrival of these red-headed fraternal twins was a delight to their mother, Lois, a fertile producer with three previous female arrivals on her scorecard. Far less enthusiastic was their father, James "Jimbo" Dumke, who groused that he had "A hard enough job feeding and housing the first three" on his salary as a school bus dispatcher for District Sixty-Four, and assistant football coach of the Woodstock High School Wildcats. The 52-year-old Jimbo, who year-round wore his WHS letter jacket earned decades earlier, commented that "At least I won't have to pay for weddings for these two new ones." This ardent Chicago Bears fan's deepest thoughts were muttered during the long, nightly walks he took with his prized rescue dog Cutler, a creature Lois described as "Acting like a spoiled brat and looking like a tattered coyote."

***

Skip was the oldest by four and a half-minutes. At birth, the boys were very close in weight and height, but that changed as they grew. Lois was convinced Dennis was the "picture of young Robert Redford." Jimbo countered that Skip remind him of "Albert E. Neuman, you know, the guy on the cover of the old Mad magazines."

In high school, Dennis followed in his father's cleat marks as a stalwart nose tackle. His skinny brother was the head cheerleader. Both matriculated to Illinois State University. Dennis made second team all-conference his senior year. Skip, having given up cheerleading to become drum major of the university's marching band, also thrived.

The twins roomed together, frequently ate together, and double dated together. But after graduation, Dennis with a degree in business, Skip's in political science, they went their separate ways. After a very brief, failed tryout with his father's beloved Bears, Dennis moved back to Woodstock, joined the town's leading bank, and wound up marrying the oldest daughter of that institution's president when he was 28.

Skip moved to Chicago and began his sorry procession through the vocational ranks, meanwhile dating widely but not well, often thinking nostalgically about his romantic romps through the ranks of the nubile pom pom squads during his high school and college days. In the City of Big Shoulders, Skip's job failures leaped in on giant feline feet. He was eventually forced into real estate in suburban Morton Grove. He wasn't much good at that, either.

Brother Dennis, meanwhile, continued to thrive. After years of proximity, the brothers rarely saw each other, Dennis the thriving banker, Skip the screw up. On Thanksgiving the previous year, they went to their parents' home for holiday dinner. Dennis's wife Deirdre dazzled them with her looks, sense of humor, and management of family decorum. She eagerly helped Lois in the kitchen, asked Skip polite questions, and played up to the obviously flattered Jimbo throughout what Skip considered one of the longest afternoons/evenings of his life.

At the head of the table, Jimbo made his usual production of preparing the giant bird. He brooked no criticism of his methods which more resembled mutilation than carving. As he dismembered it, he pointed out special parts of the bird for the occasion. "Dennis always goes for the breast meat," he chortled, nudging his son's knee under the table while leering at Deirdre's impressive duo. "Skipper, on the other hand, well, gizzard usually does for him, or the ass end. Am I right, Skip?"

Lois finally convinced Jimbo to speed up the process. Huge servings of turkey with what Jimbo declared in his blessing was "all the goddam good trimmings, thank you Lord."

The week following, Skip was now so dejected and embittered after his PP dismissal by that bastard Bretland that he took a temp job with Homes Guarded, a security firm owned by Solly Victoria, one of his drinking buddies. Skip's assignment was to purportedly attempt to break into homes whose owners had canceled their contracts with Homes Guarded, this being Victoria's attempt to urge them to reconsider. All Skip had to do was jimmy doors or knock out a couple of window panes in the attempt to convince the homeowners they had made a serious mistake. This went okay the first week or so. Skip was on a minimum wage rate for what he thought of as "this crap job" and, after nearly getting caught twice while skulking around suburban yards in the middle of the night, Skip marched into Victoria's office and quit.

"This is dishonest work," he told Solly. "I'm not cut out for this."

Solly shooed him out the door. "You weren't any fucking good at it anyway. We never got one return customer from your efforts. Try something else."

In Woodstock, Lois worried about the son she called My Skipper. "When will he get a job he likes? Meet a nice girl?"

Jimbo said, "Don't ask me. He would have turned out all right if he'd paid more attention to all the good training I gave him, even though he wimped out of football. But look at his brother! Moving right up the ladder. He always listened to me. Not like the cheerleader."

"I hate to hear you put down My Skipper for being a cheerleader. One of our presidents was one in college, Jimbo. Do you remember?" Lois spat out.

"All too well." Jimbo snapped his fingers. Cutler struggled to his feet from his bed in the corner of the kitchen. "We're going for a little walk," Jimbo said. "I don't want to talk about this anymore."

CHAPTER EIGHT

Just after seven o'clock Friday morning at Fat City, Jack recounted to Moe his meeting with Celia McCann. It was early in their workouts, both men feeling chipper, but Jack, as Moe put it, "was looking puzzled."

"I am. I don't have any idea who would want to manipulate odds at a racetrack, much less Celia's. I can't figure a way to help her out." Jack hung up the jump rope and put on his gloves and moved toward the heavy bag for that ten minute section of his routine. "You got any ideas?"

In the past, Jack had learned that a suggestion from Moe was always worth considering. Some of them had helped Jack get needed aid from Moe's childhood friend on Chicago's West Side, Fifi Bonadio. He was the longtime head of the Chicago Outfit. On those occasions, Bonadio had reluctantly helped him, even though he had taken a definite dislike to Jack's lack of respect he was used to receiving. "I'm only doing this for you because Moe asked," Bonadio said.

Kellman finished his 60 sit-ups. "Jack, you want to get to the guts of what's going on with Ms. McCann and Monee Park? I suggest you talk to Matt

O'Connor. He knows as much about horse racing and its intriguing ramifications as anybody."

"Where do you know this newspaper guy from?"

Moe said, "I've helped him out with a couple of things in the past few years. I know a few media people. Sometimes they can be useful. Matt is a very nice young guy, probably a couple of years younger than you. And, I might add, much more well mannered."

"Thank you."

"Here's his cell phone number," Moe offered.

After he'd reeled it off, Jack nodded appreciatively. "Your old mental Rolodex is still in operation, eh?"

"Bet on it."

***

Matt O'Connor and Jack had agreed to meet in the Heartland Downs track kitchen Wednesday morning. Jack was familiar with this bustling scene full of voluble Latin-American grooms and hot walkers, several white trainers accompanied by their owners. The odors of strong coffee and huevos rancheros mingled in the large, noisy room with the alternating sounds of salsa and country and western music. This, Jack had read, was in sharp contrast from the scene here 40 years before when the room was filled with mostly white and black Americans and the long cafeteria table offered mainly varieties of fried breakfast dough and coffee.

Matt was waiting for Jack at the door. They shook hands. "Moe says to say hello," Jack said. "And thanks for meeting me."

"No problem. I hope I can be of help. Let's go to that table over in the far corner."

Jack grinned. "Where's that pretty trainer is sitting?" He waved ahead at the young woman with short-cropped black hair above her tanned face. She smiled and waved back.

The surprised O'Connor said, "You know Maggie Collins?"

"Sure. Last year, when I was working here as a jockey's agent, Ms. Collins won a few races with my rider, Mickey Sheehan." At the table, Jack reached forward to take her extended hand. "Morning, Jack," she said. "Nice to see you again."

Matt said, "I see you've got your coffee, Maggie. Jack, I'm going up in the line. What can I get you?"

"Just coffee, Matt, thanks. Black."

Maggie put aside the copy of *Racing Daily* she had been reading. Jack asked, "How many horses did you train this morning?"

"Six. I worked two of them myself, the two-year-olds. Everyone did good and came back healthy." She knocked on the plastic table top, grinning as she did so.

Jack said, "Somebody told me that you had an equestrian background. Was that any help to you for training racehorses?"

"Certainly. I rode in pony shows when I was eight. Then Equestrian shows for several years. I was lucky enough to find myself where I must have always been destined to be. At the racetrack. And what I definitely know is that all these herd animals have much more smarts than most of the public ever gives them credit for."

Matt returned with a tray that he lay down on their table. "Did I hear the start of a lecture on equine marvelousness?"

She jabbed him with her elbow. "Desist, you cynic."

Matt laughed. Nodding at Maggie, he said, "She had a good education. But even at Wellesley, she never learned there's a distinction between a cynic and a skeptic. I happen to be in the latter category. We've been together for nearly four years."

"Good years, too," Maggie responded, "for the most part." She was smiling as she patted Matt's hand before her attention turned to the nicely dressed middle-aged man who was approaching their table. Maggie smiled and said, "Good morning Mr. Holland."

Retired financier and current horse owner Steve Holland had his only two current racehorses trained by Maggie. "I got up too late to see the workouts," Steve said embarrassedly. "How'd my fillies do?"

"Dashing Diana worked great," Maggie said. "She's smart, tough, and fast. I've got a race in mind for her next week. Your little bay, Cee Cee Rider, isn't that far along yet. But she's progressing."

Matt said to the relieved owner, "Steve, you want to join us for breakfast? Or coffee?"

"Oh, no, thanks. I've got to get to work checking the markets. Nice to see you all."

Jack said, "Finance guy?"

"Big time. He loves his horses. And his trainer. But not as much as I do."

Maggie said, "Ease off, Matt." Looking across the table, she asked, "What brings you out here this early Wednesday morning, Jack?"

"It's kind of a weird situation involving pari-mutuel odds being manipulated by, so far at least, unknown parties. I had never heard of anything like this before. So," he smiled, nodding at Matt, "I thought I'd consult an expert on all things racing."

Maggie and Matt both laughed, Matt the hardest. "Experts on Racing. There are probably self-proclaimed thousands of them. Most of them useless. And, Jack, I don't claim to be any kind of 'expert'. I just dig around and unearth facts and try to write entertainingly about them."

"Fine. But what about this odds-changing scheme? Celia McCann said it had happened at Monee Park. Neither she nor anyone who works there has any idea about why it's being done. Or, if it's been done before."

Matt said, "This was new to me, too. But, Jack, understand. If you are involved in horse racing for any amount of time you will learn to continually be prepared to be surprised. As far as this caper goes, I asked around the track. Nothing. Finally, I went to my ultimate source of information about the past. An unofficial historian named Edward "Jumbo" Gural, who worked on our *Racing Daily* copy desk in Chicago since Native Dancer was a foal."

"Jumbo, eh? Big smart guy?"

Maggie laughed. "By no means, Jack. I've met this nice old man. He's retired but he still comes out here to Heartland for the workouts. Always says "It's the best time of day at the track. You can't lose any money.""

"He's called Jumbo," said Matt, "because he has a tremendous memory. You know, like Jumbo the Elephant in those old children's stories. He can name the jockey on the third finisher in any Kentucky Derby since 1930, and every jock in order who finished in front of him. He's the unofficial racing trivial king of the U. S. Amazing guy."

Jack waited while Matt finished his coffee. "So? What did Jumbo say about this strange odds deal?

"Jumbo said he'd never known anything like this to ever happen in

American racing."

"Ah, shoot." Jack sat back in his chair.

Maggie said, "Jack, you look disappointed. Can I get you another cup of coffee? How about a Krispy Kreme?"

Jack nudged Matt. "Does Maggie have a sister, perhaps?"

Maggie got up and said, "Got to go, men. Must get ready for the morning feeding at my stable. Jack, great to see you. Good luck."

Both men watched admiringly as the slim, athletic woman worked her way to the doorway exchanging greetings in both English and Spanish. Jack said, "Man, you've got a winner there."

Matt nodded. "No question about that. Here's another question. What are you going to do next with your inquiries?"

"Haven't gotten that far yet. I was hoping for some help from you. Mind you, I'm not complaining."

Matt looked at his watch. "Jack, I've got to meet trainer Ralph Tenuta in ten minutes for an interview. I know you're a friend of his."

"Worked as his stable agent one season," Jack said. "Great guy. Say hello for me."

Matt's cell phone buzzed. "Wait, Jack. I've got to take this call from my editor." Jack toyed with his coffee cup and watched Matt, with phone to his ear, reaching for his notepad and began writing rapidly.

Matt put his phone back in his jacket pocket. "Bad news?" Jack said.

"Yeah. Woman named Marcy Darcy was killed last night down in southern Illinois. Young. Very smart. I've interviewed her several times. Damn!"

Jack sat back, waiting. "Marcy was the general manager of Cahokia Park," Matt said. "I talked to her last week, about a big stakes race scheduled there, and she was laughing when she told me she'd gotten an Internet message from Anonymous saying her track had made a quote 'big mistake.' Unless they changed, 'bad changes would happen.' Marcy laughed it off. Said the only change Cahokia Park had made was barring the famous owner, Ted Tilley."

"What happened to this woman?"

Mat answered, "The early police report said Marcy had just finished her regular hour jog through a forest preserve and entered the parking lot, where she was hit by a black SUV. There was a park policeman a block away. He saw it. Jumped out of his car and ran over to poor Marcy, who was battered and not breathing. The officer ran back to his car to call it in and get an ambulance. He reported this thing was intentional. By then, the SUV was long gone. Driver must have panicked after he hit March. No license plate, no other witnesses, nothing."

"Jesus!" Jack said. "Celia McCann knew Marcy Darcy. Was this killing the result of a threat being carried out? I've got to call Celia."

INQUIRY

CHAPTER NINE

Two nights after his dismissal by that bastard Solly Victoria, Skip entered one of his regular stops, The Local Drinking Hole. It was owned and operated by Luke Ledbetter, a Woodstock boy who had attended the famous Iowa University writing program after graduating from Northern Illinois. Luke emerged enlightened and embittered, convinced he wasn't going to make a living in the life of literature. So he pursued his second passion, bar life, first as a dedicated patron, then the owner of the Woodstock saloon left to him by his similarly inclined late Uncle Lawrence. Twenty-one years later, Luke was still there, sometimes in the early afternoon "back of the wood," usually at the large table in the rear corner where he could comfortably hold forth for a revolving coterie of art-inclined millennials eager to learn from his "life and writing experience."

Skip took his usual stool at the upper curve of the long mahogany bar. From there, he could check foot traffic, perhaps note somebody he knew who might have some idea as to what he might do with the rest of his miserable life.

At 5:45 p.m., the door banged open announcing the entrance of another bar regular, Jeff Khass, who shouted, "Put on the racing station!" Luke clicked his television remote. On screen appeared a cavalcade of thoroughbreds coming down the long stretch at Heartland Downs. Jeff was snapping his fingers and hollering, "C'mon Five. C'mon Five. C'mon five. Alllll riiiiight," as No. Five, a game old gelding named Twizzler Stone, thrust his long nose forward to win a photo finish.

The Greek-American twirled in small circles, arms raised, doing his Zorba dance but in triple time. The customers laughed and clapped. They applauded much louder after the voluble Jeff shouted, "I'm buying a round for the house. Drinks are on me!"

Jeff huffed and puffed and twirled for a few seconds more before staggering to the bar stool next to Skip. "Am I celebrating? Double damn right I am, Skipper. I made me a killing out there at Monee Park today. Topped off by that old Twizzler Stone taking the nightcap. A killing! Fourth time this week. Buddy," he said softly as he nudged Skip's arm, "I got a system that's fucking golden!"

Two hours of steady drinking later, all on Skip's tab, they decided to call it a night after agreeing to meet the next day at Heartland Downs. "I've got some steamers in here, Skipper," Jeff said, tapping his finger on the battered black briefcase he always had with him. "We'll knock 'em dead," he promised. "I'm surprised you haven't connected with me earlier."

Skip didn't see bartender Bill Sheridan roll his eyes hearing this statement. And Skip didn't want to confess he had zipped past dire straits and was heading toward the rocks of his disappointing life. He just said, "Hey, thanks man. See you tomorrow. He left The Local Drinking Hole with a bounce in his step.

* * *

Late the next morning Jeff bustled through the Monee Park entrance where Skip had been waiting impatiently for a half-hour, waving at vendors, glancing at his watch, tapping his track program in his hand. It was less than 20 minutes until the first race. Jeff was carrying his worn black leather briefcase containing what he assured Skip was, "The key to riches, Buddy. Vital stats and figures, observations, and race-watching notations gleaned from years of intense study."

As agreed upon at the bar the night before, Skip gave Jeff $500 to bet on his behalf this bright, promising afternoon. Jeff pocketed the wad and said, "I'll meet you before the second race. Up in my box. See you then. Got to see a man about a winning horse. Our score is coming in the second race."

The first race was just concluding as the puzzled Skip was informed by an abrupt usher, "There is no Box Five." An hour later, after roaming the track searching for Jeff, Skip realized that his five bills and new pal were long gone.

"That fuckin' thief," Skip muttered. He bought a beer and a hot dog and walked outside to sit on one of the wooden benches near the track's finish line. Listening to the talk around him during the next few races, he heard a cavalcade of misinformation, so seasoned with hope and ignorance that it amazed him. Out of the dozen people nearby, only one seemed to win a bet each race. But the other eleven just shrugged and turned their attention to the next race.

It occurred to Skip that he could probably outsmart the majority of these goofs. Pari-mutuel wagering, he knew, meant that one was not betting against "the house," as in casinos, but against the other people placing wagers.

In the Local Drinking Hole that night, Skip asked bartender Sheridan if Jeff Khass had been in. Sheridan tossed his bar rag into the sink. "Oh, that fucking hustler. He was in here two nights this week. Talked people into giving him money to bet horses he said 'could not fucking lose,' and never came back. We won't see him again for weeks. Then he'll roar back in. I try to warn people in here about his bullshit approach. Most listen. Some don't. I guess that's how he keeps on keeping on. If he didn't always

INQUIRY

eventually pay his tab, I'd bar him."

That night Skip spent less time regretting the loss of his $500 to the devious Jeff Khass than considering a new world of opportunity for him. Horse races…betting…gullible fans…there had to be ways to beat this game, harvest this crop.

After an Internet search, Skip signed up for two websites that supplied "sure winners" for a daily fee. He bought into both, with hope in his heart and a gaping hole in his bank account.

***

Skip leaned forward over his laptop. The closer he looked at the streaming video, the more apparent it became that his pick had lost the fourth race at Belmont by the width of a thumbnail. "Not again, great god almighty, not again!" he shouted before slamming the computer top down on the worn keys.

He accidentally knocked his can of Bud Lite from the table top, got up, then kicked it across the floor of Room 302 in Monee's Residence Inn Supreme. "How long can this go on?"

This was the third time in four days that Skip lost photo finishes with horses suggested by the tout systems he had purchased. Others of their "Today's Special" and "All-Time Best Bet" had fared even worse. He finally stopped pacing, sat down, head in his hands, and feeling as if he might vomit. How had he come to this? He vividly remembered his Uncle Dan Grissom's woeful plea for directions after a bad day of betting, "Where do you go to give up?"

As the horses flashed across the Monee Park finish line in the final race of the day, Skip jumped out of his clubhouse box seat and hurled his crumpled copy of *Racing Daily* down on the floor. A torrent of obscene descriptions of his losing horse, its rider, trainer, owner, and breeder made a dent in the late afternoon air.

Skip trudged out of Monee Park to his car. "I am cursed," he shouted.

Today marked three weeks that Skip had been betting Monee Park races while following the recommendations of two well-known tout services he had signed up for. "MAGIC MAVEN" cost him $12 a day with selections emailed to him. "SHUR THINGS" operated by Professor Sidney Shur charged a sawbuck per day. And Skip's usage of both had been very promising during the first week.

Skip did what he thought was decent due diligence. For example, after seeing an ad offering the "SECRET SYSTEM OF WORLD'S TOP VETERAN HANDICAPPER," self-described as the" BEST EVER IN THE BUSINESS," he called the phone number. He heard a raspy old voice. "Yeah?"

Skip said, "I have a question."

"Yeah?"

"If you're the world's top handicapper as you claim, why are you selling your system?"

Loud racking coughs. Extended wheezing. Then, the grating sound of "Why am I practically giving away my amazing system? Because I am dying of lung and colon cancer. The doc says I've a couple of weeks to live, tops. Could be less, an overlay. None of my children or their children want to go into this business. So, I am putting together a good inheritance for the uninterested ingrates. Get it?"

Skip sighed. "You're so full of shit," he said before hanging up.

He enjoyed small but regular profits with MAVEN and PROFESSOR SHUR for the first six days. Then the bottom dropped out.

If Skip played exactas, his picks seemed to inevitably finish first and third, not first and second as required. Growing increasingly desperate, he concentrated on trifectas. Their usually large payoffs could definitely right his listing ship. But, no. For the most part, those bets extended his pattern of "Oh, So

Close" results. Instead of running one-two-three as required, they often finished one-two-four, or one-four-two, or, on occasion as Skip put it, "No-fucking-where."

On a cold Thursday afternoon, Skip had an hour or so of introspection sitting at the end of the long mahogany bar. How did he get into this? At first, he fondly remembered his first day at a racetrack and old Sportsman's Park in Cicero. He went there with his favorite uncle Duane Dumke, his godfather and owner of a thriving plumbing service. What a great afternoon for a newly-turned teenager! Crowded track buzzing with conversations and loud speaker reminders "Four minutes 'till post time." Enticing odors of grilled hot dogs and tap beer, horses careening around the five-eighths mile track referred to as a "bull ring."

With a cursory look at his uncle's *Racing Daily*, Skip bet two dollars on a daily double. It paid $228. Holy shit! Thus, the hook was set. So many years ago. Those were the days.

After years of relishing the memory of his first day at a racetrack, he started to wince at comparing it to this rainy April day at old Sportsman's Park in Cicero. Deep in his slump now, Skip could compare it only to his disastrous experience at Washington & Morgan, the military -themed college his father insisted he attend. As Duane told his wife, "Discipline is what that kid needs. Toughness. He won't be able to prance around like a damn cheerleader down there."

Skip found the Washington & Morgan all-male bastion stultifying with class mates so crew cut and fit they looked eager to invade, well, some foreign country. It took him nearly two weeks that first semester to learn how to strip his rifle. It took him two more weeks to finally meet a live prospect from Wellington, the nearby women's college. Pauline Brooks was the

INQUIRY

only child of Washington & Morgan's dean, August Brooks.

One late autumn Saturday night, after sharing a succession of strawberry tequila shots at the off-campus Boom Boom Room Saloon, Skipper persuaded Pauline to lead him to the third-floor dorm room she shared with a now absent roommate. He'd no sooner gotten the eager Pauline disrobed, on the bed, and was tugging down his trousers when her old man, enraged August Brooks, barged through the door.

"I got a call about you, Dumke. Get the hell out of my daughter's room and life, you pervert!"

Skip had just managed to pull up and button his striped, W&M issued gray pants, when the enraged Brooks grabbed his shoulders from behind and propelled him down the nearby stairs. Skip hit the wall. Blearily, he looked up to where Dean Brooks stood, face as red as a hydroponic tomato, shouting "You'll be thrown out of W&M for this. I'll see to it!"

Skip staggered to his feet. "Fine with me, you old bastard. An exit from this cesspool is just what I've been looking for." He turned away, shot a middle finger salute back up the stairs, then hollered, "Tell your daughter for me she should hope to be kidnapped in order to get the hell away from you and all this."

***

Trying to find a way to emerge from his current slump, it dawned on Skip that the profits from these supposedly fool-proof betting systems went primarily, not to the hopeful buyers but, to the sellers. Perhaps some were actually okay. He had neither the time nor cash to determine which ones actually fell into the latter category. Skip decided to join the ranks of system sellers who evidently knew that the fish were out there, waiting to be hooked.

He started going to the Extended Stay gym every morning before anyone else was there. A few minutes on the treadmill, enough to break a sweat. Some jogging in place, a shower, then back to his room. Time on the computer reviewing that day's racing entries. Kind of up and down results lately, but not too discouraging. Not quite at bust out time. But, needing a cash infusion, Skip called his brother Donnie. He described in detail to him his new strenuous regimen of self-control. "I've become kind of a health nut," he said. "Sworn off Bloody Marys. Now drinking V-8 with the vodka!"

Donny stifled an impulse to hang up on his aggravating twin. He agreed to advance him another $1000 against profits despite knowing very well all the previous advances had turned into financial retreats.

Skip spent the next month working to devise his own saleable betting system. He checked into an Extended Stay Facility just blocks away from Monee Park. the *Racing Daily* was emailed to him every morning reporting past performances as well as announcing the next day's races. His great new life-salvaging venture was about to begin. He could feel it.

CHAPTER TEN

"Rudy, my man. Hey. It's Gary."

"Gary, all right. Give me a minute. I've got to shoo away, bribe, or threaten another annoying county inspector off my ongoing Mc-Mansion project. It's the first major one I've got since I started my own construction company."

Gary waited patiently for the return call from a man he had admired and relied upon since they first met after he transferred to Kenosha's St. James Parochial School and entered seventh grade at age 13.

The first morning recess period of his first day, Gary knew he would be tested in what were those days Kenosha playground challenges at these schools filled primarily with kids from working-class families. He had spent the previous night sweating in bed as he envisioned the next day's scenario—spindly, skinny Gary meeting whoever the seventh-grade physical kingpin was. At that point in his young life, Gary's strengths were mainly mental, not physical.

It was a very warm, early September day. The recess ball rang. Gary left his seat in the last row and slunk silently into the nearby cloak room. He quickly felt a serious grip on his left ear from Sister Benedict. This dedicated disciplinarian was always referred to by the class wise guys as "Arnold. "C'mon, boy, it's recess time. Everyone goes outside."

"Outside" was a 60 by 100 foot concrete expanse bordered by chain link fences and filled with girls playing jump rope or hopscotch, boys idling or tossing a softball back and forth. Gary sidled out the door, praying for a gift from God of invisibility. No go. With other seventh grade boys pointing at him, Gary watched a tough looking, stocky boy smilingly trotting toward him.

"Hey, new boy, you think you're tough?" He felt his assailant, Richie Picasso, poke him in the chest.

Gary had never thought of himself as being physically tough. But he knew that now, on this day of important first impressions at his new school, facing the grinning Picasso, he could not back down or he'd be branded.

"Tough enough for you," Gary squeaked.

Picasso laughed. The circle of watchers did, too.

Gary took the initiative. He leaped forward and threw a right cross that missed but startled the glowering Picasso, who shouted, "You're gonna pay

INQUIRY

for that, New Boy." Picasso raised his fists and moved closer, an advance that was immediately halted.

Gary looked with relief at another seventh grader, big Rudy Ozinga, who was holding the aggressive Picasso by the scuff of his neck. "Leave the new kid alone, Picasso." He gave Picasso a teeth rattling shake. Then they both walked away, leaving the relieved Gary to be surrounded by all-of-a-sudden respectful classmates.

"Rudy says he's okay," he heard, "he's okay."

Nobody messed with Rudy, he got that right away. Gary watched several times that year as Rudy interrupted an eighth grader pushing around a weak underclassman, then pounded the older student into the pavement of the St. James playground.

After witnessing one of these events, Gary walked up to Rudy as they were exiting school one afternoon. He touched him on the arm. "I like what you do for those kids that get bullied."

Autumn raindrops began descending. Gary took off his glasses, protecting them from the drizzle, and looked up earnestly at Rudy. He said, "Do you charge for your work? I'm serious. I've heard about kids paying to be protected here."

Rudy said, "Come with me." They walked across the street to a bus stop and sat down on the bench under the roof away from the now-pouring rain. Rudy continued, "No, I don't charge anybody anything. I do it because I just don't like seeing kids get pushed around. Okay?" He paused before adding, "Truth is, some of the little spoiled pricks I protect probably deserve a little slapping. So, I step in a little late sometimes.

"Plus"…he hesitated… "I get a big kick knocking the shit out of people who deserve it. Jerks that have it coming."

Gary smiled. Looking at this impressive figure next to him, he felt admiration for and a sure connection with Rudy. Gary said, "Darned good for Rudy." He offered a handshake. Rudy's huge hand enveloped Gary's.

Rudy said, "I saw you step up and try to fight that asshole Picasso. Good to know a stand-up kid like you." He stood up. "Gotta head home. See you tomorrow." Gary watched him go, thinking, well I do think I've got a good new friend here.

***

In their subsequent years as classmates, at St. James, then Lincoln Junior High, finally Kenosha High School, Gary thought that sometimes Rudy maybe went a little bit too far in his self-appointed role as an order keeper. Like the noon recess in ninth grade at St. James, when Rudy accidentally broke loudmouth Dickie Kamin's arm in their touch football game. Or when, standing in line for communion at a post-Lenten Mass in front of their class's brightest and most annoying female student, Rudy's right elbow "accidentally" blackened Susan Dilday's left eye as she was loudly upbraiding him for not moving forward fast enough.

Gary guided Rudy over some difficult educational shoals, especially spending hours tutoring him on how to diagram sentences for eighth grade martinet Sister Phyllis, a scholastic demand that flummoxed the otherwise capable Rudy. Those sessions cemented a friendship that continued after Rudy left Eastern Iowa and Gary graduated phi beta kappa with a business degree from University of Wisconsin-Madison.

Post-college years, these friends kept in touch and made a point of meeting every Fourth of July weekend in Kenosha with dinner at the Bartley House, then a drive down to the lakefront for the fireworks show. Rudy always had a local date and provided one for Gary. Great times.

As Rudy started piling up a small fortune building houses in a development seven miles from Lake Michigan, incongruously termed " White Caps," Gary first played minor league professional baseball, then worked for a Chicago investment firm for a nearly a lucrative decade. His last year there, bored out of his active mind, he spotted a tremendous growth promise in a small, profitable, New England hardware chain. "This one is completely under the radar," Gary assured his boss, who said, "Okay, go out there. Vet this Ted Tilley, the CEO. Do your usual good job."

Gary smiled as he left that office. He sure as hell knew Ted Tilley. They had been battery mates on the Oshkosh Braves for two desultory summers in the Badger Double A league. They had jointly decided that their futures did not lie in that sport and went their separate ways. They barely kept in touch until Gary made his visit to the Tilley Company corporate office.

Resuming the friendship cultivated during their baseball days, Ted and Gary clicked again at this meeting at the Tilley Company headquarters. Ted assuredly answered every due diligence question from Gary, who was again impressed by Tilley's candor, open personality, and now by the numbers on the company's balance sheet. The two men went to lunch that day, had a couple of beers, renewed many common interests: classic movies, Jonathan Winters' comedy genius, pro football, Ted a New England Patriots season-ticket holder, Gary, a diehard Green Bay Packers backer.

Outside, in the middle of a fun afternoon for them both, they shook hands as Ted walked Gary to his rental car. Ted said, "You know anything about horse racing?"

"Just enough to know that I don't know much."

"My hardware company now can pretty much run on its own," Ted began. "Very boring for me. I want to do something new. I've always loved horse racing, ever since that day when I was a kid and watched on TV as the great Secretariat won the Belmont Stake stakes by a record 31 lengths. That started the fire for me.

"You might find that surprising," he continued. "And I hope what I'm telling you about my passion for horse racing doesn't influence what your investment firm thinks about my company. Hardware is one thing for me, horse racing is another. I intend to keep those financial entities completely separate. The thing is, Gary, I want to start a racing stable, maybe a breeding operation, too. I'd need a real smart, energetic, forward thinking, quick study person to help ne run it. How about you?"

The stunned Gary said, "Hey, I'm flattered. About all I know about horses is that they are beautiful and that they can be eating when their owners are sleeping. But, let's say I'm interested in your offer. Why would you think I could do a job like this?"

"You know, Gary, even up here in upstate New York we know how to look into things before we leap. Due diligence. I've done it—on you."

Ted paused. "For my planned racing operation, I need a bright and reliable right-hand man to help oversee the kind of sizeable, ambitious operation I've got in mind. Our hardware business can pretty much run itself. But not the racing. Gary, I know you're a quick study. I've done as much diligence on you as you have done on my company. Found your career, thus far, to be very impressive. Do you want to learn about thoroughbred horseracing? Try something different? Come along with me on this project?"

Gary said, "Well, hell. This is an intriguing proposition. But, at some point, we've got to talk money."

"Certainly," Ted smiled. Then he named a number that tripled Gary's Chicago salary.

That sealed their deal. With Gary acting as stable manager and Ted selecting both horses and trainers for them, the Tilley Racing Stable began an impressive run of success, one that was threatened by the sudden decision of tracks to bar Tilley horses from their races.

Gary was as astounded as Ted by this boycott. They filed unsuccessful law suits against the five tracks. Ted's usual upbeat disposition was eclipsed by a depression that alarmed Gary. That's when he devised his odds-manipulation scheme that so disturbed the targeted tracks. After each one, Gary emailed each of those tracks' general managers the message that this would continue, "until a certain stable is allowed back at your track."

Gary drove several miles to use various library computers where he sent the messages signed, "A Concerned Citizen." Gary never informed Ted of this campaign of threats. But Gary's emails failed to produce any change in the tracks' anti-Tilley policy. Increasingly frustrated, he almost informed Ted what he had done and how disappointed he was in his failed efforts. But he then thought better of it. He knew Ted would never endorse such a plan.

Late on a summer Sunday night, his family asleep, Gary picked up his laptop and got into his car and drove seven miles to the parking lot of a restaurant he'd patronized, one that offered free Wifi. "This is the time to step up the action," he said to himself.

To the three racetracks that had banned the Tilley stable, Gary emailed this message: "Halt your Black Balling of America's LEADING OWNER. Or ELSE pay the Consequences." He signed it "A Friend of Fairness."

And then he called Rudy Ozinga in Kenosha. "Not too late to call you, right?" he asked. "How you doing?"

The call had awakened Rudy from one of his fitful sleeps in his lounge chair in front of his huge, flat-screen television. Sleeps of the sort he'd suffered ever since his work place accident. That was one problem stemming from that painful experience. Others included intermittent memory loss. Grocery lists Rudy used to keep in his head he now had to jot down on pieces of paper. Same thing with once familiar phone numbers, even sometimes the names of people he supervised at the construction sites. Aggravating as hell, but not as much as the pains that frequently flashed through his skull.

Rudy said, "I'm getting by, man. So, what's with you, Gary?"

"I got a little project I think you could help me with, Rudy. It involves scaring the shit out of people who need it. And it pays good on a case-by-case basis. All of it would be done at Midwestern locations not terribly far from you. What do you think? Interested?"

Rudy rose from his lounge chair, grinning. "Well, scratch my balls, man. This is the kind of new thing I feel like getting into."

Gary said, "That's great. I figured I could depend on you, Rudy, just like I did in seventh grade. I'll get back to you with the details on this project in a few days. Take care, my friend."

CHAPTER ELEVEN

Having finished his five-mile run along Chicago's beautiful lake front at 7 a.m., his usual seven miles per hour pace, Jack paused at the back entrance to his condo building, stretched for a couple of minutes, then relished the early morning view of a bright azure sky graced by wispy white clouds.

As he opened his condo door, he heard the land line ringing. Two quick strides and he said, "Hello."

"Hello, yourself. Top of the morning, Jack. Do I hear you breathing a bit heavily? From your morning dash about? Or just normal excitement at hearing my voice?"

Jack laughed. "No need to flatter yourself, Nora. You've never left me as breathless as you have exhilarated. Why in God's name are you ringing me at this hour?"

"It's just early afternoon here in Dublin. I wanted to reach you before you were out and about for your day. Ignoring, as you usually do, your cell phone, which I know you regard as a major irritation."

Nora Sheehan, older sister of the talented young Irish jockey Mickey Sheehan, was one of the major highlights recently in Jack's life, no matter how rarely seen. They had spent enjoyable times together two years earlier when Jack, acting as Mickey's jockey agent at Heartland Downs, had guided her into a very exciting and rewarding season, and journalist Nora was feeding a popular Irish blog about the progress of her precocious sister. Nora and Jack had hit it off at once, two very independent, outspoken, people without the remotest intention of carrying a romance out of the bedroom and into the future. They had gotten together the previous year in Ireland and found themselves grateful that their relationship was spiced by good humor, good sex, and no hint of commitment.

Jack listened to the lilt of Nora's accent as she said, "I've been hired by the Irish Times and the new Internet news startup Mashable to cover some important events in your arm of the woods. Like…"

He interrupted her to say, "We call it neck of the woods. But go on."

"Thank you. Always nice to be corrected or enlightened by a person who relishes such responsibilities."

Jack laughed, then heard Nora say, "I'm to cover Irish Fest in Milwaukee. It's the biggest such event in the U. S. Then I go on to the second biggest Irish Fest held in Minnesota near the Twin Cities. Each event lasts a week. I doubt I could lure you to Minnesota, but I thought you might accompany me to the Irish Fest in Milwaukee. It's supposed to be a great old-fun affair.

"Now," Nora continued, you know my work schedule. How about yours'? Last I knew you were helping your FBI capture the so-called mercy killer of retired racehorses that had been donated for research purposes. What are you on to now?"

Jack said, "Nothing special. I've got kind of a small project with my former employer at Monee Park, Celia McCann. Remember her? She has a problem she could use some help with."

"Ah, yes, the beauteous track owner you told me about. The woman I believe you were quite smitten with as I recall. Do men still get 'smitten'? Even men such as yourself?"

He heard her muffled laughter and waited until she'd stopped. "You know, there was a horse that ran at Monee last week, might have been named for you, Nora. A filly called Mischievously."

Nora said, "You've not answered my question."

"As far as I know, there are still probably people who get smitten. But don't tie that word to me and Celia. That good woman remarried following the sad death of her husband. Celia and I don't keep in touch. But she asked me as a favor to deal with a situation that is currently a problem for her.

"Other than that," Jack continued, "I'm kind of in between adventures. Fine with me. Especially now that I know I will have time for you. Nora, how long will you be here?"

"I can't say. I've got an open-ended assignment sheet and expense account for this trip. The Mashable company people are convinced that U. S. news on their Internet site will open the door wider for targeted advertising. I know nothing about the business end of this. I just write. What do you think about this approach? I know you came from the world of advertising."

Jack laughed. "Yes. Sadly, I missed the golden 'Mad Men' era. So, I don't miss advertising. I leave those exercises in allurement and deception to others. This leaves me time to reserve my attentions for gems such as yourself. I'd be delighted to host you, Nora. Even though you're putting a bit of housekeeping pressure on me. I'm trying to recall the location of my vacuum cleaner. But don't worry. I promise clean sheets and eager arms."

Nora's laughter rang out. "Years ago," she said, "one of my Dad's favorite Americans on the telly was your Dick Cavett. He once said that when he first moved to a big city, New York, or maybe Philadelphia, he stayed in a very cheap hotel where, as he put it, 'they changed the sheets every day—from room to room.'"

"Not to fret about that here in my place, Nora. As you know, I've just the one bedroom."

"I remember it well," she laughed. "And I'm very much looking forward to spending time with you, Jack Doyle, no matter how irreverent, irascible, iconoclastic, and occasionally irritating you can sometimes be."

Jack said, "You left out intriguing. Not to mention irresistible." He smiled at the welcome prospect of again spending time with this lively, super smart, ambitious woman, who had once advised him, early one morning in bed, to not be considering any ties that bind.

"Just concentrate on what fun we have together," she had whispered.

"I'll be delighted to retrieve you from O'Hare. When will you come?"

"A week from Monday. I can spend a couple of days in Chicago before I go to Wisconsin." There was a pause before she said, "So my chances of staying with you?"

"Aw, I'd have to think about that," Jack said slowly. "Days of consideration might be called for. I…just don't know…"

"Jack Doyle, you continue as such a jokester. I know you'll be panting to see me at the airport. Aer Lingus flight 772 next Monday."

"Probably salivating as well," Jack responded. "I'll be there."

Nora said, "Brilliant!" before breaking the connection.

Jack hung up the phone and decided it was time to shower. He felt a surge of promising times on their way. Every appearance of Nora Sheehan in his life had been a welcome boost.

CHAPTER TWELVE

After their workouts early that Monday morning at Fit City, Moe and Jack, both showered and dressed for the day, sat at the health club's food bar. Moe worked his way through a large fruit plate. Jack cream-cheesed a toasted bagel before saying, "So, what do you want to talk about?"

"I need a favor. You know my daughter Sarah's husband, Scott. You were at their wedding."

Jack nodded. "Who could forget? Probably set you back a couple hundred grand in that ritzy hotel. I think the huppa was trimmed with gold plate."

"If you ever marry and have a daughter and marry her off, and the chances of that are slim on both counts if I do say so, you'll understand that money was no object for that major Kellman family event. But what I'm concerned about is my son-in-law's new involvement in horse race betting."

"Why? There are worse diversions."

Moe said, "Look, Scott is a very nice young man. Has a thriving dental practice in Lake Forest. He's done very well while not managing to placate his mother."

"What's her problem?"

"Like many Jewish mothers," Moe said, "she doesn't consider a doctor of dentistry to be what she calls a 'true doctor.' Anyway, he's done very well. An expert on implants and dentures. But I'm concerned that he's out of his depth with his new interest in betting on horses. I asked him why he was doing this. He said he was 'bored silly' with his vocation and was looking for an avocation. That makes people nervous. His wife, his mother-in-law, and me."

Jack said, "Perhaps the lad needs a diversion from probing around peoples' palates?"

"You call his betting a diversion," Moe continued. "No. It's become an obsession with this otherwise solid young yanker of molars. Sarah says he now starts every morning retrieving some tip sheet picks on his computer. Then he hurries home at night and checks the results and either whoops or whimpers. It's driving Sarah nuts. He used to be fun. Had kind of a routine about how he could have put a smile on the George Washington dollar bill face instead of the closed mouth over the wooden teeth. What I would like is for you to find out about this tip sheet. It's run by some guy named Dumke. Skip Dumke. You ever hear of him?"

"No. I don't pay attention to those guys," Jack said. "If they really knew what they were doing, were actually successful bettors, why would they share their knowledge and hurt their prices?"

Moe said, "That's pretty much what I've tried to get across to young Scott. But he's not a good listener as far as that goes. This Skip Dumke has got his hooks into Scott pretty good. And he won't let go. Like all those hustlers, if the fish are on the hook they play them."

Jack paused to finish his bagel before saying, "Well, I understand your concern, Moe. But what am I supposed to do about it?"

"How about you having a nice talk with this Skip. Subtly supply him reasons why he should get his clutches off of my son-in-law. The guy's probably a light weight up and down. You have a talent for getting important points across. Would you do this?"

Jack said, "I am flattered. But what about your goombah Fifi Bonadio's? Why not send a squadron of his goons?"

"Jack, my connection with Fifi, who has been my friend since we fought school yard battles on the West Side, is primarily one of friendship. But I don't like to utilize Fifi's resources when I don't have to. Also, some of his 'resources' I understand tend to overdo matters. Various beat downs and crunchings that invariably bring in the police. Not good."

Jack said, "C'mon, Moe. What the hell, with all those deeply discounted fur coats you sell, Bonadio should be in your debt."

Moe speared the last piece of cantaloupe, shaking his head as he chewed. "You obviously don't understand, my friend, that Fifi Bonadio is in nobody's debt. They're in his. I only resort to asking Fifi's assistance in very, very dire situations. This isn't one of them. There are only so many bullets in that gun, Jack. I use them sparingly."

"Like you often use the truth?" Jack laughed. "Sparingly?"

Moe shook his head. "Fifi has told me that the talent pool for Outfit strong arm guys has shrunk tremendously in recent years. Very depressing, he says. I know that he has had to employ unguided missile ballbreakers who aren't nearly as proficient as their predecessors. That's why I am asking you for this favor. You should be able to get a meaningful message across to this Skip."

"Let me think about this."

Moe fielded a cell phone call. The conversation was brief. He told his gorgeous assistant, Cecilia Martin, to "sit that fat fuck's ass down, ply him with a cocktail or two, and several looks at you. I'll be there soon.

"Got a guy coming in from the Big Apple this morning," he told Jack. "A real putz, but a major client."

Moe's face flushed. "You know, sometimes Jack you piss me off major league. This is one of those days." He grabbed the check and signed it.

"Okay, okay, Moe. Let's do this. Give me a chance to talk to young Scott. Find out exactly what he's doing with this Skip. I don't want to interrogate him in your office."

Moe got up and gave Jack a hearty slap on the back. "I knew you'd come through. Dino's tomorrow night for dinner. I'll have Scott there. How's that?"

"I guess we'll find out, "Jack said.

INQUIRY

CHAPTER THIRTEEN

After his conversation with Gary, Rudy Ozinga had paced his living room floor that Tuesday night, drinking beer and planning, now that he knew the name of his target, a woman named Marcy Darcy, an executive at Pleasant Prairie Racetrack. Up early the next morning, Rudy dialed her work phone number. When he called, her secretary laughed. "No, she won't be in for awhile. She's probably on her daily run in the Harms Forest Preserve. Try back in about an hour. Or should I have her call you?"

"No need," Rudy said. "Thanks." Shortly after 7:30 a.m. he drove into the parking lot of the forest preserve. There was only one other car there. "Must be hers," he said to himself. He backed his black van into a shaded space at the rear of the lot. And waited. And watched as a young couple jogged along behind an expensive looking stroller, alternating being at the controls, chatting and smiling at each other and frequently peering forward to check on their child passenger.

As the minutes dragged on, Rudy got increasingly jumpier. He impatiently tapped his hands on the steering wheel. He felt like getting out of the van but rejected that notion. He could not risk being seen by anyone. He watched a couple of senior dog walkers at the end of leashes attached to comparably aged pets.

Even at 8 a.m., the mist lingered under dark gray clouds. The few runners still in action were hustling along, striding out. Then a woman came into view. She was wearing a light green rain jacket. Her head was uncovered. He compared her look to the photo he had on his phone. Nope.

Seven more minutes went by before he saw Marcy emerge from the wooded running path and come toward him. She was ten yards away when he started his engine and pivoted the van so that his side was near her route. He stopped before she reached him and watched appreciatively. Pretty woman, tight runner's body, long legs. Too bad she'd have to suffer a little hurt and a major scare in the next few seconds as he carried out Gary Grunwald's instructions to emphasize the seriousness of the warning she had ignored.

Marcy jogged past him and stopped at the end of the deserted parking lot. She bent over and stretched. The drizzle was picking up. Rudy slid his van closer to the blue Volvo he knew was hers. She took some deep breaths and began to walk toward it. He drove up behind her and blasted his horn. Startled, she turned just in time to see him opening his driver's door. "Scare the shit out of the bitch with this move," he said to himself. That was the plan. Come close to hitting her but then veer away and get the hell away.

Rudy was surprised that Marcy didn't jump to the side as he started to speed closer to her. She stood transfixed, mouth open. Before he could turn his steering wheel his door thumped hard into her, sending her flying. He braked and looked back. Nobody else in the wide parking lot now but the two of them. He hurried out of his van and ran to Marcy. She was flat on her back. Blood streamed from her battered face and her left arm angled oddly. He bent down and felt her neck for a pulse. Nothing. "Shit!" That wasn't the plan.

As he knelt over her, Rudy heard a yapping dog approaching with its owner from the forest. The owner's head was down, her eyes concentrating on her cell phone texts. When they left the parking lot, Rudy ran to his van and quickly drove out on Golf Road. His right hand shook on the steering wheel. He looked back. Not a vehicle in sight.

Three miles later he pulled into a shopping center parking lot. The sun had now blazed through the morning mist and he pulled down his visor against the glare. He turned the radio on to his favorite rock station. Sat up straight in his seat feeling an adrenaline rush he hadn't experienced since his championship wrestling days.

A few minutes later and five miles down the highway, Rudy shifted lanes and pulled into a McDonald's drive-through lane where he ordered four Egg McMuffins. All of a sudden he was hungrier than hell. He briefly considered getting the black van painted another color. But then he dismissed that idea, aware that no one had seen his forest preserve actions. Except, of course, the late Marcy Darcy.

As he sped toward his construction project, grinning and singing along with a Neil Young standard, he suddenly shouted, "Fuck me! I've got the old tingle back in my fucking balls!"

INQUIRY

CHAPTER FOURTEEN

Jack walked through the front entrance of Fit City on a July Chicago morning that was already nearing sweltering levels and nearly bumped into Moe, who was exiting in a hurry. They both laughed. Moe said, "Jack, you've got to stop spending so much time on the heavy bag in there and start improving your footwork."

"Very funny. What the hell are you doing leaving here before our workout time?"

"I had to get mine in early," Moe said. "I've got a breakfast meeting with a major client from the Big Apple. So, I got here at six. Listen," he continued, "I need to talk to you about something important." He glanced at his Cartier watch as his driver, the ex-Chicago Police detective Pete Dunleavy, pulled the maroon Lincoln Town Car up to the curb in front of the health club.

"Jack, can you meet for dinner tonight? Dino's at five?"

Jack responded, "What kind of Early Bird Special does your pal Dino provide you with at that hour?"

Moe ignored this jibe at his septuagenarian status. "I'm in a hurry, Jack. I expect to see you there."

"I'll be on hand, hungry and thirsty. Good luck peddling expensive pelts to the visiting New Yorker."

Moe paused at the car door. Looking back at Jack, he said, "Luck has nothing to do with how I play this fish from the waters of Gotham."

***

Dino's Ristorante on a Chicago Friday night hosted the usual bedlam involving many of the City's movers and shakers in search of good Italian food. Plus there was exposure to others of their ambitious ilk at this popular near North Side spot. A great deal of business got done here over the plates of pasta and/ or platters of chicken Vesuvio. The noise level in the main dining room accelerated by the clatter of chatter and culinary utensils hit high on the decibel meter.

As usual the customer list was made up of pols, money moguls, television notables, plus a sprinkling of actors and actresses either on their way up or down. Jack spotted one of the latter who gave him a cutting look as he brushed past her toward the hostess station. It was a tall black woman, once a regular on a soap opera series that had been recently cancelled. He heard her snarl, "Where you going Big Time? You. Whitey, I'm talkin' to you. The line starts back there."

Her companion and long time agent, a short middle-aged white man, stepped forward to block Jack's progress. Jack stopped, looking bemused, grabbed the man's left wrist and squeezed it heartily, and said "Shorty, cut the shit. Get out of my path before more hurt ensues." He released the man's wrist. Jack moved closer to him. "And tell your date back there," he continued as he nodded toward the incensed actress, "not to get so snooty even with that great booty she's got."

There was a ripple of laughter from the bystanders. Jack dropped the man's hand and stepped forward.

The air-conditioned interior was a relief. Jack tucked his sun glasses into his sport coat pocket and heard the resonant voice of Dino's veteran hostess, Marilyn Donato, Dino's wife, say, "Hi Jack."

He moved closer to her podium. Leaned forward to kiss her cheek, said, "Be careful how you say that, Marilyn."

She pulled back. "What? Why?"

Jack said, "Hearing the words hi and Jack might disturb some of the customers here. Reminding them of recent actions by some of their thieving employees. You know, trucks pulled over at the dead of night and emptied of their contents. It's called hijacking."

"Oh, Jack," she laughed. "Worry not. Look at the line of people stretched out to the door. You spot any criminal types?"

"I don't have to look, Marilyn. It's pretty much the regular crowd, several of them on the muscle to start a new promising hustle. I would say the number of white collar crooks on any day or night here outnumber the nocturnal type. Am I right?"

"Shoo," Marilyn said. "Go join Moe."

At the regular Kellman booth, located at the quiet rear area of the large room, directly beneath the huge black and white photo of Frank Sinatra with his arm around the shoulder of a young, obviously awestruck Dino. Moe's wife, Ida, welcomed Jack with a smile. She resumed conversing with daughter, Sarah, whose husband, Scott, was in earnest conversation with Moe. Moe looked over the top of his Negroni glass at his son-in-law with a skeptical expression. He looked up and smiled at Jack and motioned to him to sit next to him in the roomy, red leather booth. Immediately, Moe's regular waiter for some 20 years, Dino's cousin Bruno Savaglio, appeared to say, "Your regular, Mr. Doyle?"

Moe had become a regular at Dino's years earlier. As he once explained to Jack, "This is a convenient, comfortable place with good food and an interesting clientele. The owner, Dino, is the nephew of an old friend of mine from the West Side. Dino grew up there. He started his working life as a second-story burglar. He was terrible at it."

INQUIRY

"A great disappointment to his near relations, I am sure," Jack commented.

Moe said, "Well, of course it was a career setback. Dino had been recognized early on as a bright, personable young guy who got along great with people. Except, of course, when he was attempting to steal from them."

"Not, I presume," Jack said, "attributes useful to what you say was a bungling burglar."

"Exactly. So, they set up Dino in the restaurant business. Started with a small place on Taylor Street. Dino hired a topnotch chef, Damon DiCastri. Then he opened another restaurant in the South Loop before starting this northside place. It's gone gang busters from the start."

***

Moe said, "Jack, thanks for coming. You've met my son-in-law, Scott. I'd like him to tell you about a little horse racing project he's involved in."

Scott said, "Oh, Mr. Doyle, it's fabulous." His handsome young man's face flushed with enthusiasm. "I was just telling my wife and Moe about another winning day. Thanks to this new Racing Advisory Service I've discovered."

Moe signaled for the advance of appetizers by the attentive Bruno. Jack said, "Scott, how's it going - this new betting venture of yours? You know," he said, nudging Moe, "as I have often pointed out to your esteemed father-in-law, betting on stocks and betting on horses is the same deal. Although society somehow considers the former exercise in gambling much more acceptable than the latter."

Scott leaned forward, enthused, nearly planting his left elbow in the newly arrived platter of calamari. "I've been using something I discovered on the Internet. This Racing Advisory Service I started with a few weeks ago. The success rating is blue chip. The selections sent to me are for me only, directed to my personal account."

"I see," Jack said, thinking how crafty crooks have used the Internet to carry out the same touting scams employed for so many years by similar hustlers at racetracks. The so-called expert goes around giving a different "winner" to different people in the same race. If he's "given out" ten horses in the race, the one that wins will find its bettor, hurrying back for yet another. If this "personalized" flow of information works the same way, having been adjusted to modernity, then it is personalized advice bullshit, Jack thought.

"Scott," he said, "tell me about this service. Who runs it? What do you pay for your daily specials?"

"A fellow who identifies himself as Skip the Hip Horse Player. I learned his name is Dumke. Just a $100 a day is all I pay. Bargain time compared to the results!"

Moe asked, "You ever hear of this guy, Skip Dumke, Jack?"

"No. But I really don't pay any attention to any of the hustlers in that field. I learned that years ago when I walked out of the track after the last race, no matter what track I was at, and see guys holding up tip sheets and shouting 'Six winners here today!' The ink was hardly dry on the sheets that had just been printed up a little while earlier, using that day's results to lure the gullible. I'll tell you this. I have grave doubts about these tout outfits. Grave, as in leading to the financial cemetery."

Scott smiled. "Okay, I hear you. But I don't doubt this Skip is anything but on the level. I'm sticking with him." He reached for the breadsticks. Moe groaned. The entrees arrived.

An hour later, the Kellman party waited outside Dino's for Moe's Lincoln Town Car and driver, retired Chicago policeman Pete Dunleavy.

Jack said quietly, "Moe, I'll see what I can find out about this Skip the Hip. Maybe the guy's on the up and up. Though I think that's a longshot. But I'll let you know."

"Thanks, Jack."

Moe said, "How about doing something for me? Like asking your old buddy, Fifi Bonadio, if he knows anything about the screwy odds happening in some races at a few tracks, Monee Park among them."

"I suppose Ms. McCann, the beauteous Celia, has asked for your help in this matter?" Moe's sly grin prompted Jack to respond, "My friend, Celia, has a new last name. She's married to a guy named Calvin Douglas, a friend of her late husband. Which you probably knew, but just wanted to yank my chain anyway. Nice try."

Pete nestled the big Lincoln next to the curb and got out to open the door for the women. The men waited until Scott Epstein returned from the corner newspaper kiosk where he bought a copy of *Racing Daily* with information on the next day's races. He leaned against the car and opened the paper while starting to talk on his cell phone. Pete said, "Busy young man there, Moe."

Moe answered, "So it appears. We'll be ready to go here in a minute, Pete."

Moe turned his attention to Jack, "As to your question about odds manipulating? Only thing Feef mentioned to me was that it was happening only at tracks that had banned some owner named Ted Tilley. Feef was no way involved. His, ah, associates have very little financial interest in horse racing anymore. It's too well regulated. Old avenues of occasional chicanery no longer exist."

Scott said, "Ted Tilley? Yeah, big news when these tracks barred his horses without giving any reason to the public as to why. He has a major league stable, wins titles all over the place. Kind of puzzling," Scott said, before returning his attention to the entries in the *Racing Daily*.

Pete waited a couple more minutes until Scott got into the front seat passenger side. Then Pete turned and shook hands with Jack. "Haven't seen you in a while, Jack. You're looking tip, top. By the way, did you

INQUIRY

men hear about the death of Marcy Darcy, Pleasant Prairie Racetrack vice president?"

They said "no."

Pete said, "I just heard it on the radio. The woman got run over in Forest Preserve parking lot. That's where she usually went to jog. She was evidently hit by a car nobody saw. Sad story."

Jack said goodbye and walked briskly the ten blocks to home. Banging the front door behind him, he dialed Celia McCann, a number he knew he was fated never to forget.

"Jack, what's going on?"

"Did you hear about Marcy Darcy?"

Celia said, "Yes. That bad news is all over our racetrack. Marcy built Pleasant Prairie up to be a true success. Horrible to think of her gone."

Jack said, "First report said her death was an accident. I wonder about that."

"For heaven sakes, Jack, why?"

"I'm told this woman had received advice to rescind the Pleasant Prairie decision to bar the horses owned by Ted Tilley," Jack said. "Which she didn't do. Then, she's killed by some hit and run driver in a damn forest preserve parking lot. This is after she'd gotten the same sort of message your friend Nancy Roth told you about. This suggests cause and terrible effect to me. Scares the crap out of me. Because I know you also received one of those threatening messages."

"Oh, Jack," Celia sighed, "You seem to always come up with worst case scenarios."

Jack said, "I haven't been very far off the mark with those, my dear. Keep that in mind. I have a question. Is Monee Park one of the tracks that have refused stabling for the Ted Tilley horses?"

Celia said, "Well, yes. I was kind of talked into that by some other track operators. Yes, including Marcy, if you're wondering. They thought the way Tilley operated was detrimental to the sport. He only had a small string of horses here at Monee Park. I don't know the man at all. But I took the advice of my racing secretary, Tom Senzell, and went along with the others."

"Did you ever meet with this Tilley? Or his people? Explain the reasoning for your decision?"

Celia said, "I'm embarrassed to say I did not. I got a letter protesting my decision from Tilley's friend, a man named Gary Grunwald. He works for Tilley. I just politely wrote that what I was doing was in the best interests of my racetrack. I never heard another word from him."

Jack frowned, but instead of expressing his fear of another violent act of apparent retribution, said, "Okay then, Celia. What's done is done. I've got to go. Give my best to Calvin. I'll keep in touch."

CHAPTER FIFTEEN

Jack, who usually slept soundly, able to bat away the beginnings of bad dreams, failed to do so that night. After tossing and turning, he got out of bed right after six a.m. The hint of sunlight brightened the carpet on which he began his morning regimen of 100 sit ups and 100 pushups. The exercises failed to excise the concerns that had ruined his sleep.

Showered and dressed, he called Calvin Douglas's cell phone. The recorded message was of Calvin informing that he was to be "out of town and unavailable today. Please leave a message. I will respond when I return tomorrow."

"Well, shoot," Jack said. He put coffee on to brew, then glanced at his watch. He knew it was kind of early to make this next call but went ahead anyway.

Celia McCann picked up on the first ring. "I'm already in my office as usual, Jack, this time of day. What are you up to at this early hour?"

"Celia, hear me out. I know you're not going to like what I say. I was hoping to talk with Calvin before I brought this up to you. But he's not available."

Celia said, "He's in his hometown, Cleveland. Attending the funeral of his favorite aunt. I couldn't accompany him. We've got a big weekend of stakes racing coming up here."

"Well, I'm sure you know your husband and I are concerned about your safety after Marcy Darcy's death. When I spoke to Calvin the other day, he agreed with my idea. Has he mentioned it to you, Celia?"

"He has not. What is it you're talking about?"

Jack said, "About your safety. It's damn worrisome that Marcy, from one of the tracks that tossed Ted Tilley and was threatened with harm, is dead. Calvin and I are both concerned that there may be some kind of plan to harm others, too. Including you."

She laughed. "Oh, Jack, relax. Certainly the death of poor Marcy concerns me. But as far as anyone knows at this point, it was an accident, a hit and run, and the cowardly driver got away. An awful, one-time deal. So I'm not about to start cowering in the corner because of you two worry warts."

"Celia, I know you are a brave woman. Stubborn, too. All Calvin and I have in mind is that you might rescind your ban on Ted Tilley. There is nothing to tie him to these deaths, but such a move might be effective. Why not try it and see? That's all we're suggesting."

"I know Ted Tilley," Celia said." Not well. But enough to believe he's not any kind of person who would authorize murders. At the same time, I'm sticking with my decision regarding him not racing at Monee Park. I'm not backing down."

There was a silence. Then Jack said, "Celia McCann, you are a prime example of Irish stubbornness."

"Hah! As if you don't fall smack into the middle of that category."

"I guess I've not changed your mind," Jack said.

"By no means. I'm holding the line."

"No surprise to me there, Celia. I guess Calvin and I are going to be forced to take steps."

"Steps," Celia said. "What steps?"

There was no answer. Jack had hung up.

CHAPTER SIXTEEN

Ted Tilley was on his annual summer vacation on Upper Clear Lake near Antigo, WI. He and his family relished their two weeks each summer at this comfortable cottage that his late father had purchased some 30 years earlier. An avid fisherman, the senior Tilley had discovered Upper Clear Lake in the course of his lifelong pursuit of a mighty muskie. "Best fishing lake I've ever found," he told friends and family. "And the prettiest darn summer sunsets you'll ever see."

Ted made his regular morning call to Tilleys for Tools and More headquarters at 9 a.m. After six rings, Gary picked up his phone. "Hey, buddy," Ted laughed, "I thought maybe you'd skipped a day at the office."

Gary wiped the sweat from his forehead and leaned forward to look again at the news item on his computer screen. The one he had found when he turned on the Racing News channel minutes earlier. The one with the Marcy Darcy obit.

"So, anything new today, Gary?" Tilley continued. "I'm ready to launch a family attack on the Bass Lake walleye population."

Gary muffled a groan. "All is well, Ted. Yesterday's business reports are great. Have fun, boss. You deserve it."

"Thanks. Talk to you tomorrow. Keep the faith, Gary. And the ship on course. I'll be back in the office Monday."

Gary sat back in his chair, still sweating. "Christ, what is going on with my man, Rudy? Why hasn't he called me about this?"

***

Rudy abruptly sat up in bed when he heard the phone ring at 9:30 that morning. He ignored it. Any message, he'd retrieve later. As with every morning the last few months, ever since the "industrial mishap" as the lawyers termed it or "the catastrophic clunk on my head" as he called it, he found it more and more difficult to remember how to think or even say "catastrophic." He'd sustained a couple of "minor concussions" during his wrestling days. But nothing like this. He knew himself to be a seriously changed person. He had no idea what to do about that, except to go on.

Next to him, Treasure Defee stirred, shifted on the bed, her tee shirt having crept up her muscled back. The contrast between that white flesh and her sun-browned face, neck, hands, and arms was startlingly impressive.

They'd met early during a tequila fueled evening at Wee Hope, a bus-

INQUIRY

tling bar a few blocks down the street from his apartment. Rudy recognized a live wire when he saw one. He bought her a bunch of variety-flavored margaritas and watched admiringly as this slim, excited young woman danced her ass off in front of the aged juke box. He'd bought her a drink when she came off the dance floor and took the only open seat at the bar, the one next to him. Two half-drunk young men scurried over to talk to her. Rudy gave them one of his dark looks and they retreated.

"Good going, big guy. What do you do besides scare off guys?"

Rudy said, "I'm in construction. How about you?"

"I'm in horse racing," she said. "I work horses and groom them for trainer, Ralph Tenuta, at Heartland Downs."

Rudy grinned. "Cool. I'm kind of involved with racing myself."

Treasure looked at him appraisingly. "Yeah? Considering the size of you," she laughed, "I figure you to be a blacksmith. Seriously, what's your connection to racing?"

He ignored her question as he signaled the bartender for another pitcher of margaritas.

As the night shrank, so did the distance between them. After midnight, Rudy said, "Treasure, this has been great. Should I drive you home? You've downed a bunch of drinks."

"Hah! I can handle a bunch more," she said, almost toppling off her bar stool. "Besides, I don't feel like going home. And I got a ride here anyway. From that loser sitting over there in the far corner. I'm not going home with Skip Dumke. I'm dumping him for tonight," she giggled.

Rudy saw a concerned young man looking imploringly at Treasure, who continued to ignore him. "Who is that guy?" Rudy asked.

"Just a harmless goof who's crazy about me," she answered with a smile before draining her margarita glass. "I may have some use for him some day."

"Any use for me," Rudy said as he tossed a chunk of cash on the bar. "Like, you want to come spend the night at my place?"

After a brief hesitation, Treasure said, "Why the fuck not?"

She shimmied and shook her way to the door, many patrons at the tables raising their glasses in approval. It turned into a memorable night for both. This morning, he knew was her one day off each week from early work grooming, walking, and exercising horses at Heartland Downs. He didn't want to disturb her sleep, so well deserved after the sexual calisthenics they'd gone through the previous night.

Rudy, getting disability payments following his accident, eased out of bed. He was in no hurry. His construction crew, he knew, would already be working on the million dollar Arlington Heights McMansion they'd just begun. They didn't need him there. He closed the bedroom door, washed his face, and made a pot of coffee before returning Gary's call.

"Hey, Gary. What's up?"

"What's up?" Gary spat. "It's not what's up I'm calling about. It's what's down. Like the racetrack executives I hired you to frighten. Intimidate. Not fucking kill one of them!"

"You're talking too fucking loud Gary," he muttered through clenched teeth. "Hurting my head." Rudy clamped his large hand on his skull as another sharp pain dashed across it. It was one of the many now plaguing him sporadically day and night. The physician his insurance company sent him to, Dr. Isaac Lipman, advised Rudy, "Unfortunately, you are experiencing obvious signs of PTSD. Post-traumatic stress disorder. Very serious."

"Doc, what can I do?"

"Medically? Not much," Dr. Lipman said. "Legally? Get a good lawyer and sue the crew and company that carelessly dropped that object onto your head and into your life."

Gary said, "Rudy, listen carefully. Those things I wanted done against the track executives, stop now. Give it up. Ignore the remaining targets I gave you."

"You think I'm giving any of that money back now that you've changed your fucking mind? No way, bro."

Gary said, "I'm not talking about the promised money. I'll pay the agreed-upon contract price in full."

Silence. Gary finally said, "Is that a deal, Rudy?"

"Gary isn't going to tell me what to do," Rudy snarled. He slammed the phone down, cursing. Then he remembered his guest. He walked quietly to his partially-opened bedroom door and watched Treasure inspect his pants pockets. When he coughed and entered the bedroom, Treasure said, "I dropped my lipstick. I was looking for it."

"In my pockets?" Rudy laughed. "Weak explanation."

She moved close and put her arms around his back. "Let's take a little break for bed fun, big fella. Okay?"

In his office in upstate New York, Gary laid his head in his hands. "How can I tell Ted I've put into motion this screwed up enterprise? God help me."

INQUIRY

CHAPTER SEVENTEEN

Skip had watched, an arrow in his heart, as the entrancing Treasure had left the Wee Hope in the company of some big, tough-looking guy.

He'd been hooked on Treasure three weeks earlier, a Thursday afternoon at Heartland Downs. Race number two. He concentrated on his pick, Homey Hollis, the huge favorite in this field of bottom-level claimers. In his shirt pocket was a daily double ticket combining Doctor Kirby, winner of the opener, with Homey Hillis. To the delight of very few on hand, Doctor Kirby had scored odds of 21-1. Skip's $30 daily double ticket with Homey Hillis was worth major bucks.

A few minutes later Skip looked on in horror as Homey Hillis, after opening a long early lead, began to run out of steam in deep stretch. Skip was on his feet, waving the favorite on, shouting "Hang on you gutless bastard." Homey Hillis lost by a half-length. Skip sat down, feeling as if a Floyd Mayweather right cross had landed just above his heart.

Even being tortured by his hopes flaming out, Skip had been aware of a short, slim, very pretty and very vocal young woman seated three rows in front of him. She wore a tight white tee-shirt that emphasized her muscular, tanned arms and perky breasts. Her jeans were tight, too, showcasing her impressively rounded rump. He had a hard time looking away from her. He had to smile as she circled, arms raised, stopping only so Skip could make out the lettering on the back of her tee shirt. There, beneath the large head of a brown horse, he saw the words, "Don't Mess with the BOSS MARE."

What Skip did not relish were this girl's howls of triumph after this race and two of the three prior races. In each case, she'd shouted, "That's my horse. Come to me baby!" as the field thundered to the finish line. Her horses' average win payoff was $16.

"What the hell?" was all Skip could think.

He saw her leave her seat after the conclusion of each race and skip down the steps toward the winner's circle. There, she waved her rolled-up copy of *Racing Daily* at the victorious jockey who waited aboard his horse for the track photographer to take pictures for the delighted owner. Skip noticed that the riders all waved back at the girl, some smiling at her. He watched her jump around in a kind of victory dance.

John McEvoy

The final race on that afternoon's program was a mile and one-half marathon over Heartland Downs' grass course. All of Skip's research, all his laboriously arrived at speed numbers and pace fractions and class rankings screamed out Number Seven! A veteran turf horse named Special Shane being saddled by Heartland Downs' leading trainer, Ralph Tenuta.

Seven minutes before post time, Skip trotted up the steps into the clubhouse and found an open computerized betting machine. These devices had pretty much taken over the wagering area. They were popular among track management because they eliminated jobs held by unionized pari-mutuel clerks who had worked there for years and were paid top scale. They were also popular among the aging baby boomers and rising millennials who preferred not dealing with humans as they bet. Nearby were two betting windows manned by veteran clerks. They were primarily patronized by older customers since they had long ago developed a connection with them. They would ask, "What do you hear? Anything?" Questions machines could not answer. Skip sneered at these oldtimers as he approached the machine. He made his big win bet and hurried back to his seat overlooking the track. It was just in time to see Special Shane stumble so badly when coming out of the starting gate that his nose hit the turf. In a split second, his rider was catapulted off the horse's neck. Both horse and rider scrambled to their feet, apparently not seriously hurt.

Not as seriously hurt as Skip. Minutes later, oblivious to the between-race pony show featuring children riders, or the cooling breeze wafting in from the west on this gorgeous afternoon, Skip tore up his Racing Daily and dumped the remnants on the seat in front of him. He was going to throw down his expensive binoculars, too, but caught himself.

Inside the air-conditioned Heartland Downs Clubhouse, he continued to sweat, a combination of frustration and fury. He stopped in a men's room to wash his face, take deep breaths. Then he walked down to the next level to the Woulda Coulda Shoulda bar, a haven for bettors in need of alcohol and commiseration. He heard the man on his left say to the guy to his left, "That fucking winner of the last race was my original pick. But I got off him."

Skip thought, they could rename this bar, "My Original Pick" and still serve the same, sorry clientele. This was a perfect, disappointment-sodden oasis for losers such as himself. Bad bettors and, in his case, an unsuccessful Internet "Turf Advisor." In that venture he was now down to a lone customer, S. Epstein. And, he'd gotten a threatening phone call from some guy named Jack Doyle advising him to leave Epstein alone.

Midway through his second vodka, he felt a tap on his shoulder. It was the attractive young woman he'd watched vociferously celebrating her winning bets out in his clubhouse seat. A bright white smile in a tanned face and lively brown eyes made him think his lousy afternoon might improve.

"Hey, hello," Skip said, smiling.

INQUIRY

"Want company?" The young woman extended her small right hand and gripped his so strongly it surprised him.

"Jimmy," she said to the bartender, "hit me again. Put it on this handsome dude's tab." She poked Skip in the arm. "You're game for that, aren't you?"

Feeling he was being hustled, but happy for the diversion, Skip rapped his fingers on the bar and hollered, "Jimmy, make that a double. And I'll have another of mine.

"I'm Skip Dumke," he continued, "broken down horse player after the racing gods, yet again, pissed all over me today."

She said, "I'm Treasure Defee."

"Did you say, 'Pleasure Defee?'" he asked, leaning closer.

She laughed and patted his hand. "No, I said Treasure Defee. Yes, an unusual first name. Maybe someday I'll tell you about where it came from." She paused before saying, "So, you had a bad betting day at the racetrack? It can happen."

Skip shrugged. "After the disaster I just experienced at the end of the second race, things couldn't get much worse. And won't," he added, raising his glass, "now that I've met you." Skip gave her an edited description of his involvement with racing. Then he said, "What about you?"

"I'm from Cajun horse country in Louisiana. I grew up riding quarter horses on bush meetings for my daddy when I was six years old. He'd tie me on for those sprints on the weekends. Light as I was, I won a lot of them, and he won a lot of bets. He trained his own and ran them at the small tracks, cranking out a pretty good living there where just about anything goes."

"What do you mean?"

She took a drink of her beer before she said, "Down there a lot of times you don't get a lot of supervision. Many a night at Lafayette Park, after the last race when the stands are empty and the track lights are off, you'll see people bumping into each other on the track, in the dark, on the first turn. Using flashlights, like they're searching for night crawlers. But they aren't."

"What are they looking for?"

She reached over and patted his hand, saying, "Skip, darlin', they're out there to retrieve the buzzers, you know, batteries, joints that their jockeys dropped after crossing the finish line."

"Ah, hah." Skip thought he knew what she was talking about. "You mean those little things jockeys can hide in their hands and use to jump a horse forward? I think they call them machines. But they're outlawed in racing."

She laughed, "Illegal. As they should be. But not every user is caught."

"Do they work? I mean, I heard they're supposed to give a short, quick, electric jolt."

She said, "Only sometimes. They can work on some horses once or twice, but that's pretty much it. But when you're down there at one of those little night tracks where the purses are small, you're best shot is winning a bet. Many people tell their jocks to use the machines. At those tracks, well, they don't get caught all that often. Way of life, man."

"When did you leave Louisiana?"

"About five years ago. That was years after my daddy got killed." She took a swig of beer. Skip waited. Treasure finally said, "He was putting bandages on a mean old mare one morning, down on his knees in her stall, when she got it in her mind to kick him. Right in the head. Killed him."

"Jeez," Skip said. "What did you do?"

"I fuckin' celebrated, man. You gotta understand, down where I come from, the people's main specialties are eating, drinking, making zydeco music, and racing horses. I wasn't much good at the first three, but from the time my daddy tied me onto one of his quarter horses in a Sunday match race, I was good. You're talkin' quarter horses going two-hundred yards on dirt match races between wooden chutes. I won a bunch of races he'd bet on when I was hardly six years old. When I was eleven, maybe twelve years old, Pa started coming to my bedroom at night and putting his hands on me. Booze breath, gripping and groping. Second time, after I'd told Ma about the first, she heard me squealing and came in and sliced a piece out of Pa's hairy bare ass with a cleaver. That was the last time he came after me.

"He was a worthless son of a bitch. As soon as he won a bet, he'd start drinking the money up. Showboating, buying drinks for people he barely knew, then missing his job fishing in the bayous. If it weren't for Ma, we would have starved. She was a great cook. She ran a little carry-out restaurant out of the back of our trailer. Sold red beans and rice, gumbo, catfish, and po' boys. That got us by. Then she keeled over one hot Sunday afternoon, right at the stove. Heart attack. After she was buried, I packed my bag. No way was I going to stay in that trailer with Pa. There ain't much I miss about that life. Except…"

"Except what, Treasure?"

She thought for a minute, shook her head, and said, "Christmas season down there. Our neighbors built these small wood cabins weeks before. Laid reeds of sugar cane on the roofs. And on Christmas Eve, they threw gasoline on them and burned them down. You could see the fires in the night sky all around where we lived. I was told this started with the Cajuns 300 years before. The legend was that the fires would light the way for Papa Noel, that's what we called Santa Claus, to find them with his gifts. I can still smell the way those oak cabins and sugar cane burned.

"Christmas Eve down there was a big celebration. Folks open their homes Louisiana style to anybody, strangers or neighbors, on that special night. I don't know if it's right, but they believe this kind of thing doesn't happen anywhere else in the world. Hospitality like that, homes opened up to not only friends, but hundreds of strangers.

"Ma would squirrel away money from Pa all year so she could buy what she needed to be part of it. She was famous down there. Had picnic tables set up all around the trailer yard. She served up quarts of alligator sauce piquant, red beans and rice, jambalaya, chicken gumbo. Hundreds of people would come by and eat and laugh and sing through the night into the morning. This was my Ma's highlight. She only had one a year. Her food was loved, she was a legend down there."

Treasure sharply tapped her empty glass on the bar. Bartender Jimmy, who has been quietly listening, hurried to fill it.

Skip said, "Wow. You've had a lot of things happen in your young life. What'd you do when you finally left Louisiana?"

"First, I went to Kentucky and started working as an exercise rider at tracks there, then a couple of others in Ohio. Made a big mistake then. Got married. A young guy from Puerto Rico, Juan Salazar. He started to get lazy and put on weight and spent more time snorting cocaine than winning races. Nice guy, really, but the cocaine captured him. After a couple of years of that with Juan, bored and miserable, I got a divorce and drove up here to Heartland Downs looking for work. Took me just two days to get hired by one of the top trainers, Ralph Tenuta. Good guy. Ready to give me a new start at a new track.

"I make a pretty good living here. Trainers know I can work their horses like they want them worked. That I'll tell them what might be done to improve them—blinkers on or off, same thing with tongue ties and shadow rolls. I get on about 15 horses every morning, seven days a week, most of them for Tenuta."

Skip said, "I don't want to be nosey, but I will be. How much money can you make doing that?"

"Twenty bucks per horse. Sometimes a little more if it's a green two-year-old that needs good educating or an ornery old gelding that nobody wants to get on. I get along with horses, always have. That's why Tenuta pays me to work mainly for him, although other trainers will use me."

She got up, saying, "Excuse me a minute. I'm going to the john."

He looked on admiringly as Treasure, shoulders back, pulled down her tee shirt into her close-cut jeans, and walked off, saying quietly to himself, "What a great ass on her."

"No argument from me, man," Jimmy the bartender said. "Another round?"

Minutes later, Skip, buzzed now by the booze and Treasure, said, "How about I buy you dinner?"

She squeezed his arm. "What a great offer. But, sorry, I've got to go back to Mr. Tenuta's stable and help with the night feeding of the horses. Part of my job. They need me to do that every once in awhile when a groom calls in sick."

She stood up, reached over, and patted his cheek. "Thanks for the drinks and the talk. Hope to see you around."

Walking westward on the Heartland Downs backstretch road to the Tenuta stable, she smiled as she thought of her meeting with Skip. Nice looking guy but with "loser" written all over him. Prime for manipulation. She might have to let Skip screw her a few times, but that was okay, part of her modus operandi.

At the barn, she met Tenuta's longtime chief assistant and stable manager, Paul Albano. He was a man that, no matter how hard she'd tried, she couldn't win favor with him. He occasionally complimented her on her work but always seemed to regard her with suspicion. When she tried to come onto him one late, rainy afternoon in the stable office, Albano rebuffed her loudly. "Don't try that slut stuff on me, miss. It probably worked elsewhere for you. But not here." She hated him for this disdainful dismissal.

Her employer, 61-year-old Ralph Tenuta who she thought of as Old Man T, treated her with respect. She had nothing against this talented, well respected, veteran horseman. But in his open, trusting manner, she saw opportunity. He was tremendously proud of his reputation as the complete professional horseman, untouched throughout his long career by any suspensions or sort of scandal.

Treasure had read with great interest of a famous racing scandal on the East Coast a few years earlier. A carefully-edited video, purporting that a well-known trainer employed help that abused horses, led to a huge uproar in the animal-rights world. Nothing, however, ever came of it. The accused trainer was cleared after the investigation revealed the video was the product of a young man working for that stable and for two months had surreptitiously video recorded on his cell phone damaging, inflammatory scenes involving the woman he'd gotten involved with, the stable manager, who had thrown him over for a sensational young jockey.

Treasure had given a lot of thought to that case. Perhaps the intention of the young male animal rights advocate was to embarrass and expose disturbing stable practices. Didn't happen.

What Treasure had in mind was a similar scenario, but with a much different intent: blackmail. Even of kind hearted Ralph Tenuta.

However she set it up, she knew she'd need an accomplice.

Laughing to herself as she walked down the shedrow with a bucket of feed, Treasure thought she'd met an absolutely prime prospect that afternoon.

CHAPTER EIGHTEEN

This one was more challenging, he thought, grinning at the prospect. Not dawn this time, but dusk. Not a sparsely populated forest preserve, but a racetrack parking lot. Cahokia Park's twilight program was over. The exiting crowd had turned to a trickle, some laughing in boisterous moods, others walking with heads down and defeated looks toward their vehicles.

Rudy trained his binoculars on the Employee Entrance door. When people began emerging, he turned on the quiet engine of his stolen SUV. He'd nabbed it the night before without a whole lot of trouble after learning its owner, a neighbor of the Ozinga Company's Arlington Heights project, had taken his family to Disney World on vacation. The guy's garage security was a joke and the car was unlocked. He yanked the ignition, crossed the wires, and slid silently out of the driveway.

Rain began to fall. Three young men came out of the employee entrance. They stopped briefly to say goodbye before hustling to their cars. Three minutes later the track vice president scurried out and toward his BMW. Minutes ticked off with Rudy impatiently tapping his fingers on the steering wheel. Finally, out came Nancy Roth, a tall middle-aged woman in a stylish gray dress carrying a laden briefcase in one hand, an umbrella in the other to help shield from the now more incessant rain.

Rudy slowly drove forward 20 yards in her wake. He briefly considered using the same tactic he'd employed in the forest preserve parking lot when he'd crashed his door into the unsuspecting victim. He'd messed that up, no question - killing instead of delivering a bruising threat. His idea had been to frighten Marcy, the early morning runner. But he'd accelerated in the last few seconds and sent her on a fatal flight to the parking lot pavement. Death by vehicle. Driving away that early morning, his usual slashing headaches declined. A surge of adrenaline hit him.

His window down, he heard the woman in gray click her car door to open as she approached it. Rudy took two deep breaths, briefly closed his eyes, then stomped on the accelerator. Nancy Roth was six feet from her car when she heard him coming. Startled, she turned, dropped her umbrella and briefcase.

"Here's our deer in the headlights," Rudy shouted triumphantly as he sped forward and sent the woman in gray hurtling into the air in front of him. Right after the collision, Rudy hit the brakes and got out. The woman was motionless as he looked down at her. Papers flew out of her smashed briefcase and flew in the rain-filled wind. A few attached themselves to her bloody, battered head.

Back behind the wheel, Rudy scanned the empty parking lot. He floored the car and aimed his left wheels over the prone form in front of him. The bumping that resulted sent a surge of thrill through him. Speeding out of the track entrance parking lot, Rudy checked the rearview mirror. The only thing visible was the woman in gray's body next to her car.

He zipped onto the street, juiced now, happily pounding his big right hand on the steering wheel.

"Fuck me," he laughed, "that was a kick and a half."

Fifty-five minutes later, Rudy had returned the stolen, or borrowed as he phrased it, vehicle to its absent owner's garage. "Hope he's having as much fun in Disney World as I am here," Rudy said. He closed the garage door and walked unhurriedly the three blocks to his SUV. He wasn't hungry, he wasn't pumped. He drove home, opened a six-pack of Coors Light, and lay on his couch watching Fox News.

INQUIRY

CHAPTER NINETEEN

St. Louis, Mo—Funeral services were held here Friday for Nancy Roth, general manager of Park Racetrack.

Ms. Roth was killed shortly before midnight Wednesday as she walked to her car after the conclusion of the Cahokia Park night program. She was fatally struck by a vehicle that sped away without stopping.

The lone witness was parking lot attendant, Diego Velasquez, who said, "Ms. Roth got hit by a black car with no license plates that I could see. It sped up right at her. I shouted for her to watch out, but too late. I couldn't believe what I was seeing. That car just ran her down and then ran over her. It was awful."

Ms. Roth, 61, served in several capacities in thoroughbred racing over a career spanning four decades. She held her most recent post at Cahokia Park for the last five and one-half years.

She created a racing industry uproar a couple of months before when she angrily complained about damage "being done to my track and others by people manipulating the odds via computer just before the start of races. We have been hit by a barrage of criticism from bettors who feel they are being manipulated. It's like some weird outside force has taken malicious control. Whoever is doing this must be tracked down and stopped.

"The step I have taken is barring all horses owned by Ted Tilley from competing at Cahokia Park. I'm not saying Mr. Tilley has anything to do with this betting scandal. But the presence of his horses, as dominating as they can be, helped create this situation. I can't tell you how angry this situation makes me."

Among the eulogists at the funeral Mass was Celia McCann, president of Chicago's Monee Park race track. She described Nancy Roth as, "a great friend, outstanding racing executive, devoted wife and mother. Wherever Nancy worked, she made friends and stimulated progress with her outstanding forward approach to horse racing. Her death, of course, is a great loss to her family…and also to the racing industry that Nancy served so well for so long."

CHAPTER TWENTY

"I've got to see you. Quick."

Celia, startled, got to her feet and said, "Jack, where are you?"

"I'm in your track parking lot. Meet me in the clubhouse dining room. You can buy me lunch while I upbraid you."

"About what?" Celia said. But Jack had hung up. "That man can be so exasperating," she said to herself. She strode into the outer office. "Shontanette, I'll be in the clubhouse dining room if you need me."

"Really? Kind of early for lunch for you. Should I hold your calls?"

"Please do. I'm meeting Jack Doyle down there." She turned and hurried out the door.

"Oh, my," Shontonette murmured.

***

Five minutes later Celia hurried to her regular table in the far corner overlooking the racing strip. She saw Jack, head down, reading some papers that were spread before him on the white tablecloth. He looked up, got up, pulled out a chair for her.

"This better be good, Jack. I have a very loaded agenda today. The racing commission chairman, head of the Jockeys' Union, plus some parking lot attendants complaining they're underpaid.

"My husband, Calvin, will be joining us. He was coming out for lunch anyway. He just called me from the parking lot. He would like to meet you and find out what this urgent meeting is all about."

Jack said, "Fine."

She took a sip of water. Reached across the table to lightly tap his hand. "You're looking well, Jack."

"Not as well as you, Celia."

Monee Park's longtime head waiter, Harry Himmelblau, smiled as he delivered their drinks, an ice tea for Celia and black coffee for Jack, and said, "Good to see you, Mr. Doyle."

"Visa versa," Jack said. He watched the spry septuagenarian scurry back to the kitchen. "Harry is the only Jewish food deliverer I know who doesn't work in a deli."

"My late uncle hired Harry the first year he owned Monee. As you know, he died. But Harry keeps going. Terrific man. We are so lucky to have him. There isn't a clubhouse dining room patron who doesn't ask for him."

INQUIRY

She turned and smiled as Calvin walked to their table. He bent down to kiss his wife. Jack got up to greet Celia's smiling husband, then felt his normal size hand being enveloped by the ex-basketball star's hand. "Heard a lot about you, Jack. Glad to meet you. What brings you out here today?"

"Well, Calvin, it's about important information that has been withheld from me by your lovely wife."

Her face flushed, green eyes narrowed, Celia barked, "What are you talking about?"

"I'm talking about the fact that you, Celia, as head honcho of Monee Park, some weeks ago barred Ted Tilley's stable of horses. Which you never mentioned to me the last time we talked."

Celia shrugged. "Well, it just didn't come up. You called me about reserving a box seat one Saturday for Moe Kellman's son-in-law. I did."

She signaled the observant waiter Himmelblau for a refill of their drinks. "I just didn't think it was that important. That it wouldn't much matter to you."

Jack said, "Harry, cancel my black coffee. Bring me a Bushmill's on the rocks."

"Water back as per the usual?"

Jack nodded. Shook his head admiringly as he watched Himmelblau hustle off. "That man surely doesn't miss much. That, my dear," he continued, looking at Celia, "is something you could learn about from him."

Calvin plunked his forearms on the table, leaning forward, black eyes blazing. "What the hell is that supposed to mean, Jack? My wife is as smart a woman as any I've ever met. And the best! Who are you to be questioning her judgment? Damn!"

Jack bristled. "Don't start ragging me, man. What I'm here for is in all your best interests. You better hear me out, Calvin."

Celia threw back her head, laughter erupting. "Gentlemen, please, cut down on testosterone time. Jack, tell us what this is all about. Calvin, we'll just listen."

Jack said, "My concern is this. Two executives at tracks that rejected Ted Tilley's stable have recently died. Marcy Darcy and Nancy Roth. Odd circumstances. Marcy was jogging near a forest preserve. Roth got run over in a track parking lot. According to Matt O'Connor's story in today's *Racing Daily*, both victims had received threatening and, of course, anonymous emails warning them in effect to 'Play Fair With Tilley. Or else.'

"So," Jack continued, "I have some questions for you, Celia. One, why didn't you tell me that Monee Park was one of the tracks barring Tilley's horses? Two, did you receive one of those anonymous emails? Finally, if you did, why the hell didn't you tell me?"

Calvin said, "Jack, lower your voice. We can hear you. The kitchen staff doesn't have to."

"Okay, Calvin, you're right. But I tend to get worked up when a good friend of mine, such as your wife, seems to ignore threats, ones that I could try to help her defend against. As a player known in his days at Northwestern as a great communicating team captain, I'm sure you can understand that, right?"

Calvin smiled and said to Celia, "You didn't tell me Jack was such a sarcastic son of a bitch."

"I thought you'd pick up on that first time you spent a few minutes with him."

She turned to Jack. "Yes, Jack. We did receive a strange email complaining about the ban on the Tilley horses. Suggesting that we reconsider 'or else.' Whatever that was supposed to mean. I talked about it with my management staff and our legal advisors. They all agreed we were in the right by keeping Tilley out. And we didn't think this sort of threat should be taken seriously."

Jack asked, "Do you know Ted Tilley?"

"Not really. I mean I met him once in the winner's circle here after a horse of his won a stakes race. Seemed to be a pleasant sort."

Jack said, "This is where I admit to some confusion as to why you and those other tracks barred him. According to what I've read, he never broke any rules, except, maybe rules of decorum. This new guy comes into the game and starts to dominate. He wins race after race, often with horses that he claimed and then dropped down in class. He was sucking up purse money. So, what I'm asking, is why did you decide to blackball him?"

Celia signaled the attentive Himmelblau for more coffee. She paused, looked out the nearby window before saying, "I did it because I thought it was the right thing to do for Monee Park business. The Tilley stable was running roughshod over its competitors. Their horses were usually the favorites. A lot of our bettors just got bored. Stayed away from these low-paying winners. That badly hurt our pari-mutuel handle. I mean I know this sounds strange, but Tilley's success was costing us money. Very unusual, not for just Monee Park but for others where Tilley had horses. Those others finally concluded that barring Tilley was in their best interests. I eventually decided to go along with them."

Jack said, "So, it was nothing personal. Just business. That's what you're saying?"

Celia said, "Don't go all Godfather on me, smart guy. I did the right thing for Monee Park. It was perfectly within my rights to do so."

Himmelblau poured more coffee, substituted a new Bushmill's for Jack's empty glass, and Jack pushed it aside. "Calvin, you ever been to Vegas? Do any gambling there?"

A rumble of laughter. "When I played in Vegas, it was for good old Northwestern in a little holiday tournament with three Pac 10 powerhouses. We got our Big Ten asses kicked. Not a fond memory, Jack. Why do you ask?"

Jack said, "I presume you student athletes had no time to devote to card playing?"

"You gotta be kidding. Of course not. Our coaches wouldn't let us within blocks of the casinos."

Jack continued, "My point is that if you had played cards there, blackjack, and you wound up winning a lot, night after night, casino managers would tab you as a 'card counter.' Somebody who had managed to beat their system honestly. No cheating, just superior playing. And, they'd never let you play again. You'd be barred. Not because you were doing anything illegal, any cheating. No, but because you were too good at it. All the gamblers I know find that corporate practice to be self-serving, reprehensible, un-American, and fucking awful.

"If you're good at winning their games, too good for too long, they're gonna toss your ass out of there. This happened to a couple of smart, honest, resourceful friends of mine, Don Gutfriend and Tom Botzau. They were doing great until they were told to pack up and stay out. That was a few years back. But as far as I know, that remains the Vegas Policy. 'If you're too good at the game, we won't let you play.' A wonderful way to run a business where the odds are always against the bettors in the first place."

He turned to Celia. "What you and the other tracks in your little group have done is the same thing the Vegas masters do in barring card counters. Not because these winners were doing anything illegal. Just because they were too good at it. I find this approach repugnant. Penalizing legitimate successful efforts. That stinks. Celia, I'm surprised you would go along with this weak-kneed practice."

Celia said "I admit that decision has bothered me. But I heard very convincing arguments from the other tracks that closed down Tilley."

Jack leaned across the table toward her. "Let's keep in mind that two of those convincing colleagues of yours are now dead."

Celia, eyes down, replied softly, "Yes, Jack, I am aware of that."

"Of course she is!" insisted Calvin. "We both are."

"I've got to admit," Jack said, "this whole thing baffles me. I researched Ted Tilley. Found his decent baseball career, his tremendously successful management and expansion of the family hardware chain. He's a family man. Outstanding citizen by all accounts. There's nothing in his record to suggest he'd resort to anonymous threats attempting to get his way.

"Of course," Jack continued, "nobody's public record ever contains the whole story. That's why I asked Moe Kellman to use his considerable resources, some of them even legal, to vet this Ted Tilley. With the help of his lifelong friend, Outfit boss Fifi Bonadio, Moe was able to dig deep. When he did, he found nothing to indicate Ted Tilley is anything other than a truly model citizen. That's what makes this situation so strange."

Calvin asked, "Have you ever met this guy?"

"No," Jack said. "But I think the time has come." He moved his chair back from the table and got up. "I'm going to book a flight to Ted's hometown tomorrow. Thanks for the drinks. Great to see you, Celia. And good to meet you, Calvin."

Celia and Calvin walked with Jack to the clubhouse elevator. She tugged at his sleeve. "Can I, well, finance your trip? Retain you, your services? As I've done in the past?"

Jack laughed. "Yeah, that last time almost got me killed. Calvin, ask her to tell you about that some time. Seriously, Celia, I probably need more to be restrained than retained. This whole thing pisses me off. Calvin, I'm sure you'll keep a protective eye on your wife. Who knows? She may be on some asshole's hit list."

Calvin placed one of his long, strong arms around Celia's slim waist and pulled her close. "Count on that, Jack."

The elevator door opened and Jack entered. "I'm sure I can, Calvin," Jack said.

As they walked back to the dining room, Calvin said, "You never told me this Jack was such a, well, character."

"That hardly begins to describe Jack Doyle," she said.

INQUIRY

CHAPTER TWENTY-ONE

Jack exited the elevator and began to walk to the parking lot when a gastric rumble reminded him he hadn't had breakfast. He was only a few yards away from a place he knew he'd be fed well. So, he walked around the side of the clubhouse to the entrance of the jockeys' room. At the door, which was usually guarded against irate bettors who might seek vengeance, he was greeted by the familiar voice of Harry Schwartz, long-time member of the Monee Park security force/team.

"Hey, Mr. Doyle," the old fellow croaked, struggling to his feet from the park bench on which he had been reclining. He was shakily holding a can of soda in one hand, a large submarine sandwich in the other. Jack had advised Celia McCann to retire this notorious bumbler years earlier, but to no avail. Her late uncle Jim Joyce, from whom she'd inherited Monee Park, hired Harry years ago, she'd told Jack, adding, "Why, I do not know. But he left strict instructions Harry was to remain on the payroll as long as he wanted to. As you know, that old fart will never quit a job this easy. Plus, he's very sociable. The jocks all like him."

"Harry," Jack said, "you're looking…well, like you look." He took in the soiled gray jacket and recognized food spots on it that appeared to be in the same places he remembered from their last meeting. Harry's face had several days' worth of gray stubble. His glasses were so smudged Jack could barely make out the eyes behind them. That, too, was a traditional Schwartz look.

They shook hands. "Catching any winners, Harry? With your access to the riders, you should be getting some good tips, right?"

"Oh, Mr. Doyle, if only that were the case. I'm on very, very good terms with these fellows. But I learned years ago to ignore any 'hot tips' they might come up with. The thing is, they really believe in those tips. Years ago, somebody told me that the great rider Eddie Arcaro said he could retire and make more money booking the bets from the jocks' room than riding horses. After burning money for years, I finally came to the point where I saw his point. But, I still love these guys. Little men strong enough to guide 1,000 pound animals. Most of them really good guys. Not all, of course."

Jack was tempted to ask Harry to name the others, then thought better of it. "Harry, I'm hungry. Want to come along to the room and I'll buy you breakfast after you finish your lunch?"

Harry took a giant bite out of his sandwich, sat down, and patted the midsection straining the buttons on his uniform. "Naw, but thanks." He nodded toward the jockeys' room entrance. "Those young fellas take good care of me, bringing me whatever I ask for. Go on in. Clarence is still the best chef ever."

Jack paused at the entrance to the jockeys' room, this athletes' sanctum sanctorum. The scene was familiar from his previous time working as publicity director at Monee Park. All the riders had finished their morning work on horses for trainers who employed them. Now, they were relaxing. The two ping-pong tables were alive with action and Jack once again marveled at the reflexes of the competitors. Two tables were packed with players of racecourse rummy, loud and frequently profane comments being exchanged. Through the window to the exercise area, he saw treadmills humming. In the far corner of that room was the hot box, a sauna-like contraption designed to sweat water weight off the nearly zero body fat on these athletes.

First time Jack ever gave much thought to jockeys was when, as a teenager, his uncle Art took him to Heartland Downs one summer afternoon. After the first race, they stood at the railing to the path where the riders, having dismounted, walked to their room. He was astounded at the vituperative statements being hurled by a small section of the crowd. "Martin, you pin head, where'd you learn to ride. On a hobby horse? Don't grin at me, pea brain... Another major mistake by a midget. You stink, Valdez."

Uncle Art tapped his nephew on the shoulder. "You hear these idiots? They lost their bets. Now, they want to take it out on their jockeys. What a joke they are! Jockeys are some of the best conditioned, strongest pound-for-pound athletes in the world. Most weigh less than 114 pounds, some far less. Yet they control 1100 pound animals traveling 35 miles an hour." Uncle Art shook his head. "At least a half-dozen, on average, are seriously hurt each year. I'm not talking about the hundreds of broken collarbones, arms, wrists, ankles, and concussions resulting from falls during the races. I'm talking about the ones that are thrown off horses and wind up in wheel chairs for the rest of their lives. Yet, these goofs," he said, pointing at the very vocal critics nearby, "have no idea."

Jack headed to the small lunch counter at the far end of the room and took one of the half-dozen stools. In a chair next to a sizeable grill, he saw a pair of short legs sticking out from behind an upraised *Racing Daily*. Rapping the counter top with his knuckles, Jack said, "What does a man have to do to get service around here?"

Clarence Meaux lowered the paper. Grinning, he got up and walked to the counter. "Jack Doyle, as I live and still breathe. What are you doing here in your old haunt? Great to see you, man."

INQUIRY

"Great to see you, too, Clarence."

Clarence, a short, stocky man with slicked-back black hair and a pencil-thin mustache, extended his hand. They shook. Jack said, "I see you've kept that 'stache that makes you like a Bourbon Street pimp. I guess they can take the boy out of Naw Awlans, but…"

"Hasn't hurt my love life one bit," Clarence shot back. "I've cultivated a small string of fillies here better than I did when I was the country's leading apprentice rider."

Jack said, "I remember that. It was many years and many pounds ago." Clarence was a riding sensation at age 16 and 105 pounds. He won a national award as leading apprentice of the year. Then reality stepped in. He grew three inches in one summer and expanded to 135 pounds, which ended his career as a jockey. But not as an ardent appreciator of great food.

"What are you hungry for, Jack? I've fed all those boys over there."

"Something not on your jockey diet, Clarence. How about a couple of scrambled eggs, two pieces of bacon."

The Clarence Meaux-designed jockey diet was carefully controlled, calorie-measured meals, "Much better than what I came up on," Clarence said.

U. S. jockeys, regardless of where they plied their trade, usually could not get mounts if they weighed over 114 pounds. To get down to that level, many were forced to spend hours in a hot box sweating, or running around the track in the mornings in heavy jackets, or, as a last resort, "flipping" or "tossing", which meant regurgitating food recently ingested.

Clarence had employed all those methods in his abbreviated second year of riding. Without the advantage of a five-pound allowance for an apprentice, he struggled, both getting mounts and keeping his weight down. Finally, track owner Louie LaCombe called him into his office. "Clarence, here's some advice. Retire."

"And do what? Riding's all I know. It's the weight thing that's ruined me. I just can't get it down without starving myself, getting so weak I can hardly hang on to a horse. I just turned 20. I got nothing going."

Louie said, "I understand you put on some great crab boils and barbeques for your friends on the backstretch. That you make a great jambalaya and seafood gumbo."

Clarence smiled. "Yes. That's true. I like cooking. It's fun for me and fun for the backstretch workers."

"Well, how about this? My chef in the jocks' room kitchen has just quit on me. No notice, no goodbye. What about you taking over his job?"

Stunned, Clarence said, "Whoa, boss. I don't know…I've never really cooked in a real kitchen. I don't know…"

Louie convinced him to try it, thus launching Clarence's career as a specialist in effective, healthy, tasty diets for jockeys. He worked La-

Combe's Fair Grounds in the winter, then Monee Park in the summers.

"Jack, I'll start your breakfast." Looking past him, Clarence said, "Here comes a prime example of my work. Look at this oldster," he grinned. "Pull up a stool here, Eric. Say hello to Jack Doyle."

Jack said, "I know Eric. I wrote a lot of press releases about him a few years ago."

Eric Broussard, perennial leading rider at Monee Park, shook Jack's hand before taking an adjacent stool. His tanned face was agleam. He used the towel he had around his neck to wipe his face and closely shaved head. "Pardon the perspiration. I just finished my workout." Then he toweled off his muscular arms before tossing the moist cloth right into the middle of a laundry hamper located next to the wall.

Jack said, "I've heard about those workouts of yours. Very, very impressive."

"Well, good enough to allow me to keep doing what I love at age 48," said Eric. "Clarence, pour me some water. Did you hear anything new about Vasquez?"

"No, Eric. The update on the Paulick Report this morning said the kid was still in critical condition."

"Are you talking about Juan Vasquez? The youngster from Puerto Rico who used to ride here?" Jack asked.

"Yeah. He got in a bad riding accident at Gateway Park in California night before last," Eric replied. " Remember, he went out there a few months ago. In the feature race yesterday, his horse snapped a leg and fell. Juan got thrown off, then trampled by horses that had been behind him. Goddam sad situation."

Eric was a racing legend. A winner of more than 4,500 races and hundreds of millions in purses. Multiple jockey championships at Midwest tracks. This in spite of numerous riding accidents, broken bones, even a punctured lung three years previous. But, on he went.

Jack said, "Eric, what did you do today already?"

"Started out of my apartment at 5:30. Rode my bike here ten miles as fast as I could. Got in the exercise room and did an hour on the treadmill."

Clarence said, "Jack, I gotta tell you what this man did after that. I've watched him in wonder many a morning. Most of them, he lays his 114 pounds down on a weight bench and starts lifting. Every day Eric presses a 200 pound bar at least 20 times. Seeing this small fella shoving metal more than his weight toward the ceiling time after time, well, it's something to see. Like watching a squirrel throwing a shot put," he laughed.

Eric said, ruefully, "A few years back I could rip off 30 reps. I guess I'm weakening."

"Ah, cut the shit," Clarence said. "These younger jocks here look at you like they're looking at an old super man."

Eric said, "You know what I tell those boys? Well, the few that ask me for career advice. I tell them stay away from all the broads that come on to you when you're going good and making money. It took me two very costly divorces to learn that lesson. Plus, I tell them, don't drink alcohol or use drugs. Stay off fatty meats and fried food. And work as many horses in the morning as you would love to ride in the afternoon. Winning races! That's what it's all about."

Clarence turned around from the griddle and said, "Years ago I heard an old, retired jock tell me that the best advice for a young rider can be found on the lid of a mayonnaise jar. It reads 'Keep cool, but don't freeze.'"

"Good one," Eric laughed.

Jack said, "Eric, one of my favorite racing writers, Matt O'Connor, has called you the best conditioned jockey in the country."

Eric laughed. "I wish. Anyway, Clarence, would you make me that vegetable smoothie? And give Jack what he wants. Put it on my tab."

Clarence got up and turned to the grill, saying, "You've got no tab with me, my brother." Their bond was long and strong. Two products of Louisiana's Cajun country, famous for the many star jockeys who came from there.

Eric asked, "What brings you out here this morning, Jack?"

"I came out to talk with Celia McCann about her ban on the Ted Tilley stable." Eric shook his head. "Gotta tell you, Jack, I just didn't understand that. I rode a lot for the Tilley outfit here, won a ton of races. None of their horses ever tested positive for any drug. When they got the boot, I was amazed."

"Do you know Ted Tilley?" Jack asked.

Eric smiled. "Sure do. Whenever I won a race for him and he was here to watch, he'd lead his horse into the winner's circle and reach out to put a $100 in my left riding boot. Now, mind you, this was on top of the normal ten percent of the purse I earned. Me and all the boys over there," he said, nodding toward the large area of the quarters, "sure as hell wish all owners were as generous as Mr. Tilley. Believe me, I was sorry to see his horses thrown off here."

Jack said, "Well, bad things have happened since that happened. Two track executives dying recently. Tilley protesting his innocence and filing lawsuits." He reached for a napkin as Clarence brought a platter of eggs and bacon with wheat toast on top of the fried potatoes.

Eric looked at the food and groaned. "Gotta get out of here. That's too tempting for me." He shook Jack's hand and headed for the showers.

Clarence waited until Eric departed before shaking his head, then saying, "That guy is super special, Jack. One of the most determined individuals I've ever known, or known about. These younger jocks in here," he said, gesturing toward the bustling room behind them, "have the sense to respect the hell out of Eric Broussard. Not only for his self-discipline, but his decency. If any of these guys have the sense to ask him for advice, to critique what they are doing in races, Eric never holds back. That's something you don't see too often in professional sports. A top guy generous in that way to people who are competing against him and trying to take money out of his pocket.

"And the other jocks, for the most part, don't resent Eric Broussard's mastery of them. That kid just coming out of the workout room, Billy Baird, said to me last week, how impressed he was with Eric. Billy, come over here. Say hello to my friend, Jack Doyle. I'll get you some tea. Tell Jack about Eric."

Billy, still in his workout clothes, took the stool next to Jack and they shook hands. Jack said, "Clarence, here, was just telling me about Eric. He said you were a rival of his. I see in the paper you're second to him in the standings at this meet."

Billy grinned. "Let's be on the square here, Jack. I'm a distant second to that old fella." He sipped his tea, started to reach out for a saltine cracker, but brought his hand back.

"Let me say this about Eric," Billy said. "I can't believe, at his age, how strong and competitive he is. Last Wednesday in the feature race, Eric came boiling up the rail that I thought I'd closed off. I had tightened it up, man. Most of the jocks won't go into those narrow traps. But Eric does. And he beat me in a photo finish, and we're galloping our horses back, and he's laughing about it afterwards. I couldn't even get mad about it. He's too good a guy."

Billy said ruefully, "Someday that old fella will hang up his whites and give the rest of us a chance. But," Billy continued as he got up and reached to shake Jack's hand, "I do not believe that day is anywhere close to near. Nice to meet you."

***

Clarence said, "Don't bother with the hot sauce on those eggs, Jack. I hid some lively hot pepper pieces in there."

"Fine with me. You don't do much wrong there, chef."

"What about this Ted Tilley, Jack? Do you think he's done wrong? Something we don't know about?"

Jack grimaced. "There's something wrong with these eggs, Clarence?"

"What?"

"Yeah," Jack smiled. "There's not enough of them. As to your question about Ted Tilley. Well, I'm going to do my best to check him out. I'm going to go see him."

INQUIRY

CHAPTER TWENTY-TWO

Jack rented a Ford Focus at the Albany airport and drove 120 miles north to Ted Tilley's Freedom Farm, one of upstate New York's equine showplaces. His appointment with Tilley was for nine o'clock that morning. As always, Jack was on time. Tilley wasn't. He had left word at the farm gate apologizing, saying he'd be there in a half-hour, and suggesting that Jack take the long drive to the Stallion Barn where he would be met by farm manager Wardell Simmons.

Jack, or "Mr. Excessively Punctual," as he was called by Nora Sheehan, shrugged off his irritation and followed directions. He parked in the large graveled lot east of the rectangular barn complex. It was flanked by two long structures for broodmares, yearlings, and runners back from the tracks now with time on their hooves. Jack whistled softly at the sight of this obviously very expensive and carefully maintained home for Tilley's horses.

Out of the car, he put on his sunglasses and waited as a stocky, middle-aged man in work shirt, blue jeans, and boots came toward him, his hand extended. "Mr. Doyle, good morning. Ted said you might be along. I'm the farm manager, Wardell Simmons. Glad to meet you. I'll be happy to show you around."

"Good meeting you, Wardell," Jack smiled. "Yeah, I'd love to see the place. Where are you now in your morning schedule?"

"We're just about to work a few head over on our training track on the west side of the property. Come along," he said, pointing to a green pickup truck with Freedom Farm emblazoned on both doors. "I'll drive you over there."

Wardell whistled softly as he started the truck. Jack noticed the man's lined, tanned face and the powerful hands on the steering wheel. A workman's hands, Jack thought.

Driving along the long concrete roadway past white wood fences and lush pastures, Wardell asked, "Ever been to a thoroughbred horse farm, Mr. Doyle?"

"Yes, Wardell. And please call me Jack." As they continued, he looked at the broodmares and this year's crop of their foals. Dozens of them. Some of the youngsters dashed away briefly before returning to their dams' sides. Others, heads down and tails swishing, grazed avidly.

John McEvoy

Jack said, "A friend of mine and I owned a very good racehorse named Plotkin. He stands at a farm in Kentucky. I've visited him there."

Wardell turned to Jack and said, "Oh. I didn't know you had that horse, Plotkin. Hell of a runner. Now making his mark as a stallion. Well, sure, I guess you'd know all about breeding farms."

"Ah, my partner and I got super lucky with Plotkin. We bought him for $50,000 as a two-year-old. Turned out to be one of the best bargains ever. Over the next two years, he won stakes and purses of just over $300,000. Now, he's breeding to 80 mares per year at $20,000 a pop. His first foals come to the races next year. People who have them say they look and act good. Like their daddy. Anyway, we'll see."

"I'm sure you know, Jack, in this business the proof ain't in the pudding. It's in the first year the stud's offspring gets on to the racetrack."

Jack said, "I know that very well. But until they do, Plotkin is providing my partner and I with a very nice annual profit. Serving 80 mares a year as he does now, Plotkin brings us $1.6 million every breeding season."

"Nice numbers! How many partners did you say you have in Plotkin?"

"Just one. Moe Kellman, great friend of mine. And he'd be the first person to say how lucky we were with this modestly bred, yet very talented, horse. Actually, Wardell," Jack continued, "I worked one summer on a farm in Kentucky. It was owned by a man named Rexroth. I was there undercover to help the FBI convict that bastard for insurance fraud. Rexroth was killing his own less productive stallions. Fortunately, it worked. Rexroth is in federal prison in Wisconsin for a good long stretch."

Wardell said, "Sure, I remember that now." He shook his head. "I will never understand why anybody would intentionally harm a horse."

"It's beyond me," Jack said. "Starting when I got there, I loved the horses and liked, no, I'd say loved some of the honest workers who were inadvertently caught up in Rexroth's criminality. I have some great memories involving them. As for Rexroth, I take pleasure picturing him behind walls in an orange jump suit."

Wardell pulled the truck up next to the wooden railing that surrounded the half-mile dirt training track. "Let's see what we've got going on here, Jack."

Jack closed the truck door behind him. He lifted his face to the morning sun and took deep breaths of the familiar and welcome odors of newly cut grass. The sounds of horses exercising also sparked his spirits, their feet pounding the loam, the sounds of their exercise riders urging them on.

Wardell said, "That dark bay moving up the rail toward us, that's our current best hope. There's one every year. He's got good pedigree and looks, all the promise in the world. We're really excited about him. Mr. Tilley has decided to name him We'll Get Back. Look how nice he moves."

INQUIRY

"Impressive, Wardell." He recognized here the kind of passionate involvement in horses he'd observed so often before, not just in Kentucky but at the Chicago tracks. For many of the workers in the thoroughbred business, it was truly a labor of love. For most, Jack knew, the pay wasn't great and the hours were long. Many stable workers were there because it was the best job they could find and be hired for. Many more were exercising, hosing down, hot walking, cleaning manure from hay-strewn stalls, and soaping saddles because they loved being with these frequently fey, four-legged creatures.

They turned to look up the track, both men with their forearms on the wooden railing, as a pair of two-year-olds came sprinting down the stretch. The chestnut filly on the rail was running straight and true. But the dark brown colt on her outside was attempting to bite her on the neck despite the strong effort being exerted by his exasperated rider trying to keep him from her.

Jack asked, "Does that colt have love on his mind with the filly?"

"Hell no," Wardell said. "He's just a mean-spirited son of a bitch who's been like that all his life. Tries to savage anything running near him, in the paddocks or on the track. He'll be a gelding soon. And then better mannered, we hope."

Jack walked with Wardell along the railing to the four-stall starting gate at the beginning of the track. "Look at that," Wardell said enthusiastically. "We just got it last week. Brand new. State of the art. I guarantee you it cost Mr. Tilley a bunch of money. But the gates open great when a bell rings, which helps us train these youngsters for what happens when they reach the race track."

"I take it Tilley spends a lot of money on this place."

Wardell snorted. "Does he spend big? You kidding? He spares no expense. The operation we've got here is as good as it can get. Same thing when he had his horses at the tracks. First class from day one and 24-seven. Before," he stopped to expel a chunk of chewing tobacco onto the grass, "the bastards threw him out. Sure as hell isn't fair because Mr. Tilley is the best boss I've ever known, both for his horses and his workers.

"You see that pretty blond woman standing over there next to the gate?"

"I do. Hard to miss her. What does she do?"

Wardell said," Mr. Tilley hired her several months ago. She's a veterinarian with a new approach to horses. Dr. Kristine Janks. Very nice lady. When our horses come of the track after their workouts, she checks their vital signs using heart rate monitors she's got strapped to their chests. She told me a good horse's heart can reach 220 beats a minute when they are on the track going full tilt. Then it falls to right around 30 beats when they are at rest. She keeps charts on this. Mr. Tilley is convinced what she discovers with these measurements can help him to know which horses are doing well, which aren't, and who is ready for racing. That, of course," Wardell spat, was when Mr. Tilley's horses were racing."

Jack knew he had to be careful here. "You know, Wardell, I've heard a lot of good things about Tilley, not just from you. What bothers me is that some people who run the tracks that barred him have suffered sudden, mysterious deaths." He paused, seeing Wardell's jaw tighten, eyes boring into Jack. "I'm just wondering, like a lot of other people, whether your boss could be kind of responsible for those tragedies."

"Stop right there." Wardell glared at Jack. "You're way off base thinking that. Mr. Tilley loves and respects both horses and people. He'd be the definition of straight arrow. I've been alive long enough to recognize the few qualifiers for that title. There is no damn way Ted Tilley would go into the kind of crap you're suggesting."

Jack smiled. You're a loyal employee, he was thinking, but confined himself to saying, "Wardell, I get your point."

He watched as Wardell, still steaming and nowhere near mollified, walked to the truck. He got in and slammed his door.

Wardell started the engine and looked straight ahead as Jack got in and shut his door. The truck jumped forward. Jack buckled his seat belt. "Look, Wardell," he said, "I wasn't insulting or accusing your boss of anything. Chill out, man. Take it easy."

The truck zoomed up the long drive to the huge house. Wardell skidded to a stop outside the front door. Not looking at Jack, he said, "Mr. Tilley should be waiting for you in his office right now."

"Thanks for the ride, Wardell." Jack shut his truck door behind him before Wardell gunned the truck away. It was obvious to Jack that Mr. Tilley had inspired extra-strength loyalty in this one of his employees. He just didn't know yet if it was deserved.

CHAPTER TWENTY-THREE

Ted got up from behind his cluttered desk, walked around it, and extended his hand. "Jack Doyle, welcome. Sorry I had to push back the time of our meeting. Come in and sit down. Would you like coffee or something else to drink?"

"No thanks, Ted. And I didn't waste my time waiting for my appointment. I had a very interesting tour of your impressive farm, courtesy of Wardell Simmons."

"I knew you'd be in good hands with Wardell," Ted said. "Glad he could show you around. Next in line after my family, Freedom Farm is my pride and joy. But I know you didn't come all the way from Chicago to take a farm tour. What actually brings you here?"

Jack said, "I've been asked by my friend, Celia McCann, at Monee Park to ask you a few questions. Some of them I'm sure have been asked before. And you've answered them. What we're looking for is a bit more detail, depth.

That's why I'm here."

In the next few minutes, the slightly exasperated Ted emphasized that, "One, those tracks have no reason to ban my horses. And, two, I have no connection to any of the threats that have been made to track executives on the Internet. For God's sake, Jack," Ted said as he got to his feet, "I've played by the rules all my life. In school, in baseball, and in horse racing. One, just one of my trainers, old Charlie Carpenter at Cahokia Park, incurred just one minor medication violation. The trainers I use are dedicated to a hay, oats, and water regimen for my horses. What other stable the size of mine could match that record of clean racing?"

Jack said, "I don't believe Celia McCann would disagree about you not having violated any rules of racing. She explained her decision to ban you by emphasizing the harmful effects your stable's success had on the Monee Park pari-mutuel totals."

"You know, Ms. McCann and those other track honchos seem to ignore the fact that I help them fill races. Yes, I run a lot of horses. By doing so I increase the size of their fields. As I'm sure you know, the larger number of horses in a race, the larger the betting on that race."

"Yes," Jack said, "I understand that was helpful, but only up to a point. When your stable became so dominant, there was a negative effect on the total betting. Seems every other horse you ran went off as the big favorite. Lot of bettors stay away from them. Chalk eaters, they're called."

Ted said, "I don't control the odds. All I do is place my horses in races I think they can win. If I have to drop them down in claiming prices, fine. I want the wins and the purses that go with them.

"No question," Ted continued, "that I shook up the game with this approach. If I claimed a horse for $20,000 and dropped him down and ran him for $15,000, and he won, that was what I was after. The purse he brought home made up the difference in his value. How this is perceived as something perverted is beyond me. What really worked up many of my rival owners was I would claim one off them, drop him down, bet my money on him, take the purse, and wave 'goodbye' when somebody claimed him off me.

"I've been in the retail business with our hardware company for a lot of years. I've always been able to recognize value in products and price them for volume sales at attractive prices. I've grown this chain of stores successfully for 20 years. When I wanted to turn my attention elsewhere, I got into horse racing. Using the same scheme. All this did, because it was making me a lot of money, was piss off the racing establishment bluebloods who resent the hell out of me as a not-member- of- the- club newcomer and interloper. And I think those big shots put pressure on the tracks where I raced to get rid of me. This has no more to do with free enterprise than I have to do with free range chickens. It makes me sick."

He took a deep breath. "Excuse my venting. I need some coffee."

Ted walked to the small adjacent kitchen, asking, "Sure you don't want anything, Jack?"

"I'll take some water, please."

Back behind his desk with his composure regained, Ted sipped his coffee before saying, "This whole thing they've done kills me. That they are concerning themselves with the Tilley stable when their main target should be elsewhere. I read about the various symposiums on the future of horse racing held around the country. From one year to the next, it's the same brand of hand wringing from the same clueless contingent of so-called industry leaders."

Jack asked, "What do you mean about their main target not being you, being elsewhere?"

"You know what CRW is, Jack?"

"Nope. Sounds like a hospital test I wouldn't want to be taking."

Ted said, "CRW is the acronym for Computer Robotic Wagering. Very smart people use computers programmed to identify value in pari-mutuel betting pools."

"So, what's new about that?" Jack asked. I had an uncle, one of my mother's brothers, who used to go to the races at old Sportsman's Park in

INQUIRY

Cicero, take a table in the clubhouse, and chart the changes he could see on the odds board in the infield. Used an old hand held Cascio calculator to identify what he thought were mismatches. He'd sit there all afternoon, drinking coffee and filling in sheets of numerical tables. Every other race or so, he'd dash to the $50 window to bet. Back at the table, he only looked up at the race in question when the leader reached the finish line. I spent two of the most boring afternoons of my life with him. I didn't think what he did was 'going to the races.' I liked going around the grandstand, smelling the grilled Polish sausages and onions, listening to guys argue with each other about what was the best bet of the day. My favorite thing was going outside, down to the rail near the finish line, and see these amazing animals battling to win. Sportsman's Park is long gone now. But not my memory of it."

Ted smiled. "I can see that you, like me, appreciate the attraction of horse racing. What I'm concerned about is the impact of CRW on it currently. You've got these sharpies using computer programs to identify value. With the instantaneous knowledge of probable payouts, they can make bets of various sizes on hundreds, even thousands, of different combinations just a few seconds before the race in question goes off and the odds are settled. The poor saps at the track don't have time to dash to the windows or the computer bet takes with this brand new information about what the best betting choices are. Or even, if they're sitting at their computers at home, have enough time to type in bets based on this sudden information.

"The goal of smart horse players is identifying overlays, horses with good chances, whose odds are high. This is a strong attraction for veteran bettors and new ones that the sport needs to attract. But these CRW players have helped reduce the instances of such overlays. They recognize them through their analytics programs and jump on them first. That weakens the betting product for everybody else. I'm sure you've heard of the 'Flash Boys' who used brilliant computer programs to make fortunes in the stock markets a few years ago. These CRW guys are right from that family of sharpies that veer the probabilities their way every day. It tends to discourage potential new racing bettors who are looking for a new challenge, a game of real skill other than pushing slot machine buttons. "My point, Jack, is that the CRW guys cause more damage to track business that I ever could with all my wins. Yet they are still operating. And I've had racing's door slammed in my face. Go figure."

Ted's intercom buzzed and his office door opened almost immediately. Jack got up and turned to see a tall, serious looking man, probably in his early forties like himself, but far better dressed in a bespoke charcoal colored suit. He approached Jack with his hand extended. Ted said, "Jack, meet my right hand man, Gary Grunwald. Gary, you want coffee?"

"No thanks, Ted." Gary placed his bulging brown briefcase on the carpet. "So, Jack Doyle," he said with a smile, "I understand you came a ways today to talk to Ted. And me, I guess. How's your visit been?"

Jack sat back in his chair, relaxed. "It's gone very well. Had a great tour of the farm, courtesy of Wardell Simmons. Then a very informative talk with Ted."

Gary looked at his Rolex. "Nearly lunch time, fellas. Jack, if you're finished here, how about joining us?"

Jack said, "I guess I'm finished here as you put it." He paused. "But not finished with my concern over the threats being delivered to track owners since Ted's horses got the boot."

Gary, Jack thought, didn't look like a guy given to twitching. But he saw a hint of one, even some beads of sweat on Gary's forehead. But he still assured him, "We share your concern, Jack. What right-thinking person wouldn't?"

Jack stood up and made a show of looking at his cheap Timex. "Thanks for the lunch invitation. But I've got to drive back to Albany to catch my flight." He shook hands with the smiling Ted, then the frowning Gary.

"Thanks for your time, gentlemen," he said.

The door had barely closed behind Jack when Gary said, "What do you think, Ted?"

Ted shrugged as he pulled on his sport coat. Gary hid his annoyance at his friend's nonchalant reaction to Jack's visit. "About what, Gary?"

"About this Jack Doyle. What did he tell you? What was he here for?"

"He represents the Monee Park owner, Celia McCann. Jack said he came to see me at her request. To ask me about my banishment, how I felt. Also, what I thought about any emailed threats, or the deaths of those two track executives. I was up front with him about everything. Emphasizing I knew nothing about how those poor people died. How could I?"

Gary said, "You think he believed you?"

Ted, shocked at the question, said "Why the hell wouldn't he? It's the damn truth isn't it? You know that." He started toward the door. "C'mon man. I'm starving. Let's get lunch."

Gary hesitated and stood looking out the office window for a few seconds thinking about Jack's visit. The man's questions of Ted posed a possible problem, no doubt about that. When he heard Ted say, "Gary, let's move," he paused, still shaken.

"You know, Ted, I'm not all that hungry right now. But I'll join you." Actually, he thought, "I could use a couple of goddam stiff drinks about now."

INQUIRY

CHAPTER TWENTY-FOUR

A week after Skip had suffered watching Treasure Defee leave the Wee Hope with that bruiser, he felt a tap on his arm as he sat in his Heartland Downs grandstand seat. Rain was dousing the bedraggled jockeys and horses in the post parade for the fifth race on this dark, humid afternoon. But Skip's day brightened when he heard, "How goes it, Skipper?" Treasure bent down to delight him with a kiss on his cheek.

"Geez, you look good, Treasure," he stammered.

"Maybe, but I'm not feeling that good." She took the seat next to him. Skip didn't remember ever seeing anyone pout before, but he thought this might be it. "Treasure, what's going on? What's the trouble? I doubt it can be compared to mine," he said bitterly.

"Really?" She leaned closer, frowning. "What's going on with the Skipper?"

"Nothing anywhere near good," he answered. "My career as a racehorse bettor came to a crashing halt. Both in bankroll and confidence. Then, I don't think you know about this, I opened up an Internet tout service. I got up to two dozen clients each paying a $100 a day for my betting advice. Which, sadly enough, turned out to be no better than my betting. Every one of these suckers jumped out of the pool except a nice young guy named Scott Epstein. I had him on the hook for a few more weeks. A tribute to my salesmanship, if I say so myself."

Treasure said, "Or to this Epstein's gullibility. But go on."

"It was kind of crazy for awhile. I made some encouraging phone calls to Scott Epstein's house. He'd be whispering into the phone saying, 'I can't talk to you now. My wife could hear. She wants me to cancel my membership in your Winner's Club. Thinks it's a scam of some sort.'

"Of course," Skip continued, "I tried to talk him away from that attitude. Told him I could show him detailed records of my success as a selector, even though I didn't have them. I'll mail them to you, Scott, I told him.

"But Scott said, 'Better not. My father-in-law, Moe Kellman, took a look at our situation. Advised me, very strongly I must add, to stop dealing with you Skip. Moe knows a lot about betting and gamblers.'"

Skip said, "Listen up, Scott. Tell your father-in-law there are no worries! This temporary bad trend in our business will pass. I'll keep sending you my picks, at a discounted rate, let's say half-price."

Scott Epstein was silent for several seconds before he said, "Skip, I don't think that's the way I'm going to go. Because Moe Kellman said you are going to hear from a friend of his."

Skip leaned forward in his seat, took two deep breaths, then told Treasure, "Scott Epstein is related by marriage to a big shot Chicago furrier, a guy named Kellman. He's some kind of mobbed up. Hell, I didn't know. Anyway, I get a nasty visit from some hard looking guy named Jack Doyle. He came to my motel. Just opened my door somehow and walked right in. Pushed me down in a chair. Tells me he knows a lot about betting scams, hustlers, touts." He shuddered at the thought of it.

Treasure leaned over and put her hand on his arm. "So, Skipper, what went on then?"

Skip said, "It was a tough situation for me. This guy, Doyle, laughs and says something about giving me credit for what he called, 'Ballsy entrepreneurship. Probably driven by desperation.' I'm pretty sure that's what he said. It was all happening so damn fast. He didn't say a whole lot, but scared the crap out of me, especially after he grabbed my shirt with one hand and lifted me off the rug. Wow. What the fuck! Made me promise—promise-- to never again contact Scott Epstein."

Treasure said, "Wow. So, what did you do?"

"I never again contacted Scott Epstein, that's what."

They both looked up hearing the sound of the bugle calling the horses out for the seventh race. "Well, I'm sorry to hear that, Skip."

He buried his head in his hands, on the verge of a whimper. "I got nothing going for me. I can't try to go back to real estate. I know I'd never be hired. And I can't make a living either betting on or touting horses. My life is a fucking disaster no matter what the hell I do."

Treasure began to soothingly stroke Skip's back, gently back and forth as she said quietly, "Listen, my friend, I have an idea involving you. You and me, I mean. Want to hear it?"

He looked up and smiled at her. "It's the 'you and me' part that interests me. What've you got in mind? I'm about game for anything at this stage of my horrible summer. My horrible life."

Treasure said, "Listen, Skipper. Are you afraid of horses?"

"Only of the losing variety. With which I am depressingly too well acquainted."

Treasure put a hand on his forearm. "I'm serious, Skip. Do you think you're capable of getting up very early in the morning and coming here to Heartland and spending about four hours hot walking horses that have just had their workouts?"

On the verge of snorting out an emphatic "no," Skip paused. His unemployment had run out. His credit cards were maxed out; his bank account was on financial life support. Instead of saying, "Are you kidding me? Why would I do that?" He sighed, "Okay, Treasure. Tell me more."

She said, "I work for Ralph Tenuta, one of the top trainers here. I exercise his horses in the mornings, sometimes help with stable work late in the afternoon. Very honest gent. He pays real well. Everybody knows that."

"What does 'real well' mean?"

Treasure said, "As a hot walker you'd get 350 bucks a week."

"Let me get this straight. That's for four hours every morning, every day?"

"Yeah. It also covers the two hours per day you have to be there for the night feeding."

Skip said, "You're talking about six hours a day, seven days a week, for that money. Hah!"

"I can see you don't know shit about backstretch economics. You laugh at what Tenuta pays? You should see what most of the other trainers dole out to people very accustomed to living under the poverty line. And glad to get the work, I might add."

He shifted in his seat. Thinking for a moment that he might tap his brother Donald for another loan, then recognizing the futility of that, he said, "Okay, let's say I take this horse tending work for a few weeks. Until I get back on my feet. I've got some pretty good ideas…"

She slapped his wrist. "Skip, stop dreaming. Start scheming along with me."

"Scheming. About what?"

Treasure sat back and smiled as she looked out at the track. Then she jumped to her feet. "Let's go. I'll tell you later."

They bypassed the Original Pick Bar, Treasure insisting, "Let's go to your place. Where we can talk real private."

CHAPTER TWENTY-FIVE

The desk clerk at Skip's residence inn did not acknowledge them as they walked past him to the elevator. Past Skip's doorway, Treasure looked around. "Nice. You got any liquor in that little refrig?"

Skip locked the door. He watched Treasure extract two short bottles of tequila, the cost of which he hesitated about adding to his mounting bill. But he was in no mood to stop this exciting woman.

She shook a few cubes out of the tray and placed a cube each in the plastic containers serving as glasses, then poured the tequila. Smiling she handed one to Skip.

Skip, his heart pounding, managed to say, "This is great. But, Treasure, what's your plan for me at the Tenuta barn? What can you tell me about that?"

Treasure grinned. She walked up and put her palm on his chest and pushed him backward toward the bed. He happily complied, sitting his butt on the end of the queen-size bed, looking up expectantly.

"Skipper, I've got a plan. Thought about it for months. I'm positive it'll work. You and I will get it done. And, babe, this will be major money for us both. And I know you need yours."

Semi-stunned by the tequila infusion, sitting on the edge of his long bed, intrigued by the thought of any new possibility that could improve his life, Skip said, "Well, Ms. Defee, you've got my interest. But I've got a lot of questions. Details and so forth. What do you say?"

She drained her drink, stepped back, quickly unbuttoned her jeans, and shed them. Turning away from him, shaking her ass as she did, she stripped off her white tee shirt with its "Racing Lover" inscription. He gawked as she cupped her breasts that, as she stroked, produced extended dark pink nipples. He could hardly swallow. She slowly moved toward him. As he reached for her, she ordered, "Skipper, honey, lie back there. I'll explain everything in good time. Now," she whispered in his ear, "let's make this a real good time."

"Oh, yeah. Oh, yes," Skip murmured as she unhooked his belt. He was going to say it to himself again, but then Treasure and he got busy.

INQUIRY

CHAPTER TWENTY-SIX

As they did almost every work day, Ted and Gary met early in the morning in the company's cafeteria. They sat at their regular corner table. Gary had once asked his boss why they couldn't have breakfast in his office. Ted had replied, "I like to make myself available to any person who works for me that wants to say something to me. I like giving them a daily chance."

A hardy summer rain lashed against the picture window that overlooked the beautifully manicured grounds. The men always served themselves, coffee for Ted, some citrus concoction from the juice bar for Gary, the tall glass of which Ted always regarded with suspicion.

"What the hell is that you've got in there this morning?"

Gary answered, "I'm on a new diet. This one is guaranteed to curtail my appetite, cleanse my colon, and give me an overall big-time uplift. I figure it's worth a try. I'm about 20 pounds over my old baseball playing weight."

Ted laughed. "I believe that weight estimate may be a bit low, Gary. But that's not what I want to discuss. I want an update on where we are with our attorneys working to convince the racing commissions in the states where I've been barred they've made a mistake. What's the latest?"

Gary reached into his briefcase. He flicked through a thicket of papers, extracted two, and said, "Here's the story so far. The racing commissions say they cannot prevent racetracks, private entities, from barring whoever they want. That's current law.

"Item two," Gary continued. "Our written pleas to the managements of the race tracks in question have been either ignored or rebuffed. They're not bending." He sat back and closed his briefcase, a look of resignation on his face. "Ted, they just won't let your horses on their grounds. That's the deal as of now."

Ted sat back in his chair. "This is the damndest thing I've ever run into. They don't say why, they just say stay the hell away. I've tried to talk face to face to these track people, but they refuse." He got up and walked to the wide window. A big man, his shoulders were slumped in a posture of defeat Gary had never before seen.

Gary said, "We've got something else to figure out. Like, what do we do with all the horses that have been thrown out of those tracks and placed on nearby farms. Sell them? Slaughter the slow ones?"

"That's not funny, Gary. I've never been in the horse killing business. We'll put them out to pasture until this problem is resolved."

"What about all the stable help you've employed? The trainers, grooms, hot walkers, exercise riders?"

Ted said, "I've made it clear to our three trainers involved at the tracks against us that they are welcome to resign from working for me. To move on. Find new clients. Two of them said, however reluctantly, that they would have to leave. I don't blame them. The third, young Jason Moore, said he'd stick with me."

"Doing what?" Gary asked. "What are you going to do with Jason if he doesn't have any horses to train for races?"

Ted said, "I'll treat him as if he still trains for me at the track. I told him to keep his staff intact. I'll pay all of them like I do on a regular basis. Exercise riders, grooms, the whole bunch."

Gary groaned. "So, your charitable work now extends to the backstretch?"

"Gary, why the hell not? It's not their fault they're out of work! Just as I did nothing wrong, same for them. I don't know why I'm being punished. But I know they shouldn't suffer just because I am. They did good work for me. If they can find other jobs, fine. If not, I'll keep them on the payroll until we get this mess straightened out."

"Ted, you already pay the highest wages on the tracks. Other stables' workers are paid $350 a week tops. You've always paid $450! That's way above the norm."

Ted sat back in his chair and paused to rub his hands over his drawn face. *My friend is being beaten down by all this,* Gary thought. *Damn those tracks.*

"Gary, since I got into racing, I've become quite familiar with the lives of its backstretch workers. Their long hours, their low pay. As you know, the majority of workers on American backstretches are Latino, mostly Mexican, but other south of the border strivers, too. They've taken over this tough work because Americans won't do it. Wash and feed and clean up after these large creatures for small pay and long hours.

"These people," Ted continued, "are for the most part housed in on-track, rudimentary conditions. Small rooms, shared toilet facilities. The defenders of the status quo point out that these workers pay nothing for their housing. And their housing is worth about nothing, too. But this work force can't afford better housing outside the tracks' property, even if they could find it.

"Their children? Brought up in stable areas dangerous to the unwary. Some are schooled at spring and summer programs I've helped finance at several tracks. In the fall, they are bused to nearby schools that hardly

INQUIRY

receive them with open arms. Then their parents, many married couples - but also many single mothers, have to move to get work. To Florida, or Louisiana, or Arkansas, where the fall and winter tracks are open and there are jobs available. The kids are pulled out of schools they've gotten used to. This happens year after year. Meaningful education for these children, if it exists, is short-lived.

"So, my friend, if you assume I'm running a charitable program for my employees, who now have no work, my answer is, you're damn right I am. They deserve it."

An hour later, Gary sat in his office for the next hour after telling his secretary, "No calls." What a tangled web he'd put himself in! Hiring the now-out- of-control Rudy Ozinga to intimidate the track executives that were abusing Ted Tilley. Now, he feared Ted could get wind of his misguided operation, although designed to help him. An operation that, Gary knew, Ted would abhor.

He was watching races in TVG when an announcer broke in with what he termed "An alarming news bulletin." Another racetrack exec, Nancy Roth, had been murdered. Gary clicked off the television and buried his head in his hands. Then, he took a deep breath and dialed Ted who was on the golf course. "This better be good, Gary," Ted said, a smile in his voice. "I've birdied the last three holes. Gotta keep hot."

"What I've got to tell you, Ted, will cool you off in a hurry. It's about Nancy Roth at Cahokia Park."

"Tell me she's changed her mind and is inviting my horses back to her track. Or that she got fired for not doing so."

Gary said, "She didn't change her mind. And she didn't get fired from her job."

Ted said, "Well, what the hell happened to her, then?"

"She was murdered. Much like Pleasant Prairies' Marcy Darcy."

He could hear his startled friend pull in his breath before saying, "Dear God almighty. What the hell is going on?"

CHAPTER TWENTY-SEVEN

Jack stood among the eager dozens at O'Hare Airport international's arrival area waiting for passengers on Aer Lingus Flight 1506 to emerge from Customs. He well remembered the last time he'd stood here waiting for two arrivals from Ireland, young jockey Mickey Sheehan and her older sister, journalist Nora. He had signed up to serve as agent for Mickey. He wound up doing very well at that. Another success was the establishment of a beautiful relationship with Nora, one of the very few women in Jack's life who combined physical attractiveness, lively intellect, and a built-in ability to laugh at either herself or others.

The Aer Lingus passengers began bustling through the exit from Customs. Whoops went up from members of the crowd as they spotted arriving relatives or friends. There were whistles and calls and happy faces. Jack watched as the sharply dressed stewardesses led the group, chatting as they pulled their wheeled bags along. Then came a couple of elderly women being pushed in wheel chairs, smiling as they saw their greeters, followed by the rest of the swiftly- moving passengers.

Jack remembered Nora being in the forefront the previous time he'd waited here. But, dozens of people came through with no sight of her. He was about to give up, thinking maybe she'd missed the flight and hadn't informed him when he heard her familiar laugh. It was directed at a tall, well-dressed man walking beside her, head bent attentively.

Relieved, Jack said to himself, "She's charmed another one." When they reached the exit barrier, Nora shook hands with the tall man who attempted to hand her his business card. She politely shook her head no and scanned the crowd for a couple of seconds. That's all it took for her to see Jack.

He moved toward her as she stopped her bag of luggage, raised her arms, and gave him an enthusiastic hug. "Right on time as usual, eh, Jack? You're a marvel to see, indeed." She kissed him heartily.

Jack lifted her off her feet and swung her slightly around. Some of the other departing passengers smiled as they saw this strong looking, sandy-haired man bury his face in the black hair of this delighted woman, her face crossed by a wide grin.

He put her down. Nora said, "You never change, Jack Doyle. It's a wonder and a great one!"

INQUIRY

"But you do, Nora. Every time I see you, you look even more beautiful than ever. It's like a small tradition. Let me take your bag."

Nora slapped him on the arm, saying, "Oh, your reputation, as a full-fledged blarney boat, remains intact."

"Let's move on," Jack said. "The escalator's over there."

He picked up her bag and let out a groan. "Smuggled gold bars in here from some secret ancient Celtic site, did ya?"

"No such luck. Just my usual traveling-to-America inventory. I brought you some grand Irish cheese and rashers. My reference material is in there along with the changes of clothes my work requires. I also have a print of our great racetrack, the Curragh, that Mickey wants me to give to the trainer, Ralph Tenuta. Mickey remembers him very, very fondly. My sister rode a lot of winners for him as I'm sure you recall."

"Remember? Hell, as her agent I got her mounts on those live horses. I don't suppose," he said, "that young Mickey sent any fine gift for me, eh?"

"Only me," she said, stepping off the escalator. "Now, Jack, take a look. I've been practicing at batting my eyelashes." Her infectious laugh spread to the smiling arrivals near them.

Jack said, "You're batting percentage has always been very high with me. Turn right out of the door. I'm parked in the second row."

"Are you still driving your gray Accord?"

"Sure am. Old Reliable continues to abide."

As he walked happily alongside her, Jack, the twice-divorced heterosexual iconoclast, who vowed years before never to again engage in any serious relationships, felt Nora's presence threatening that stance. In its own way, not a bad feeling, he thought.

Out of O'Hare and headed to Chicago, Nora said, "Jack, I've got to check some emails. Would you mind turning down the radio?"

"And stop the sound of the great Johnny Hartman? With Coltrane? Oh, well, just for you, Nora." She patted him on the arm and went back to her emails.

Jack felt great. It was a beautiful afternoon. He zipped through the southbound traffic en route to his northside Chicago condo, remembering how much he'd missed having Nora in his life. She was bright, fun, adventurous, and had no more desire for permanency than he did. Nora's only marriage, to a once promising, now nearly-forgotten, Irish-ballad singer, had ended badly. That experience had soured her on marriage. Great by Jack, who heartily endorsed the same view.

Glancing over, he felt his heart jump as he looked at her earnest face in profile. When they got off the Kennedy and headed east, she shut her phone off, turned to him, and said, "What's on the agenda for tonight?"

Jack said, "Why, joyful revelry, as always."

They entered Jack's condo just before seven o'clock. While Nora unpacked, Jack checked his answering machine. Nothing memorable there. Same thing on his email. It being an election year, both devices were rife with earnest appeals from ambitious candidates. He ignored them all.

"Jack," he heard Nora say, "Do I have time for a shower before dinner?"

"Sure. I have a question, though."

"What's that?"

Jack asked, "Would you like any help in there? Perhaps back rubbing, front massaging, other pleasing sensory maneuvers? They are my specialties, you know."

Nora waved him off. "No, laddie, not at this time. I'm travel-grimed and famished. I need cleansing and feeding. Of course, an interesting request will undoubtedly follow later in the night. I'm sure you can help me with that."

"I promise to do my very best," Jack said.

Twenty minutes later Nora came out of the bedroom, dressed and glowing.

Jack said, "Damn, woman, international travel certainly agrees with you."

"It brings a surplus of hunger pangs, probably sparked by a sense of relief." She adjusted her dress, checked her makeup, and started walking to the door. "You might be surprised, Jack, to learn that long ago I discovered a collection of articles by your late Chicago newspaper columnist, Royko."

"Mike Royko? You're kidding. How would a Dublin-based person get on to that genius?"

Nora said, "Pure luck. I was researching for an article about the so-called City of Big Shoulders and I stumbled upon this collection of Royko's columns. Once I read the first entry, I kept going. And, no matter how many times I walk down the ramp to an airplane, I never can forget his views on flying."

"Which were? My folks were big fans of Royko. They were always quoting him," Jack said.

Nora explained, "He wrote about his deep seated fear that a huge metal device such as an airplane could somehow rev its engines and thrust itself into the clouds. He said he was never able to convince himself to have much faith in that concept, especially when he was aboard. He probably wasn't a very frequent flyer. But he certainly was a very entertaining writer."

As they exited the building, there was a police siren wailing a few blocks away. "Ignore it," Jack said. "That's just Chicago on a summer night. Now, let me ask you. How about Mexican food? There's a great

INQUIRY

place just five or six blocks away. Taco Diablo. It's owned by a guy I know from racing, Juvenal Marquez. He's got a son, Juvenal Jr., who is a pretty good young jockey. Nice kid. His old man's nice, too. And the food he serves is outstanding. Wait," he said, stopping. "I forgot to ask. Do you like Mexican food?"

"If it's good, I guess, but I'm pretty sure I've never had any fitting that description in Dublin. The so-called Mexican restaurants in my hometown I think are run by Croatians."

"Well," Jack said, "in that case you're in for a treat."

A half hour later they'd shared a pitcher of margaritas and a basket of freshly-baked chips with guacamole. Then, as Nora enjoyed her chicken flautas and Jack an expansive combination platter, she said, "This is marvelous. I love the beans and rice, too."

Owner Marquez came to their table. "Everything okay, Jack? Miss?" he added as he bowed slightly to her.

"Great as usual, Juvenal. This lady from Ireland is impressed."

"Indeed I am," Nora said. "Really wonderful food."

Strolling back to Jack's condo, they appreciated the soft summer breeze on this Chicago night. He let go of her hand when he heard rapid footsteps coming from behind him. He quickly turned, realizing he was about to get jumped by two young white guys. One was short and stocky, the other tall and lanky. The tall one was grinning as he shouted, "Toss me your wallet, pal. Your watch, too. The bitch can keep her purse."

"Well," Jack said, "here's a hearty fuck you to you and shorty."

He motioned Nora to stay behind him, never taking his eyes off this advancing twosome. Shorty ended the suspense when he planted his right foot and grunted as he launched a sweeping kick with his left that was intended for Jack's face.

Jack slid forward and grabbed the advancing leg with his right hand. He momentarily held Shorty up, one leg down and precariously balanced, the other up in the air. Then Jack pivoted to his left, set his feet, and propelled the squealing Shorty into the nearby bushes.

Tall and Lanky lunged forward. Jack moved in and pounded him with his favorite combination from his boxing days, a stiff left jab, right cross, then left hook to the kidney. Down he went while emitting a high-pitched yelp.

Jack grabbed Nora's arm. Her eyes were wide, her mouth open, as she held a trembling hand to her face. "We'll just go on from here now, Nora," Jack said as he walked her briskly away.

At the corner, Nora said, "Are you going to call the Garda? I mean, your police?"

"No. They wouldn't be much interested in a little scuffle like that. Although I may call in to report a possible muggers' threat on this street."

Nora said, "That was pretty impressive, Jack Doyle, the way you handled matters back there. Maybe this is where I should kind of lunge at you and say, 'Oh, my hero.'"

"There are other, more preferred ways of appreciation I have in mind. But, in truth, those two goofs were out of their league. Shorty with his stupid slow kick must have considered himself a karate black belt. I'd put him, maybe, at the chartreuse level. His buddy is a walking punching bag. They're going to have to prey on seniors using walkers to advance their mugging careers. Hope they saw the light tonight and will go on to something different."

In his condo he poured them nightcaps of cognac. They relaxed on his couch. He put the television on with sound off. That night's news could all be discerned without need of sound: another gang shooting in Englewood, truck and car collision on the Dan Ryan, then the clips of the presidential candidates attacking each other, as was their daily practice.

He turned the television off, got up, and started his CD player. "Check this out, Nora. It's a recently discovered, long-ago recording of the great jazz pianist, Bill Evans." He sat down beside her, arm around her.

Ten minutes into the Evans CD, they were in his bedroom. It had been too long since they'd been together, he thought, and Nora enthusiastically agreed. When they finally lay their heads back on his pillows, he pulled her close again and she laid her head on his chest. He gently stroked her face. They had never said anything like, "How was it for you?" in years past. Jack smiled. He wasn't about to begin now, except to offer, "Cosmic fireworks? Earth movement? There was for me."

Nora said, "Settle down, Jack. And go to sleep."

CHAPTER TWENTY-EIGHT

They were up and out early the next morning for breakfast at Jack's favorite neighborhood greasy spoon Petros's. "We cannot advance northward without sustenance," he told her.

As they walked Nora took his arm. "This place, Petros's, I remember you mentioning it when I was here a year ago. 'An easy spoon,' I think you called it?"

Jack laughed, "I said 'greasy spoon.' It's an American term for places that are not upscale, not bottom scale, but in the middle. They do the basic things right. If you ever see what Petros calls Eggies Benedicto on the menu, ignore it."

Owner Peter Petros was behind the cash register near the entrance, licking his right thumb as he used it to count currency from the previous day's business. "Good morning El Greco," Jack said. "Engaged in your favorite pastime I see. How about spending some time improving the fare here?"

"Jack, do not make jokes at me. Especially when you are in the company of such a beautiful young woman come to improve my morning. She must have lost her way to be coming in here with you."

Jack took Nora's arm and ushered her to his favorite front window booth. "This is why I come in here. Not for the food, which is pretty good but available elsewhere, but just to rattle that Greek rascal's cage."

Nora said, "Shall we ask for a menu?"

"No need. Eggs are good here any style. They actually serve a good Irish oatmeal. And you can't go wrong with their Nueshke's bacon."

Waitress Vera Siger hustled forward and handed a menu to Nora. "Hello, miss," she said, "welcome to Petros's. This fella here," she added, poking her order pad at Jack, "has never come in here with someone as great looking as you."

"I think I saw you blush, Nora," Jack said. "Vera, you're in fine form this morning."

Orders in, they reviewed their schedule for this beautiful Saturday morning. Up HY. 94 to Wisconsin and 60 miles more to Milwaukee. "I figure two hours tops," Jack said. "I checked the weather. Supposed to be good all day up there."

"Well, that's promising," Nora said. Vera came to the table with their breakfasts. Orange juice, oatmeal, and tea for Nora. Nora looked at Jack's breakfast platter of two scrambled eggs, two pork sausages, two bacon strips, hash browns, and two slices of buttered wheat toast.

"A meal like that would floor me for the day," Nora said, "if I could even finish it. I don't know how you do it."

"Practice, my dear. I've been blessed with a hearty appetite and a system that ignores cholesterol. I run three days a week and work out in the gym at least two more, so I'm sure that has something to do with it. But genes are involved. Of that I am convinced. My grandpa Mike, my mother's father, was a rotund insurance man who, after he retired, kept to his usual diet, which featured at least two pieces of pie every day. He sat in his living room chair watching television for hours every day. Never exercised a minute during all his retirement years. And he lived to be 97. What can I tell you?" Jack grinned. "It's in my genes. I'm obligated to take advantage of it. Can I finish that oatmeal for you?"

***

Thirty minutes later they were on their way. Traffic was unusually light for a weekend morning. "Maybe all of my fellow residents have already beaten us to the path leading up there. There are thousands of Illinois people who vacation in the Badger State."

"The what? Badger State did you say?" Nora asked. "What does that mean?"

Jack said, "All 50 of our states have nicknames. For a reason I am not familiar with, Wisconsin chose a rather unappealing looking animal that preys on moles, gophers, and squirrels. That's the badger. A couple of times, I questioned why this creature was chosen. The cheese heads I asked got very irritated and defensive."

"Cheese heads? Is that what you said?"

Jack said, "I'm sorry I mentioned it. Wisconsin residents take pride in being called that which refers to their famous dairy industry. At the Green Bay Packers football games, yellow foam cheese hats are, pardon the expression, spread all over the place. And these folks don't mind being called cheese heads. They're proud of it. And keep in mind that they refer to me and my fellow Prairie Staters as Illinois nuisances. And sometimes something worse."

He moved to the right lane out of the way of a couple enormous semis, their drivers ignoring the posted speed limit for trucks. "Nora," he said, tell me more about this event we're going to. I understand why, as far as you're concerned. You're reporting on it for some newspapers back home as well as internet company. Right?"

"Yes. The internet company is called Cashable. Rather an exciting new company. Their London-based news editor called me to ask if I would be interested in covering Irish Fest for them. I told her I'd be delighted as long it was all right for me to file some separate stories for some of the papers I string for in Ireland. She said, 'no problem.' I'm getting expenses plus a rather generous story rate."

Jack said, "Why is this event such a big story for people in Ireland?"

"Well, my coverage is not just for the folks back home. There are Irish people all over the planet. Cashable aims to attract them to their website."

They passed an exit for Racine, Jack smiling, said "I was briefly in jail there once in my youth."

She turned to face him. "What was the charge?"

"Street fight. An argument over a pretty girl. Familiar story for young bucks. No, I didn't spend a night in jail. The booking officer just looked at us sadly, shaking his head. Told us to get our sorry asses out of there. That he didn't want to clog up the judicial system with the likes of us. He was a good guy."

As they approached the outskirts of Milwaukee, Jack said, "I trust you've got directions to the Fest."

She opened her reporter's notebook "It's on the lake front. So take something east. It's in Henry W. Maier Festival Park. That's at 200 North Harbor Drive. Do you want to put that in your GPS?"

Jack laughed. "You see anything resembling a GPS in this veteran of the roads?" He used his right index finger to tap his temple. "I have a JDPS. Right in here. The Jack Doyle Global Positioning System. Anyway, what more should I know about this event?"

With another glance at her notes, Nora said "Today is the first of four days of what has become the largest Irish festival in the world. More than 150,000 people coming from all over attend each year. They'll have more than 250 musical acts on multiple stages. A man named Dennis Ward started this in 1981. They get visitors from Ireland, England, Scotland, even Pakistan and Egypt! One year, I think 2005, Ireland's President Mary McAleese attended. This event went from an acorn to a stand of oaks in just a few years. And every year, some 4,000 volunteers work it. Pretty amazing."

"Agreed."

Nora continued, "Mr. Ward wrote early on that his mission was to celebrate numerous aspects of Irish, Irish-American, and Celtic cultures. 'To create in future generations an appreciation of their heritage,' is how he put it. A noble cause, I'd say."

Jack exited the expressway and turned right on Wisconsin Ave. "I see you've done your homework on this project," he said.

"That's one of the things I like about my work. It involves learning and sometimes appreciating new things. So much of a journalist's life," she sighed, "is afflicted with depressing, dismaying subjects." As Jack entered an already nearly-full parking lot, Nora perked up at the sight of Lake Michigan in the foreground. "A giant lake of azure blue," she murmured.

"What a treat! Added on to these golden hours I'm spending with the great Jack Doyle." They both laughed at that.

***

They spent the next several hours moving around the extensive festival grounds. Nora stopped frequently to question attendees. Many wore green tee shirts emblazoned with such family names as Sheridan, Higgins, Fitzgerald, O'Day in white lettering. Once informed she was a visiting journalist, most were delighted to talk. Nora also took dozens of photos with her phone which she immediately dispatched to her Dublin office computer.

At noon, they shared a plate of fish and chips and a large Guinness. "Pretty good fare for over here," Nora enthused before they continued their stroll. It was now taking longer as they had to wind their way through the growing crowd.

They stopped at a stage featuring Irish dancers. Young girls, dressed in green with tall curled hair arrangements, white knee sox, and active feet were in motion.

Jack said, "I never saw the famous River Dance troupe, and I don't know much about Irish dancing. Why are they all bouncing about with their arms at their sides?"

"That's the tradition," Nora said. "Evolved from the time when the Irish Catholic hierarchy discouraged any kind of hands-on dancing. Fearful of sexual enticements. Silly then, and silly now. But this group is from Dublin. They're darned good. I'll have to give them a little story," she said, as the troupe left the stage to a rousing ovation.

Standing near Jack were dancers from a Chicago Irish dancers club, scheduled to perform a few minutes later. He laughed as he heard the girl next to him announce to her dance mates in reference to the just concluded Irish contingent, "We're gooder than them."

Two more hours of listening to traditional Irish bands, some with singers, all devoted to Celtic traditional music, Jack said, "Nora, my dear, have you gathered enough information for the day? I hope."

She grabbed his arm, laughing. "You've been a patient angel, Jack. Yes, I believe I've accumulated plenty to work with. I'll file my stories off in the morning. Shall we leave?"

They walked around a small clump of angry young men, beer glasses dropped and fists up, in a staring and yelling match. She pulled him forward. "That's a familiar scene for me. Like some parts of Dublin on a late Saturday night."

He looked back at the noisy testosterone fueled confrontation. "You see a lot of this back home, Nora?"

"If I stay out late enough on a weekend night. Fights among young men are an Irish tradition. Like pub living and betting horses. The gargle, as it's called, is the gold medal winner in my country's Olympics of self destruction. Gambling and drugs take the silver and bronze."

"In your roster of vices, what about marital infidelity? That would be high up in our rankings here," Jack said.

Nora laughed. "In Ireland? That would be a distant also-ran."

They were wending their way through the crowded parking when Jack's cell phone activated with its first notes of the great jazz pianist Oscar Peterson's "Night in Nigeria." He answered it and continued walking, but only for a few strides.

"Damn," Nora heard him say as he abruptly stopped. She heard him say another "Damn" before he plunged the phone into his pocket.

Nora said, "What is it, Jack? What's going on?"

"Aw, damn," he said, shaking his head. "Some bad news. That was Calvin Douglas calling, Celia McCann's husband, and a very concerned man. Because there's been another death of a racetrack executive. Woman named Nancy Roth. Happened last night. She was the second woman to be killed. Calvin says he's getting damn worried. I don't blame him, Nora."

CHAPTER TWENTY-NINE

FBI agent Karen Engel hurried into the office she shared with work partner Damon Tirabassi in the Bureau's headquarters on Chicago's near west side. "Got you an Italian beef, wet, hot peppers, the usual," she said. "Took awhile. The place was jammed."

"Thanks, Karen. My turn tomorrow. Now, I have something to report. Jack Doyle is on his way here. He called about 15 minutes ago to say he wanted to talk to us. I started to tell him to make an appointment for tomorrow, but he'd already hung up. You know how headstrong that man can be."

"I sure do," Karen smiled. "Had I known he was on his way, I would have gotten him a pastrami on an onion roll, one of his favorites as I recall."

Their office was on the seventh floor of the Chicago Bureau's impressed glass-covered building on West Roosevelt Rd. "The Odd Couple of law enforcement," as Jack termed them, had partnered for six years. Damon, in his early 50s, was a super serious, by the book sort, with feathers of dedication Jack loved to ruffle. When he first got to know Damon a few years before when they worked together on a thoroughbred insurance fraud case, he'd remarked, "I've never met an Italian as tight-assed as you, Damon. You should be head of security in the Vatican."

Jack was much more at ease with the tall, athletic, attractive Karen Engel. She was a former volleyball star at the University of Wisconsin who was as dedicated to their work as Damon. The difference was she brought a lively sense of humor to it. Damon was married with four children. Karen, in her mid-thirties, and her partner, Cynthia Tepes, had been openly together for three years. This contrast in lifestyles never impinged on the efficiency of the Engel-Tirabassi team, one which had earned numerous Bureau citations for excellence.

At noon the angelus rang at the nearby St. Stanislaus Catholic church. Damon, about to unwrap his sandwich, looked at a familiar sight—a small group of aged women struggling up the steps to the church door. They were the only dependable contingent to attend the noon Mass that he'd ever seen.

The church bells recessed at a minute after noon. The next sound Damon heard was the buzz of his intercom. Their receptionist, Barbara Beer-

INQUIRY

man, said, "Karen, Damon, there's a man out here demanding to meet with you right now." She lowered her voice and whispered, "He insists he has new information on the Lindbergh baby kidnapping. And some clues about what he says is a long disappeared person named Judge Crater? I don't know what he means!"

Damon sighed. "That's undoubtedly Jack Doyle. Send him in."

He turned to Karen. "Jack's here."

She grinned. "Good. Haven't heard from this interesting man in some time."

Barb Beerman pressed the buzzer and waved Jack into the agents' office. As Jack entered, he motioned with his thumb over his shoulder, and said, "I've been trying set up a date with that gorgeous woman I just saw for the first time." Beerman grinned and headed back to her desk. Jack said, "Damon, how about giving me a good reference with her?"

Jack and the agents had a history. One often marred by conflict, confusion, and personality clashes. Yet, from that cauldron had come major convictions, starting with that of an eccentric and dishonest media mogul who had secretly ordered his own thoroughbred stallions killed to collect the insurance on them. Their most recent joint endeavor saw them uncovering a determined animal rights activist who had performed "mercy killings" of retired thoroughbred race horses.

Their association, however productive, had never been a smooth one because of personality differences. Karen got along well with the often impatient and usually irreverent Jack. Not so with Damon. When tension developed between these two strong, but very different, personalities, Karen was usually able to defuse the potential flare up and moved them forward.

After Barb Beerman closed the office door behind her, Damon barked, "Jack, mind your manners. That woman is happily married. With three or four kids!"

Jack sat in the chair closest to Daman's immaculate desk.

"Ah, Damon." Jack shook his head. "I think you've got some kind of mental chastity belt combined with moral blinders. I was just flirting with and thereby complimenting the attractive Ms. Beerman. Having a little fun with that nice woman. What's wrong with that? "

Jack looked at Karen. "It saddens me to think what kind of a strong clamp is on your partner's mental scrotum that prevents any forward thinking."

She looked away, hiding her smile from Daman. Then she said, "Guys, how about getting to the matter at hand. It's up to you, Jack, to say what it is."

"Well," Jack said, "this falls into the man bites dog category. Along with hell freezing over. You know what I mean Damon."

Damon said, "No, Jack. As is so often the case in my dealings with you, I am puzzled. And that has become a familiar source of irritation."

"Ah, Damon," Jack laughed. "Same old loveable, open minded representative of national law enforcement. Hah!"

Karen, once again assuming her role as a buffer between these two, said, "Jack, how about getting to your point."

"In sharp contrast to our past dealings," Jack said, "which have always seen me responding to FBI requests to aid in the capture of criminals, this time I'm calling to you for help. No laughing, please.

"There's a situation in horse racing that's got me worried," Jack continued. "A few months ago, a few thoroughbred tracks decided to ban from participating a prominent owner named Ted Tilley. Wouldn't allow his horses on their grounds anymore. A rather shocking development, since Ted apparently had done nothing illegal at all. Nothing except win races at a remarkable rate. These track owners saw the Tilley stable dominance as hurting the betting at their tracks. No, I'm not going to explain their thinking in arriving at this conclusion. They just did it."

Karen said, "Wow. That sounds a little bit off. Wouldn't that be in restraint of trade or something?"

"Not under current legal definition," Jack said. "Under the law as it stands these tracks are private entities that can ban anybody they want for reasons they choose. Not of course on the basis of race, sex, or ethnicity. But otherwise, they've got a green light."

Damon glanced impatiently at his Italian beef sandwich. "So, what does this have to do with the Bureau? Why are you here except to add a little exasperation to my life?" He smiled as he prepared to take his first bite.

Jack leaned toward Karen. "You know what I like about your crabby partner? His consistency. He's like a living metronome of irritability."

She said, "Jack, Damon's question is a good one. Why have you come to us?"

"There is an aspect of this Tilley situation that alarms me. After these race track bans on him went into effect, my friend Celia McCann, out at Monee Park, received a threatening email urging her to withdraw her opposition to Tilley. She shrugged it off. But her new husband, Calvin Douglas, considered it to be worrisome. That's when he called me to tell me about it."

"Calling you?" Damon snorted. "Mr. Douglas must be desperate." He took another bite of lunch and sat back in his chair, as pleased with his comment as he was with his sandwich.

Jack said, "Karen, if you don't get major combat pay for working with this man, our government is hugely remiss."

He turned back to Damon. "All I'm asking for is some advice. There have been two deaths of two track operators who received threats via email.

INQUIRY

That they would pay if they didn't lift their bans on Tilley. They were apparently murdered. Shouldn't that be against the law?"

Karen said, "Jack, of course, murder is against the law. But there's no law against what appears to be threats. They flood the Internet every day 24/7. Loonies super busy venting and rating. What could we possibly do about what you're talking about? Veiled threats? Perhaps deaths resulting? That's the province of local law enforcement, not us. These don't fall into the federal crime category."

"There is no law that applies to what you're concerned with, Jack," Damon said. What could we do for you? Surveil a phantom?"

Karen said, "Really, Jack, we couldn't possibly get involved on the basis of no evidence linking the threatening emails to the awful deaths. Sorry, my friend."

Jack sighed, got up, and walked over to the window that overlooked the church. "Tell you the truth, I didn't expect much more than this. Guess you folks don't gear up unless it's some nationally prominent person."

"Yes," Damon snorted, "that is ordinarily the case. We don't spring into action on the basis of fears expressed by the worry wart husband of a race track operator."

Karen stood up and joined Jack at the window. She patted his arm as she said, "Jack, I'm glad you came in. We will certainly remember the concerns you express. It's always a pleasure to see you. At least for me," she grinned. "Seriously, if something concrete develops regarding this matter, be sure and call us. Okay?"

Jack said, "Sure. I'm sorry I couldn't get your partner to show a bit more interest. But, as always, Karen, it's great to see you. You are looking," he added, "in absolute peak condition."

Karen laughed. "Same old Jack Doyle."

At the door, Jack turned back. "Damon, I believe you have some sandwich gravy on that ugly tie you're wearing. Actually, looks like it's improved the pattern. Ciao."

CHAPTER THIRTY

Leaving FBI headquarters, the aroma of Damon's Italian beef sandwich a tantalizing memory, Jack walked to the nearby and very popular Morrie's Deli. Seeing the line for lunch already stretched a half block from the door, he decided to head home. Parked in the condo building's underground garage, he quickly reviewed the food possibilities in his fridge. Not much was there, and what was there was a small, less than inspiring, collection of frozen entrees— the curse of a bachelor's gastronomic life. He decided to walk the four blocks to his favorite neighborhood greasy spoon Petros's.

As usual, owner Pete Petros was seated behind the cash register near the entrance. His bushy black eyebrows rose when he saw Jack. "Jeck! What time is it?" he said, pretending to look at the wall clock behind him. "You only come here for breakfast! What is this you showing up now?"

"Look, El Greco, I'm hungry and in kind of a hurry. Tell Vera I'll be at my usual spot."

Within minutes, the smiling Vera Siger bustled to Jack's table with napkin, silverware, and worn plastic menu. "Jack, this is new, you here for something besides breakfast. What can I get you? And where is that lovely young lady you brought here the other morning?"

Jack said, "She's working up in Minneapolis covering another Irish Fest. After that, she flies back to Ireland."

"You don't look too happy about that, Jack."

"Vera, I am not by any means happy about that. Anyway, let's talk food, Vera. I'm going to depend on you for advice. What qualifies for an edible lunch item here?"

Vera reached down and patted his hand. "Let me surprise you," she said. "The Wednesday four-star special from the kitchen of Petros's."

The large flat screen television on the far wall, Petros's lone improvement in the many years he'd owned the restaurant, had on the Chicago Cubs game. They were at hallowed Wrigley Field facing the hated New York Mets. Jack had a cousin in the Bronx named Gloria Feit, a diehard Mets fan, who regularly yanked his chain when her favorites beat Chicago's favorite baseball team.

Jack sipped his coffee and watched as one of the promising Cubs rookies larruped a homer that flew over the right field scoreboard, giving his team a three-run lead. "I'll be damned," Jack said to Vera who had arrived with his food. "I guess these young guys are for real. Wouldn't that be an upset! For a team that hasn't won a World Series since 1908?"

She placed the platter before him. "Cubs, schlubs," she said. "My whole family is White Sox fans."

He looked down at his meal, then reached to grab Vera's hand. "I'm reminded of something here."

She rolled her eyes. "I'll bet you are, Jack. What is it?"

"Years ago one of my favorite humorists, Dave Barry, wrote that in the case of pop star Brittney Spears, 'Our nation deserves an explanation.'"

Vera asked, "So? What does that have to do with your lunch?"

"Now, Vera, don't be prickly. All I'm asking is a definition of what's on this plate. I see white mashed potatoes peeking out from under a brown gravy layer. Some sort of tired looking vegetables lurking nearby. But at the center, nearly obscured by the gravy, is what? Mystery meat?"

"Oh, Jack, ye of little faith. That's the Petros's Number One Luncheon Meatloaf Special. Famous for, well, blocks around. And just $6.95. Before tip," she added, looking back over her shoulder.

Jack lifted his fork and started digging in. He chewed with relish.

"Pretty damn good," he murmured. "Reminds me of my Mom's meatloaf."

He heard Petros call from behind the register, "What you think, Jeck?"

"I've had worse," Jack conceded. "How about turning up the volume on the Cubs game. That's Anthony Rizzo coming up to bat for our heroes."

The Cubs had batted around, scoring six runs in the first inning. Jack laid a five dollar tip on his table. Paying his bill at the register, he heard Petros say "Those Cubs look pretty good, am I right, Jeck?"

Jack said, "Yeah, they do. But don't get your hopes too high, my host. This is a baseball franchise draped in historic disappointment. Things look promising every other decade or so. But then traditional Cubness sets in dashing all those hopes. Some years back, the great Chicago newspaper columnist Mike Royko wrote something my father never forgot and that he annually quoted to me. Royko always believed that being a Cubs fan built strong character. It taught a person that if you try hard enough and long enough, you'll still lose. And that's the story of life.'"

"But, maybe not this year, eh Jeck?"

Jack paused at the door. "Petros, keep in mind that the Chicago Cubs mantra since I've been born, and for thousands of others born before me, has always been 'Wait Till Next Year.' See you."

Strolling home Jack heard the radio broadcast of the Cubs game coming out of several houses on his block. He smiled, still amazed at the indomitable faith and hope the team's fans maintained.

In his foyer, he pulled "The New Yorker," "Atlantic Monthly," and

"Sports Illustrated" magazines from his crowded mailbox as well as the monthly newsletter from legendary Texas liberal, Jim Hightower. It was four pages of biting comment from the one-time Lone Star state's sharpest observers and establishment pain-in-the-butt about Texas current elected leaders as well as national political follies. This was the item that Jack always read first.

Included in the hand full of other mailings was a "New Appeal" from Illinois House of Representatives candidate Danny O'Rourke, a resident of Jack's ward. Looking at the smiling face of O'Rourke posed amidst his family—wife Moira and three bored-looking young children—Jack laughed aloud.

The first paragraph was an appeal for contributions to candidate O'Rourke from the "We, the Environmentally Concerned," an organization Jack had never heard of. It cited O'Rourke's "Unfailing, lifelong dedication to the preservation of our God-given natural surroundings. Clean air and clean water, have been Danny O'Rourke's golden goals over all his years attempting to be elected to Public Service. This is his time!"

Jack crumpled the flyer and tossed it into a waste basket. "Is there an Irish word for chutzpah?" he asked himself as he entered his condo.

A couple of months before, Jack was in the middle of his early morning run along Chicago's lakefront when he saw Danny O'Rourke and a burly man unloading a worn sofa from the back of a station wagon in the, otherwise vacant, parking lot.

Jack had heard that Danny's marriage had gone off the rocks. His wife, Moira, had remained silent about the blowup during Danny's political campaign. She'd moved with their children to her parents' home in Chicago's Beverly neighborhood. Danny had sublet their apartment to save money and moved in with his bachelor and recently divorced campaign manager, James O'Connor.

Jack pulled up and stepped to the side of the running path to watch these ambitious politicos at work. Danny must have had to empty his apartment, Jack thought. I guess the big guy is helping him out.

The two men struggled to carry the sofa up onto the lakeside concrete blocks. Danny slipped once and nearly dropped his end, cursing with conviction. After a restful pause, they hoisted the old sofa into the air and threw it into the lake. As it floated for a moment, and then began to sink, Jack watched as they bumped fists, and listened to their boisterous laughter. They hustled back to the station wagon and each yanked out a can of beer.

"And this conniving phony wants to join the legislature?" Jack muttered. "He should fit right in."

With a mile to go, Jack picked up his pace.

INQUIRY

CHAPTER THIRTY-ONE

Treasure signed her release form at the Lutheran General Hospital. Two hours earlier, she had been thrown to the ground on the Heartland Downs backstretch in the course of a morning workout.

She never saw it coming. As she was galloping one of the Tenuta stable's green two-year-old colts, she was crashed into on the left side by an out-of-control speedster zipping up the rail from behind her. She'd heard him coming and jerked her mount's reins to the right. Not far enough. She felt her horse being slammed, turned almost sideways, and saw the brown loam looming up at her. Eyes closed, she managed an athletic roll, heart thumping. She staggered to her feet in time to see one of the track outriders catch up with her frightened mount a furlong down the track. She wiped away blood from some cuts on her face, but otherwise had suffered nothing terrible—no broken bones, or spine injury, the latter a rider's greatest fear. Following Heartland Downs accident protocol, she was helped into a track ambulance that drove quickly to the nearby hospital emergency room.

Waiting for the results of her examination, Treasure swore softly to herself. Time for a fucking life review, she thought. I'm nearly 26 years old with no husband, no savings, working in a hazardous job because that's all I know how to do.

She met Ralph Tenuta and his wife, Rosa in the emergency room waiting area. Treasure said, "Hey, you two look too worried. I'm on my feet. Sore, but moving. I just need a ride home. Thanks so much for coming here."

"Well," Ralph said, "I guess we should be thankful you weren't hurt much worse in that fall. When I got the news at the barn, I called Rosa and we drove right over here. Come on, we'll give you the ride."

***

A half-hour later, the Tenutas waited until Treasure was settled in her room in the Extended Stay complex some three miles from Heartland Downs. She thanked them again for their concern, closed the door, and walked into the bathroom. Another look at the cuts on her forehead and bruise on her right cheek bone deepened her growing sense of depression.

Although she hadn't suffered major injuries in her violent meeting with the Heartland Downs racing surface, she was nevertheless very body sore from that incident. She ran hot water into her tub and peeled off her clothes, then made a quick trip to the refrigerator for a bottle of Bud Lite. She couldn't help but recall her late father's motto about dealing with body pain: "Get out of your duds and relax in the tub with some suds."

Treasure's horse trainer father, Shane Dupree, had been killed in a van accident while transporting two horses to Delta Downs. She was 12, his death a blow from which she would never recover. Shane was a strong, quiet, hard-working man who loved his family only slightly more than the horses he bought, sold, and trained. The respect he had earned in Cajun country was evident by the large turnout on the rainy morning he was buried.

A year and a half after her father's death, Treasure's mother married another horseman who, as it soon became clear to her, was one of a far different sort than her father.

Eric Morreale encouraged young Treasure to keep exercising horses. "Girl, you got a great seat," he frequently noted when she returned from a gallop aboard one of the bottom-level claimers he owned. Their rudimentary training track early in the mornings was a great escape for Treasure. She rose at five a.m., quickly dressed, and piloted four horses around the ring before waiting for the rural bus to take her to high school. Sometimes her mother would even be up early to fry her a couple of eggs and pack a sandwich lunch. Sorely missing her beloved father, this routine at least provided Treasure with a welcome distraction.

Becoming a far less welcome distraction was step father Eric's interest in her. Treasure's 13th birthday was celebrated in a surprise party her Rosa threw for her that early October night. Eric had strung lights on lines above the cooking area where crabs were being boiled as boudin sausages sizzled on the grills. Their small backyard was filled with friends and neighbors. A CD player boomed out zydeco favorites.

Treasure watched from the main table, surrounded by contemporaries, most of them laughing at the dances being undertaken by their parents and older relatives. Perhaps impelled by the half bottle of Jax beer she drank, she got up and joined the dancers. By herself. But feeling the power of age 13. She moved gracefully around the rim of the dance floor. She twice noticed her step father watching her, eyes gleaming over a beer, grin widening.

The last of the party guests waved goodbye shortly after midnight.

Several of them were horse trainers who had to be at their barns by five a.m. Treasure helped her mother clean up. Paper plates in the two big barrels at the end of the yard, their flames just starting, "Cajun recycling" her mother called it. Eric sat on a bench at the side of the yard watching Treasure, beer in his hand. No help coming from him, she thought. Back in the kitchen, Treasure was going to chide her mother about Eric's sit-back-and-watch-others work attitude, but she kept her mouth shut.

It was nearly one a.m. when Treasure, pleased by the turnout but exhausted, hugged Rosa and went to bed. Shortly after going to sleep, she was awakened by loud voices coming from her parents' bedroom down the hall. She heard her mother uttering sounds she'd never heard from her before. Heard Eric issuing commands that Treasure did not understand. After several noisy minutes, there was silence, and Treasure dozed off.

Thirty-five minutes later, Treasure was awakened by the feeling of a firm hand on her left thigh and a booze-blasted breath in her face. Eric moved to be on top of her. "Mama!" she shouted as she tried to roll away from him. But he restrained her with his powerful hands and pinned her down beneath him.

Terrified, she looked up at Eric's grinning face and heard him say, "Young girl, you heard that pleasure I give your Momma a while ago? Bet you did. Now, it's your turn. Lay back down there. Watching you these past few months, I just knew you were ready for this. Let the fun happen, hear?"

He pinned her flailing arms to her side. She started to scream. But one of his big calloused hands covered her mouth while the other tore off her panties. She groaned in pain as he penetrated her. Over his shoulder, she saw her mother standing in the doorway, hand over her mouth, but making no attempt to halt this assault. That realization caused more of her tears to flow.

Five brutal minutes later, Eric rolled off her and off the bed. "Sweet dreams," he muttered as he walked out her door.

Treasure lay motionless for nearly a half-hour. When she finally realized her mother was not coming in to see and comfort her, she staggered to the bathroom and toweled off over and over again, rubbing the smell of him off her. Instead of returning to bed, she walked outside and sat on one of the picnic benches. Before the sun crept onto the skyline, Treasure decided she was going to get the hell away from Louisiana.

CHAPTER THIRTY-TWO

Jack sat up with a start. He heard the buzz of Nora's cell phone on the table next to her side of the bed. He carefully stretched over her to grab it, but she awoke as he was doing so. "Ach, I've got it Jack," she said sleepily, "I've got it." She sat up in bed, naked from out of the thrown-back covers, and waved him out of the room.

This was an early wakeup even for early riser Jack. He put on his raggedy old green boxer's bathrobe which he had saved after the many years following his final bout and went to the kitchen and started his coffee and brewing tea for Nora. Dawn was just starting to lighten up his windows. He leaned back against the counter, yawning, and waiting, thinking this call from Dublin must be something important.

She entered the kitchen, dressed now in one of his tee shirts, cellphone at her ear, gesturing for Jack to pour her a cup of tea. He watched as she paced around the room, with the tee shirt rising up from her slim waist and briefly exposing what he admired as her beautiful bubble butt, thinking, "This is the best damn morning show I've ever had here."

He finished his coffee as she finished her conversation saying, "I'm on it. See you soon." She was frowning as she picked up her tea.

"Well?" he said.

Without looking at him, she said, "I've got to get some clothes on. Then I'll tell you what that was all about. You're probably not going to like hearing it."

Within five minutes she was back, dressed, pulling her carry-on suitcase behind her into the kitchen.

"Aw, shit," Jack said.

She walked up and threw her arms around him. He waited. Nothing, just her tightening her embrace on him.

"Nora, dear, what the hell is going on here? First, there was the scantily-dressed Irish journalist hinting she'd provide a receptive Chicagoan with some early-morning sex. Then this new moving-out move. How about an explanation?"

She pressed her face against his chest. "Just bad timing," she said softly. "That was my Cashable boss, Eoin Healy, in Dublin. There is a terrorist there that has the city in an uproar. He's short-handed. He begged me to get back there."

INQUIRY

Nora released him and stood back. Looking up, tears formed in her bright green eyes, she said, "I'm sorry, but I've got to go home. This is a major opportunity for me. I've got to do it, dear Jack."

Jack turned to the sink and rinsed his coffee cup. For a moment, he rested his hands on the sink. He heard her approach him and reach around his waist and lay her head on his back. She was shaking as she wept.

Turning to her, Jack held her face in his hands and kissed her forehead. Abruptly, he disengaged. "I don't think I can wear this to the airport, do you?" he said lightly. "Time to change. Time to leave. I'll drive."

He hustled to the bedroom, yanked himself into jeans and pulled a sweatshirt on. As he sat on the bed tying his shoes, he tried to duck away from the layer of sadness on him. He had long relished his relationship with the bright, insightful, thoroughly entrancing Nora. He'd anticipated having at least another week with her visit to him.

He said to himself, "So it fucking goes."

They were in his Accord and on the way to O'Hare in ten minutes, neither of them saying anything. They'd spent high quality time, as he termed it, together first in Chicago, then in Ireland. But their partings at the end of those experiences had not dug as deep a hole in him as this one. Nora was as fine a woman as he'd ever known. True, his two disastrous marriages had lowered the bar along those lines. He had chosen unwisely regarding those women, but their complicity in failure was just as strong as his. He knew that.

He wheeled the Accord in the International Departure lane at O'Hare. After nearly a half-hour of silence, Nora turned to him, reached across the seat, and kissed him on his cheek. He said, "What, no lips allowed?"

"Don't be dismissive, dear Jack," she said. "I hate to leave you. But I must."

She got out, extracted her carry-on from the back seat, and walked into the airport never looking back.

Jack sagged in his seat as he watched her go. He hadn't moved even after she'd disappeared through the door. A repeated horn blast from behind him made him sit up straight. That, and the whistle of the woman Chicago Police Dept. traffic controller. He opened his window and said to her, "Officer, I'm on my way out of here."

Before he could advance, there was another lengthy horn blast from a white stretch limousine behind him. Looking in his rear view mirror, he couldn't see the face of the driver through the tinted limo window. That was okay. He slowly turned the wheel and started away. Window still open, he smiled at the lady cop and thanked her for her patience. "Give my regards to that limo asshole behind me," he added, "plus a hearty 'fuck you.'" She dropped her whistle as she laughed and patted the roof of his car and waved him on his way.

CHAPTER THIRTY-THREE

Rudy Ozinga again woke up an hour before he'd set on his alarm clock. He wasn't sleeping worth a shit. He didn't shave, or brush his teeth, or shower. He dressed in his work clothes and walked, leaden footed, to his parking lot. A light rain was washing the dust off the fading red Ford truck.

There was a long line at the Dunkin' Donuts drive through, so he peeled away and headed for the construction site. Usually, one of the men he supervised there had a thermos of coffee.

At the intersection of Oak and First, a smashing pain in his head caused him to jerk the wheel, almost hitting the car slightly behind him in the right lane. The driver, an enraged young woman, snarled at him, her mouth moving rapidly, and her left hand raised in the universal one-finger salute.

He ignored her. When the light changed, he floored his truck for the first 200 feet before sharply turning it into the right lane. He heard her horn's loud blaring as he cut her off, then sped forward. "So long, sweetheart," he said to himself.

The smile on his face turned to a scowl when he passed the neighborhood's new car fix franchise with its huge "As Low as $19.99 Oil Change."

"What bullshit," he muttered. Just last week he'd advised Tim Tully, his new assistant foreman, that "Anytime you see 'As Low As,' get ready to be reamed. New windows, carpet cleaning, dental implants, you name it, they never turn out to be 'As Low As.'"

Neither Tully nor the rest of the crew had arrived at the job site when he got there 20 minutes before seven. Rudy got out, stooped and stretched, looked at the darkening early morning sky. "Shit. We may lose another work day here with the fucking storm coming."

The loss of a day's work wasn't the main thing on Rudy's mind that morning. Pressing forward were his thoughts about what he'd done with those two racetrack executives. Dead and fucking gone! The memories of his actions had only receded slightly. He could still feel the heartening surge of adrenalin that coincided with his murders of those women.

Yeah, sometimes deep in one of his vodka-driven nights, Rudy momentarily flushed with regret over what he'd done. But those brief moments were almost instantly replaced by surges of satisfaction that came with his thoughts of his killings, a feeling that he hadn't enjoyed since his years as a champion wrestler. God, how he needed those thrilling moments and the memories they produced!

After waiting for the storm to pass, Rudy got out of his truck and gathered the workers about him. "Not today, guys. Rain's gonna last until late afternoon. Pack up, go home, come back tomorrow. And, yes, you'll be paid for today, even though you're not working."

"Thank you, amigo," came a voice from the crowd. It was his best roof man Diego Velasquez, showing a dark brown face split by a wide white smile.

Rudy sat in his truck, like a load of lead. No work here today, maybe not even tomorrow. He picked up his cell phone and dialed Gary Grunwald's number. Gary picked up and said, "Hey, Rudy."

Rudy said, "Just checking in. Slow days here during the Chicago area's rainy season. Bro, you got anything for me?"

CHAPTER THIRTY-FOUR

Jack stepped around the waiting line at Dino's Ristorante and was waved forward by Marilyn, the longtime hostess stationed at the front of this bustling north side Chicago hot spot. "Moe's in his booth, Jack. You're late."

"Bad traffic, then a long wait for your valet parking guy." He leaned forward and kissed her cheek. "There is something so efficient about you Marilyn that inspires great respect, plus a lurch of lust."

She batted him on the shoulder with a large wine list. "Go eat, you rascal."

Moe was seated in his regular booth at the back of the large room whose walls were covered with blown up photos of owner Dino and show business celebrities, major and minor, who had dined here. Moe was on the phone. He waved for Jack to sit down. At once, a veteran waiter appeared with a Bushmill's on the rocks for Jack. He indicated Moe had already ordered lunch for both of them. Jack nodded in agreement.

A minute or two later Jack heard Moe say, "Arnie, that's great. I'm happy you survived, you putz." He laughed as he put his phone away.

"Who is Arnie, the putz?

Moe answered, "An old friend of mine. He was supposed to come into town to shop for some furs, but he had an accident. So, he postponed."

"Serious?"

"Hardly. He and his much younger fourth wife, Yvone, were on a biking vacation in Vermont. Jews peddling. Arnie hit a curb and got tossed to the road. He gets up hurting and they rush him to a nearby clinic, the only medical facility in the area open on Sunday.

"So he goes in, gets x-rayed, and is told that he's broken his right collarbone. They put him in a sling. Arnie says, 'Well, thanks doctor,' to this young black guy wearing green scrubs. The guy says, 'Thanks. But I'm not a doctor. We don't have doctors on staff on Sunday.'

"Arnie is stunned. He says to Yvonne, 'what have I done here? Getting treated by a nurse?'

"She tells him, 'If you're so worried, call David back home.' That's their regular doctor, David Yonover. So Arnie calls him."

Moe waved to their waiter and motioned for a refill of Jack's Irish whiskey and his own Negroni. "So Arnie gets Dr. Yonover on the phone and tells him all about his accident, the sling, the treatment by not a doctor, but a nurse. I think he said he was originally from Haiti. Maybe Jamaica.

"'Nice guy, but I'm still concerned.' He tells his doctor. 'What do you think about this?'

"Dr. Yonover says to Arnie, 'Well, it could have been worse.'

'Worse?' Arnie says. 'How?'

"Dr. Yonover says, 'It could have been me.' And he hangs up on Arnie. Pass the breadsticks, Jack. What do you hear from Ireland?"

Jack said, "From who? The uachlaran na he Eireann? Their president?"

Their lunches arrived, a garlic laden pasta platter for Kellman, an order of spaghetti Bolognese for Jack.

"Pass the butter. That sounds Yiddish, but I don't think it is."

"It's Irish. I learned it just recently."

Moe said, "You know who I'm asking about. The lovely, exciting, talented Nora Sheehan."

"You left out independent and ambitious. How is she? Fine. We email each other a few times each week. Her journalism career is zooming upward. She's been super busy lately doing stories for her new Internet employer, an outfit called Cashable."

Moe said, "Am I right in thinking you're not real pleased about this?"

Jack said, "Actually, I'm delighted for her. The woman works her beautiful butt off. She deserves all the great credit she's been getting."

"So, what's the drawback?"

"The drawback is that Nora's success guarantees she will remain over there. 'The rising star of Irish journalism,' as one media critic put it. I have a couple of times suggested—no, make that hinted—that it would be great if she would come to the States to work. Test her talents in the real Big Time. And, of course, spend more time with me."

"And?"

"Laughing, but polite refusals. Plus, and this was a surprise, an invitation for me to go over there! Set up joint housekeeping on a trial basis in her apartment right outside Dublin. See how our lives might mesh. Or not. She knows I've been divorced twice. She's never been married. I think she considers that invitation as part of an experiment. I declined. I don't want to be a lab rat in that."

Moe shook his head. "I think you're making a mistake. I've spent time with Nora Sheehan. So has my wife, Leah. We both think she's terrific. You haven't had much better offers than hers since I've known you? Why not move over there and give it a try? Your ancestral home. In the company of this wonderful young woman."

"Move?" Jack said. "And leave what I've got going on here? The Tilley case. The track executives' murders. I wouldn't even consider going anywhere until those matters are resolved. Plus, the prospect of possible marriage doesn't appeal to me. As you know, I'm not real good at marriage."

Moe said, "I appreciate your candor."

"Candor is my byword," Jack said. "Plus, I'm not sure I wouldn't get caught up in what I once read was the citizens of Ireland's most relished topics: the hubris and comeuppance of their own people."

Moe slapped the table. "Hell, Jack, you could join right up and become a leader of any movement like that. You've got the temperament and talent for it. You want dessert?"

"Thanks, but no."

The waiter delivered, not a check but a chit for Moe to initial. Jack said, "You're buying again? Multi grazie."

Their exit from the air-conditioned restaurant to an early, almost balmy, Chicago night made both men smile. Jack saw Moe's regular driver pull the big Lincoln into the waiting area. Pete parked, got out, and rested his rump on the back of the Lincoln.

"This is kind of early for me, Moe," Jack said. "You want to stop at Gibson's for a nightcap? My treat?"

"No thanks, Jack. I've had a long, hard day. Fifi Bonadio called in with a major order requiring the murder of numerous minks. Wants one coat for his wife for Christmas, the other for his current in Amorata. Asking for wholesale prices cut in half. Like always."

Jack smiled. "A request you can't refuse, right?"

"Hey, listen, Jack, this isn't some kind of threat pulled from the Godfather movie. Feef and I have been friends since grade school on the west side. We were even doing each other favors then and there. That's what is called a bond. He and I have one. Anyway, I'm tired. Ready to go into my Doctor Dentons." He clapped Jack on the shoulder and opened the Lincoln's door.

Jack said, "Wait a minute there, Moesy. You're planning to get into your Doctor Dentons? What does that mean. Who is Doctor Denton?"

Moe leaned over slapping his thighs laughing. Once he'd stopped, he said, "Jack, sometimes I forget our age differences. I take it you've never heard of Doctor Dentons?"

"Hell no."

"They were a brand of pajamas me and my two brothers wore as kids. Some kind of flannel with a drop seat. My mother saw it as a triumph when she was able to afford to get us into them for the night. I think they were kind of expensive for her in those days. Sometimes I forget, Jack, about terms I know and you don't. Generational gaps, I guess you could say."

Jack bristled. "All right, you got me with Doctor Dentons. So what? I keep a pretty good eye on past favorites."

INQUIRY

Moe grinned. "Is that right? Well, how about Tipping the Toledos?"

"Tipping the what?" Jack said. "What the hell are you talking about?"

Moe said, "In your amateur boxing days you were what, a middleweight?"

"Yeah. Right at just under 160 pouns."

"How many fights did you have? I'm not asking about your record, just the total bouts."

Jack walked over to Pete. "Does Mr. Kellman often get into a questioning mood after a dinner at Dino's?"

"That is not an infrequent occurrence," Pete responded.

Turning back to Moe, Jack said, "I had 38 recognized fights. First at welterweight, then at middle. What does this have to do with what you said, Tipping the Toledos?"

"That was a couple of decades back," Moe said. "When you were not the observant fella you've become. The Toledo, Jack, was the scale used in most athletic facilities. Tipping the Toledos was how guys my age used to inquire about weight gains or losses. Themselves, even some of their wives. That's it, Jack. My final tutorial of the night. I'm on my way." He entered the Lincoln as Pete started it.

It was a long walk to his north side condo, but Jack didn't care on this pleasant summer night. He smiled, thinking of Moe's cross generational anecdotes.

Crossing Fullerton he momentarily considered stopping for a nightcap at the Lighthouse, owned by a guy who knew, Bill Sheridan, and with a title that made no sense, since the building was located more than a mile from Lake Michigan. He decided not. By the time he'd reached home, he'd given a lot of thought to what Moe had said about his relationship with Nora Sheehan. He could not stop picturing when she was with him in Chicago and when they'd spent time together in Ireland.

He knew he missed the hell out of her.

CHAPTER THIRTY-FIVE

Dawn had just appeared when Treasure entered Ralph Tenuta's stable office on the Heartland Downs backstretch. The shed row was bustling with grooms feeding, watering, and cleaning up after the three dozen equine residents. Mexican music from boom boxes counterpointed the clank of buckets and shouts of workers singing along or loudly conversing with each other.

"Morning, Boss," Treasure said. "How many you want me to get on this morning?"

The normally welcoming trainer didn't even look up from his desk where he was riffling through employee work sheets. "Gotta find Diego's replacement," he muttered. Treasure shrugged, then sat down on one of the two very-well-worn leather couches dominating space in this small office. She attempted to pet the prized Tenuta cat called Tuxedo because of its black and white markings. Tuxedo responded with one of her regular imperious looks, jumped off the couch, and strolled across the room to the other couch. "That bitch hates me," Treasure said.

Ralph looked up. "What, Treasure? Are you talking about Tuxedo?"

"Yes, sir."

The trainer smiled. "Don't take it personally. Tuxedo doesn't like hardly anybody. Including me. Now," he continued, leaning forward over his battered old wooden desk, "I've got a problem here today. That's why I wasn't ready with the horses I want you to work today."

"What's the problem, boss?" she said, looking concerned.

Ralph said, "You know the groom Diego Velasquez? Been with me for years. He got word last night his mother is very sick down in Mexico. He called me right away to tell me he'd be away. I'll miss him. It's hard to find good help anymore. But I've got to find somebody to replace him right away."

"Well," Treasure said, "maybe I can help you out there. I've got a friend, Skip Dumke his name is, who is kind of between jobs right now. Strong young guy, loves horses, loves the race track, and knows his way around it. I'll bet he wouldn't mind filling in for Diego. Should I ask him?"

"I don't know," Ralph said. "Has this guy ever groomed horses? I can't be breaking in a rookie here."

Treasure said, "He's in good physical shape. I'm sure you could start

INQUIRY

him out as a hot walker before letting him groom horses."

Ralph sat back in his creaking chair, a sound that always brought a look of disgust from Tuxedo. He rubbed his eyes, looking like someone who had missed most of his sleep the night before. "I'm thinking, Treasure. I appreciate your help here."

Treasure got up. "I'd better get out there and start exercising your horses, Boss."

"Yeah. Sure. But Treasure, this guy Skip, are we talking reliable here? Show up on time, not hung over? Being careful with and around horses?"

She paused at the doorway. "Far as I know he'd be just what you need right now. Want me to talk to him about this? I'll probably see him at the races this afternoon."

"Yeah. Sure. Go ahead. If he wants the job, tell him to get here tomorrow morning at six. Okay? I'll leave an entrance pass at the stable gate for him."

"Naw, don't bother. I'll have him ride with me. You handle getting him a groom's license later in the day."

She checked the workout board with that day's schedule written in chalk. "I see you've got me on five, Boss. That's good." Treasure hesitated before saying, "Uh, oh. That green two-year-old filly, Goldielox. I've got to work her today? Shoot."

"Treasure, no other exercise rider around here will even get on her. She cost 200 grand as a yearling. Great breeding. But terrible temperament. Will you try again with her? Try to get her through a mile and a half gallop without taking an hour to do so? The people that spent that big money for her are all over me to get her started in a race."

Treasure said, "Have they ever seen this nut case in action?" She had made clear to Ralph what a challenge Goldielox was, telling him that, "Some mornings when I get her on the track, she cries out like a baby. Then whines like a child—boo, hoo, hoo. Strangest things I've ever heard. One morning she threw me off and tried to crawl under the starting gate to be close to another horse because she was so terrified."

"Yes," Ralph said, "I certainly remember all those war stories. But you wound up doing a great job with her. I don't know whether it was your kindness that cured her mental troubles, but whatever it was, it worked. Goldielox might turn out to be a real racehorse—thanks a lot to you."

Ralph closed the notebook, got up, and walked to the door. "I'll have Goldielox saddled and ready for you in a couple of minutes." He patted Treasure on the shoulder. "You've done a great job with her."

"Thanks, Boss," she muttered as he exited. "If I'm doing such great work, how about a great fucking bonus once in awhile," she muttered.

He couldn't have overheard her, but Treasure was startled when Ralph stopped, turned around, and walked back.

"That guy, your friend, Skip, you sure he'll start tomorrow morning?"

"Count on it," she said, producing a smile as Goldielox was brought to her and she got a leg up from Ralph.

They walked the loam path from the barn area and the filly threw her head as she approached the entrance to the training track. Treasure had her stop and observe the scene of dozens of horses going past, some galloping, a few walking, some sprinting. She put her right hand on Goldielox's trembling neck. "Not to worry," she said, and began to hum the Cajun legendary song, Jolie Blon. Goldielox took a big sigh. She turned her head to look back at Treasure who said, "Okay, baby, let's fucking do it."

***

An hour after the races had ended late that afternoon, Treasure knocked on Skip's door in the Extended Stay Building. It took three loud knocks before the door opened. Skip, hair mussed, face slack, said, "Hey, it's you. Come on in Treasure. What brings you here?"

She said, "Did I wake you up? Didn't you go to the track this afternoon? What's going on?"

He stumbled over and sat down on the side of the rumpled bed. "I took the day off. Felt like hell, tired and depressed. My life is shit, if you'll pardon the expression."

"Well, yeah, I guess you're in kind of a tough patch here, Skipper. But," she smiled, "I've got a proposition for you. How about you going to work for trainer Ralph Tenuta starting tomorrow morning? Short hours probably in the beginning, but regular pay. I think you'd like that kind of work. You know, fresh air, exercise, and so on. A whole new outlook for you. And frankly, you look like you need one."

Skip said, "Me? Working with horses? Hell, the only thing I know about those animals is how to lose money betting on them. You must be kidding."

Treasure walked to the bed and sat down. She began to lift her tee shirt up and off, smiling as Skip's eyes focused on her breasts. Then she reached down and began to unbutton his pants, her eyes boring into his.

"I am not kidding, Skipper. Once you start working for Ralph Tenuta, I've got something in mind that'll make money for both of us."

Skip looked on with wonder as Treasure rose and shucked off her jeans before coming to the bed and straddling his lap. "Jesus," Skip said softly. His hands circled her back as she pressed her lips on his then her tongue in his mouth.

A minute later, she broke away and leaned slightly backward as she took his trembling hand and placed it on her left breast. Smiling broadly, Treasure said, "Am I right about you now, Skipper? You'll do this favor for me, going to work for Tenuta? Am I right?"

Dumke groaned in tumescent agreement.

INQUIRY

CHAPTER THIRTY-SIX

Jack reached across Moe to pay the beer vendor for two seriously over-priced beverages. "Keep the change," he said.

"Not much change here" was the scowled reply. Jack frowned. "I used to be able to buy two six-packs for what I've just paid here in this outdoor clip joint for two beers."

At least once each summer, Jack and Moe attended a baseball game at hallowed Wrigley Field, one of the nation's oldest ballparks and host to one of the nation's least successful won and loss franchises. Last World Series win: 1908. Last WS appearance: 1945.

Moe bought season tickets each year for use by customers of his furrier business. Each year, the price rose like the morning sun, but Moe didn't wince. "People I deal with love this ballpark. When they fly in to Chicago in the summer, this is one of the main things they want to see. I oblige them. They are even excited about the Cubs this year."

"Am I correct in assuming that my butt now rests upon a seat that costs more than 90 bucks per game?"

"Yes," Moe said. "The owners raised the prices again. But, at least the product seems to be improving along with the ticket gouging."

"It sure as hell should," Jack said. They joined the 39,000 in attendance standing for the national anthem being sung by a Chicago mainstay Wayne Messmer of Cubs, White Sox, and Bulls games. Midway through the song Moe turned away from the field as he answered his cell phone.

"Batter up," they heard the announcer say as the lead off man for the St. Louis Cardinals approached the plate. Moe pocketed his cell phone and sat down.

"Bad news, Moesy? You look disturbed," Jack said.

Moe reached for his beer. "No," he said, "not disturbed. Make it distressed. That was my oldest grandson, Seamus Blittstein." He gave Jack a challenging look.

Jack said, "No comment. I am well aware of your negative attitude about your young family members using Irish first names for their children in recent years. Not a subject I feel like reprising."

They looked up, hearing the roar of the third strikeout of the first inning by the Cubs best pitcher. "All right," Jack said. "Great start."

Moe said, "My grandson Seamus is a beautiful kid. But he keeps pestering me to come to this one-night musical performance in some kind of off-the-wall sites around Chicago. Once in awhile, just for his sake, I do."

Jack patted Moe on the knee. "That's what a terrific grandpa should do. So, what's your problem with this request?"

The Cubs went down in order in the bottom half of the first. Jack signaled the scowling vendor for two more beers. He waited for Moe's answer to his question.

"Jack, what can I tell you? I love Seamus. Maybe I've not enjoyed his musical efforts, but at least I've encouraged him. Why not? I've always rooted for people who try hard and work hard."

The Cubs third batter, ace first baseman Anthony Rizzo, cracked a homer deep into the right field bleachers. Wrigley Field erupted. Inning ended with the Cubs up by a run.

Jack said, "Well, that was fun. Now, Moe, tell me what's bothering you about young Seamus."

"Jack, I don't know anything about what he's doing. Garage punk music? I think that's what he calls it. He's also starting to rap. Can you imagine? A teenage Jewish rapper? Then, he keeps changing the name of this four-person band. It went from Clean Meat to Rot Awhile to Dorsel Morsels. There's probably going to be another new name next week."

Jack said, "He'll probably grow out of it."

"Yeah. But, will I?"

At the end of the fifth inning, as players trotted on an off the glistening green Wrigley grass, there was a commotion behind them. Moe and Jack got up and turned around. Five rows up, in the aisle, there was a chubby millennial fellow on his knees before a grinning girl with her arms held wide. Cameras were flashing around this couple. The chubby lad presented a ring that was quickly accepted. He struggled to his feet and embraced his bride to be. All the younger patrons in the area applauded loudly, some whistling. A man with a video cam gave them a thumbs up and hurried back up the aisle.

"I need another beer," Jack said. "I find that brand of exhibitionism offensive."

Moe paid for their beers. "Why?"

"Because, it's so cute it could make me puke. These public proposals of marriage are all over the place because the participants are dying to be seen. Guy on his knees offering a ring to a supposedly-stunned girl. Happens on city streets. The aisles of airplanes for Chrissake. Always filmed by some buddy of theirs. One guy I know, his son arranged with a cop friend of his to stop his car one night when he was driving his woman home. Siren goes on, squad car lights flashing. The driver gets out and kneels down on the side of Dempster Street in Skokie and holds out the ring as the cop shines his flashlight on the supposedly surprised girl."

INQUIRY

They watched as the Cubs Kris Bryant slid into second base with a double. Moe said, "What do you mean when you say this guy's girl was 'supposedly' surprised before the video camera?"

"You know, Moe, for a man of your age, experience, acumen, you sometimes surprise me. Call it senior citizen naivete in your case. Supposedly surprised?' That's redolent bullshit. Very few guys have romantic imaginings like that. It's their women who design these dramatic scenes that they have recorded and displayed on their Facebook pages."

Moe drained his beer. "Jack, you may be right."

"Yet once again," Jack said.

CHAPTER THIRTY-SEVEN

Kris Bryant was stranded at second after his lead off double, but it didn't seem to matter because the Cubs ace pitcher, Jake Arrieta, continued to mow down the opposing batters and protect his shutout. The sunshine warmed the appreciative thousands.

Jack said, "You know, Moe, people are talking World Series about this team. Pretty exciting."

"I was here the last time the Cubs got into the World Series."

"You're talking 1945, right? Decades ago? You were perhaps a stripling?"

Moe said, "Don't be making light of my involvement with the Cubs. Yes, I was a kid then. My Uncle Max took me to the July doubleheader when a good pitcher named Hank Borowey arrived in Chicago from the New York Yankees after an unusual mid-season trade. Uncle Max and I were in the first row down from the left field line, right where the Cubs bullpen was. I could lean over and see Hank Borowy warm up. Jeez, could you hear the pop of his pitches hitting the bullpen catcher's glove.

"Uncle Max put his hand on my neck and pushed my head forward. He said, 'Moe, watch when he warms up his curve ball.'"

Moe paused, took a sip of his beer. "What a memory that was, Jack.

I leaned over and watched this guy Borowy, his curve ball from right to left into the catcher's glove. I had never seen a real major league curve ball! He did that for about ten minutes. Then he took the mound and pitched the second game of that day's doubleheader and shut out the Cardinals. He went on to win ten more games for the Cubs that season. Only pitcher then to win ten games in one year in two different major leagues. Got the Cubs into the Series. He was something, Jack."

"Which they lost. They haven't been back in since '45. Haven't won a World Series since memory of man runneth to the contrary."

Moe said, "Don't be such a smart ass. Yes, the franchise has an historic record of futility." He signaled the now very-attentive vendor for two more beers and again tipped him lavishly.

"I was in third grade in '45. That loss was a crusher. Our teacher was a baseball fan and she let us listen to the series on a radio she brought in. Very nice lady. Miss Eckstrom. When the final game ended, she saw that I had tears in my eyes. She had some in hers, too, and gave me a big hug. The only good thing about that experience was when I got home that afternoon. My cherished mother Pearl had also listened to the game and knew the result. Bless her, she leaped into action and baked a cherry pie, my favorite dessert then. And now, for that matter. Helped ease my pain in a big way that sad day."

They joined the crowd in standing for the singing of "Take Me Out to the Ballgame." Today's guest vocalist fit the regular pattern of being a minor celebrity with a major musical flaw leading to his being off-key throughout. Huge applause followed the last bedraggled notes. Jack said, "They must be clapping because he's finally finished murdering that song."

"Could be," Moe said. "You know, Jack, thinking back to 1945, I learned a lot about life that year because of this ballclub. How to have your hopes dashed. And even before the World Series loss, there was another memorable Wrigley Field moment for me. Get this, even as short as I was, I played first base on our neighborhood team. Mainly because I was a good enough fielder to snatch up the variety of off-target throws headed my way from third base, Buddy Lepp, and shortstop Gerry Greenberg. Not easy work.

"Anyway, my Cubs hero at that time was the Cubs first baseman. Uncle Max and I always got to the ballpark early so I could watch batting practice.

"When that was over, Max went inside to make a phone call. I took my program over to where my hero was talking with a guy. The conversation went on. I waited. When they had shaken hands at the end of their talk, I piped up, 'Mr. Phil, could I please get your autograph?'

"He'd started to walk away when I said that. Then he stopped. I thought, 'wow, he's going to sign for me.' Nope. All my favorite Cubs first baseman said was 'Get the fuck out of here kid.' It was like a kick to the heart. When I went back to my seat next to Uncle Max, I had tears in my eyes. He asked me what happened. I told him.

"I can still hear him saying, 'Why, that heartless son of a bitch.' Then he put his arm around me and said, 'Sorry to say it, but that's how life can be with these so-called heroes. Remember that, Moe. How about a hot dog and a Coke?'"

Moe drained his beer cup. "The memory of that afternoon is as clear to me today as it was then. That failed attempt to get a valued autograph was a life lesson I have never forgotten. You know, in a way it was a good thing to have learned that young."

"What?" Jack said. "How to have your heart broken when you were in short pants? That was a good thing?"

Moe said, "I'm not saying it was a good thing. It was a valuable thing and helped me shape my life, its expectations. You know, Jack, one of your fellow Irishers made a comment I've never forgotten."

"Who?"

"Daniel Patrick Moynihan. You must remember him. He was a famous sociologist, worked in several administrations in D. C. He once said 'I don't think there's any point in being Irish if you don't know that the world is going to break your heart, eventually.' I would amend that to say you don't need to be Irish to relate to what Moynihan was saying. You can quote this Jew on that."

Jack shrugged. "I can't argue with that, Moe."

There was a very loud crack of the bat and thousands of Wrigleyites jumped up from their seats to admire the flight of Anthony Rizzo's rocket blast clear the right field bleachers. Rizzo trotted around the bases until he reached home plate, where he was engulfed in a jumble of excited teammates. "Walk-off homer," Moe said. "Cubs win in the bottom of the ninth." He gripped Jack's arm, grinning. "Damn, that's fun. Maybe this team really does have what it takes after all those years of futility."

Jack, laughing, gave his friend a hug. "Great to see you so excited, Moesy."

"Hey, Jack, after decades of 'Wait until next year,' maybe next year has finally fucking arrived! C'mon, I'll buy you dinner."

They moved their way slowly through the exuberant fist-bumping, high-fiving crowd, several of the celebrating women of Moe's age. As the crowd headed toward the exits, Jack looked back toward the diamond. The late afternoon sun brought all the outfield greenery, the famed ivy on the outfield walls, to vivid sight. He smiled, thinking, pretty great afternoon.

Pete was right where he said he would be, just outside the park. He was chatting with the police officer who'd allowed him to park in this valuable spot. Moe nodded as Pete waved him forward.

Jack's cell phone buzzed and he took it out of his pocket to open it as he neared Moe's Lincoln Town Car. He suddenly stopped. He reached forward and grabbed Moe's elbow.

Puzzled, Moe said, "What's up, Jack?"

Jack said into the phone, "Got it, Calvin."

"Damn," Jack said as he pocketed his phone.

Moe said, "What it is, Jack?

"Another murder of a racetrack executive. That was Calvin Douglas. Celia's husband. He usually defines imperturbable. Not today. I've got to meet those two today."

He waved at Pete, then jumped off the curb to hail a slowly-passing, empty cab. "Moe, thanks for the game. Great afternoon. Go Cubs!"

INQUIRY

CHAPTER THIRTY-EIGHT

Jack exited the taxi two traffic-clogged streets from his condo. He sprinted the three blocks to his basement garage, started the gray Honda, and headed south out of the city to Monee Park.

Fifty minutes later, he entered the almost deserted track parking lot. Night racing was scheduled for this date, first post time at eight o'clock, so neither patrons nor most employees were present this late afternoon. He hurried through the unattended clubhouse entrance and took the elevator to the top floor executive offices.

Celia's secretary looked up as he hustled through the door. No smiling welcome from this longtime friend of Celia's. Her striking, copper colored face was set in an expression of concern. She got out from behind her desk and walked up and hugged him. "Jack! Thanks for coming so quickly. You made good time. Calvin told me he called you only an hour or so ago." She frowned. "They're in there," she said, motioning to the doorway to Celia's office.

They were standing at the broad window behind Celia's desk, looking out over the deserted track, hands held tight. He closed the door gently behind him. "Ah, excuse me, folks. It's the Jack Doyle to the Rescue squad now on hand."

Celia laughed. Calvin managed a grin. Jack kissed the former and shook hands with the latter. "Jack," Calvin said, "I'm sorry to bother you on such short notice. But Celia and I are very, very concerned about the safety of these women racetrack executives—especially hers."

"Can't blame you, Calvin. What happened today?"

Celia took an email printout from her desk. "Actually, not today, Jack. Probably late last night. Aurelio Gomez was killed. She was the recently-appointed vice president of Madison Park. Very nice woman and one of the few Latino women in a major position at an American racetrack. This in an industry which is dependent on Latinos to fill numerous backstretch jobs. She was a trail blazer. Now she's gone."

Jack asked, "What happened to her?"

Celia shuddered. Calvin put his arm around her. He said, "According to the early reports, Ms. Gomez was strangled."

"Jesus," Jack said. "Where?"

Calvin said, "In the parking lot of her condo building. She evidently had just gotten out of her car when she was attacked. No witnesses. No known suspects! The police said it didn't look like a robbery because her purse was there, intact, as well as her laptop computer which she always brought home from the track with her."

"Isn't Madison Park one of the tracks that barred Ted Tilley's horses?"

"Yes," Celia said. She moved to the chair behind her desk, sat down, and put her head in her hands. "Aurelio and I met at a National Racing Association convention about five years ago. We were among the very few women there as participants. I think there were three of his. Aurelio was outgoing, interesting, super smart. I was grateful she decided to become friends with me. I was honored. To think of her being murdered just makes me sick. Physically and emotionally."

Jack waited while Celia reached for another Kleenex. "Celia, did you ever discuss barring Ted Tilley's stable with Ms. Gomez?"

"Yes. We agreed it was in the best interest of racing. I wasn't completely convinced of that. But I went along because Peggy Vandervort was so forcefully pushing for this decision."

Jack said, "Should I know that name?"

"Peggy is president of Oakbrook Downs, which she inherited from her father who built it."

"And," Jack said, "how many others did Ms. Peggy convince to join the anti-Ted Tilley cause?"

Calvin snorted, "Jack, you should know how many. There were five tracks. And now three women employed at them are gone. That's why we're scared to death here today. Celia could be next on this list of murdered women. I know it sounds crazy. But, hey, man, we're facing this."

Jack walked to the window, paused, watching a lone racehorse going through a workout. Back still turned to them, he said, "I've got to think about this."

Celia led Calvin to the brown leather office couch positioned under the array of photographs depicting famous horses that had won at Monee Park. He was tapping his foot impatiently. Celia whispered, "Do not push this man. Just sit. It won't take him long to say something to us about all this mess." She felt Calvin squeeze her hand.

Calvin took a good look at Jack Doyle. Not a big guy. But, he'd been told, a successful amateur boxer. What he remembered best was Celia's account of Jack, in self defense one night in the Monee Park barn area, killing a threatening criminal by thrusting a pitch fork into his gut.

Jack sat down in the chair across from their couch. He spread his hands, saying, "Well, my friends this is very serious business. But what the hell are we dealing with here? This is three racetrack women dead in the course of a couple of months. Is this some kind of Ted Bundy imitator turning his attention to racing? I heard the police believe the first two cases were random killings. The death of Aurelio Gomez moves this whole scenario into another level. One that spells out specific attacks on targeted women."

Celia said, "Nobody seems to have any idea about who is carrying out these killings. The women die, there's been no trace of the killer, or killers. I'm not the only one now fearing for my life. Peggy Vandervoort at Oakbrook and I are the only two remaining women at tracks that tossed Tilley."

Celia got up from the couch, patting Calvin's hand as she did. "Well, I've alerted our security staff to be on the lookout. And Calvin, of course, is on the alert."

Jack asked, "Is that so-called security staff still headed by Barry Shulman? Your longtime employee you inherited with the track? An unpleasant old fart who couldn't find his ass with both hands behind him?"

"Now wait a minute here, Jack," Calvin said. "Celia knows how to run this business. I don't like you questioning her judgment."

Jack said, "Well, tough shit, Calvin. Celia is great at most things life demands of her. But her defending and employing this inept jerk is a triumph of loyalty over reality. Usually a bad bet.

"Looks to me," he continued, "the motive could well be some brand of deranged revenge. And who would qualify on that count? Ted Tilley springs to mind."

Celia said, "Because of his being excluded from these tracks? Well, I could see that as a motive maybe. But as far as I know, Tilley has no criminal background. It's hard to imagine him connected to this." She shook her head. "I don't why I got myself talked into tossing Tilley's stable out."

Calvin said, "I agree with Celia about Tilley. Guy seems absolutely on the up and up. I think we'd better start looking elsewhere for the killers."

"You may be right," Jack said. "On the other hand, maybe we shouldn't look too far away from Tilley. I've already had a meeting with his right hand man, Gary Grunwald. He could be running this rampage without his boss knowing about it. He and Tilley go back a long way and Gary is very, very loyal."

He looked at his watch. "If I hustle, I can get a late afternoon flight to Albany and drive to Tilley's business headquarters in the morning. I'm sure Gary will be there."

"Are you going to let Gary know you're coming?" asked Celia.

Jack smiled. "Of course not. A pretty smart fellow once said, 'the element of surprise is both powerful and productive.'"

He kissed Celia's cheek, shook Calvin's hand, and walked to the door. Calvin said, "Jack, what smart fellow was that, that you mentioned?"

"To be honest," Jack said, "it was me. I'll be in touch."

Calvin turned to Celia and said, "Our friend Jack Doyle does not lack for confidence, does he?"

"Never has and never will," Celia said.

***

Jack hustled to the distant O'Hare gate just minutes before boarding time for American flight to Albany. He'd bought an overpriced bottle of water and a similarly expensive bag of potato chips on his way, dinner on this flight. On board, he used his cell phone to make another call to Gary Grunwald. Again, he heard a recorded request to leave a message.

"Mr. Grunwald," he said, "I'd prefer to talk to you person, but I guess that's not possible now. Just know that I will be in your office bright and early in the morning. I have a serious matter to discuss with you. It would be even better if you could have Mr. Tilley join us. See you."

Minutes later, he looked out his window at the city he loved living in. When the plane headed east over Lake Michigan, he ate half of his chips, drank half of his water, and laid his head back and went to sleep.

CHAPTER THIRTY-NINE

Still troubled by sharp headaches, Rudy grew even more depressed when a succession of odd thoughts suddenly began coursing through his damaged head on a regular basis.

All of a sudden names were popping up that he had never previously given any thought to. One morning it was Rimsky Korsakov. "What the fuck?" he shouted. "Is that some Russian hockey player? I don't get it."

Two days later, song snatches began to invade, almost always of a sort he hated. "You will see a stranger across a crowded room…" plagued Rudy all of that morning. The next night, out of nowhere, his mind kept repeating, "Chicks and ducks and geese better scurry…Shall we dance bop, bop, bop..." What the double fuck!

These intrusive song remnants, he knew, could be traced to his previous year's affair with Claudia Stabler. She loved American musicals and rented them to play on her television by the score. Rudy sat on the brown leather couch in her living room snuggled close to his semi-beautiful construction company bookkeeper, eager to get his large hands on her hot little body. Glancing at the screen, he was bored as stiff as his dick was stiff. Movie over, Claudia and he would get right to it.

Claudia astounded Rudy when she suddenly decided to join her brother-in-law's accounting firm in Laramie, WY. He missed the hell out of her. He didn't miss the damn music. Now, Rudy was burdened by the frequent invasion of those damn lyrics, "When you walk through a storm…" Another product of his damaged head.

CHAPTER FORTY

Treasure hit what she saw as her jackpot early on a Friday morning at Heartland Downs. That was when Ralph informed her that stable manager Paul Albano had been called away. "A serious illness in his family," Ralph had said. "Wouldn't tell me who. You know how closed-mouth he is. Anyway, I don't know how long he'll be gone."

"Who is going to replace Albano?" Treasure asked.

Ralph said, "I've hired back a guy I fired two years ago. Max Tyson. Excellent horseman with years of race track experience."

"I'm not sure I get this. If this Tyson is good, why did you let him go?"

"Because he has a huge loud mouth on him. He drives a lot of people crazy with his attitude and opinions, including most of my staff of grooms and hot walkers. I'm not very fond of him either. But," Ralph sighed, "the son of a gun knows how to run an efficient shedrow. He knows my routines here, what I want done. So, I've got him on the payroll again."

Treasure walked down the shedrow to where a man she'd never seen before was saddling the gelding she was scheduled to exercise. He looked, to her, to be maybe three or four inches taller than her five feet four height. Blocky build, large hands. He was very efficient and was quickly finished saddling. When he turned around, he took off his ball cap that said LOYAL TRUMPSTER. Under his sandy haired buzz cut was a tanned face that bordered on handsome. She heard him say, "You must be the exercise rider. What do you know? Ralph finally hired some good looking help."

Treasure said, "You must be Mr. Tyson. Great to meet you, Max.

"None other. C'mon, I'll give you a leg up." He also gave her ass a strong pat as she mounted the gelding. "That's got a good feel to it," he said.

"I think you're leering at me Mr. Tyson. I've got work to do." She motioned to the hot walker to lead her gelding out on the path leading to the training track. He broke into a trot, Treasure standing up in the stirrups, a picture of grace and health and strength on this early morning.

"That's what I like about this place," Max said to the hotwalker whose limited command of English did not command that statement.

Tyson commandeered one of the Tenuta stable golf carts and took it to the training track in time to see Treasure starting to breeze past on an unstarted two-year-old filly named Appleton Annie. He looked at his stopwatch when the workout was over. Treasure had been told to work the filly a half-mile in :52 and that's exactly what she did. "Impressive," Max said to himself.

In the course of the next week, Treasure saw an opportunity in Max and worked to exploit it. She listened, sometimes amazed, as he talked about horses, racing, jockeys, trainers and owners in a profanity-laced monolog. He expressed no affection for the animals he made his living off of, referring to most as crow bait. He hinted of fixed races he knew about, always awaiting Treasure's shocked reaction, and a jockey he knew he described as "the master of the illegal battery." Asked to name him, Max grinned and refused.

After listening to the verbose new Tenuta employee for nearly a week, she concluded he was full of crap—engaged in a campaign to shock and impress her. That's when she had Skip Dumke secretly record on his cell phone Max's tirades on three mornings after his hot walking duties were finished.

Late that first week, Treasure accepted Max's invitation for breakfast in the Heartland Downs track kitchen following workout hours, then dinner two nights later at a nearby Applebee's.

"Big spender, eh?" she said as he drove her back to her apartment.

"Better days are coming, sweetheart, of that I am sure."

Treasure said, "How about better nights. You want to come on up for awhile? I can pour you an after-dinner drink and maybe you can tell me a few more of your war stories from the backstretch."

Max reached his big right hand across the seat and began to gently rub the back of Treasure's neck.

"Oh," she said, "that feels good, Max."

He removed his hand, parked, took the key out of the ignition, and opened his door. "I've got something thriving in my jeans here, Honey, that'll feel a whole lot better than a neck rub."

Treasure took his hand and led him to her door. Inside, she turned to give him a kiss while reaching for his swelling crotch. "Oh, c'mon big boy," she whispered walking to the bedroom. She ripped off her tee shirt and threw it on the floor. Max nearly ran her over in his haste to get close to the bed.

Two hours later Max, exhausted, left. Treasure heard the door close. She lay back on her rumpled bed, smiling. "That big prick has a big prick," she said to herself. "And I'm going to use Mister Arrogant Max Tyson."

Treasure set the four a.m. alarm on her cell phone. She walked into her bathroom and then into the shower and let it run hot for five minutes before toweling off and returning to her rumpled bed sheets still redolent of Tyson's sweaty efforts.

Head on the pillow, eyes on the gently whirring ceiling fan, she said, "Christ, what I have to go through in order to make a decent living."

CHAPTER FORTY-ONE

Gary met Jack at the Tilley Company's reception area. They shook hands as Gary said, "I told Ted you were coming. He wants to see you, Jack. I hope you don't mind."

"Fine with me," Jack said.

Ted came from behind his desk to greet Jack and the men sat down around it.

"Coffee, Jack? Water?" Ted asked.

Jack declined, leaned forward, and said, "I'm here because of the recent deaths of racing executives in the Midwest. Women, all from tracks that had barred your stable."

Ted frowned. "Those were terrible things that happened. But what do they have to do with us?"

"Ted, I'll be blunt. Trying to figure out who the killer is, or killers are, I thought of motive. What the hell would the motive be to lead to murders? Hate to say it, men, but you came up big in speculations."

Ted's large fists clenched on the desk before him. His face reddened. "Mr. Doyle you are way out of line. Do you actually believe I wouldresort to threats, to physical violence, to protest my banishment? That's a ridiculous and very insulting suggestion. I'm fighting these people through the courts, period."

Jack saw Gary turning away from the conversation to look out the picture window. He felt a tremor of anticipation right behind his breast bone. He said, "Ted, I respect your very creditable record for honesty. But let me ask you this. Is it not possible that someone in your employ, or some other admirer of yours, might get involved in what is apparently a failed blackmail scheme? One that's resulted in the deaths of three women at this point?"

Ted sprang to his feet and leaned forward with his fists on the desk. "There is no way, Jack, that anyone working for me would be encouraged to commit crimes like these. No damn way!" He walked out from behind the desk as he said, "And that's all I've got to say to you, Jack."

The door banged closed. Jack looked at Gary who stood up with his hands stretched out, shoulders hunched in a shrug. "What can I tell you Jack? The man has spoken. That's all there is to it."

Jack smiled. "Gary, I doubt that very much. So long."

INQUIRY

In his rented Focus driving to the airport, Jack used his cell phone to call Calvin Douglas. "Calvin, I just finished here at Tilley's. Not any real progress. Ted denied any involvement in the killings and I tend to believe him. His right hand man, Gary, however, I've got my doubts about. Look, I've got to cut this short. The state cops around here are famous for nailing drivers texting or talking."

"Okay," Calvin said. "But, real quick, did you learn anything solid on your visit up there?"

Jack said, "Sure did. I learned not to take a night flight out of Chicago after a hard day's work. Very tiring. Hold on while I park."

He drove the Focus into an open slot in the Rental Car Return lot. "You still there, Calvin?"

"Yes. So what else can you tell me? Don't you have anything more to report, Jack?"

Jack grinned. "Like the holder of a marked deck in a high stakes poker game, I've held something back. I'm getting on the transfer bus now." He heard an exasperated sigh. I don't know why I like to yank Calvin's chain, but I do, he thought.

"My main point Calvin is that we have to surround Celia with a tight and efficient security presence. Not that doddering old Barry Shulman she employs. We need to get some pros. I don't know who is killing these women but I sure don't want to see Celia added to that sad list."

Calvin said, "Naturally, Jack. But I don't know anybody who could recommend top security people."

"You don't have to, Calvin. I'm going to give you the phone number of a great friend of mine who will know exactly what security people you should get. His name is Moe Kellman."

Calvin said, "I understand he's a friend of yours. Why should I call him? Why don't you?"

"Because you're the one that can give Moe and his people the daily details of Celia's schedule. I don't know them. You live with her, you should know."

Calvin said, "Give me Kellman's number. I'll call him right away."

"At the start of your conversation make clear to Moe that I told you to call him." He paused as he saw the shuttle bus to the terminal approaching and heard Calvin ask, "What does this Kellman know about security firms?"

"More than you want to know," Jack laughed. "Seriously, Moe can line you up with dependable security personnel. Ordinarily you'd have to foot the bill. But I'm sure I can get Moe to waive that as a favor to me."

Calvin said, "I'll have to clear this with Celia."

"Don't waste time here, Calvin. Just tell her it's a done deal arranged by me. She'll go along with that."

"I don't know anything about this security outfit Kellman will contact. What should I tell her if she asks for details?"

Jack said, "Kellman's so-called security outfit will be comprised of trusted members of the Chicago Outfit headed by his friend since boyhood, Fifi Bonadio. Moe has called on Bonadio for help in the past, and vice versa. You can count on competence here, Calvin."

"Good. I'll make that call right now. Have a good flight, Jack."

With no luggage or carry-on Jack zipped through airport security. He looked at a large wall clock hanging over the entrance to a bar named Comfort for Travelers, laughed, and entered. He found an empty stool at the far end.

The bartender, a tall blond woman whose nametag read "Aggie" smiled at him and said, "What'll it be traveler?"

"Make it a double Bushmills on the rocks with a splash, Aggie. And make it quick, please. I've got to board in ten minutes." He watched as she quickly prepared his drink. "Good work Aggie," Jack said. "Interesting name you have. Were you named after a marble in the playground game by any chance?"

She laughed with him. "No. I was baptized Agnes Flynn. Named for the patron saint of young girls. My folks were serious Catholics."

"Agnes is not a name you hear much anymore," Jack said.

"Like Ruth and Nancy and Mary," she laughed as she delivered his drink."

Jack laid a $20 bill on the bar. "Keep the change," he said. Aggie waited while Jack quickly emptied his cocktail glass. He slid it toward her. "Nice work, Aggie. I'm off for Chicago."

INQUIRY

CHAPTER FORTY-TWO

Another Racetrack Exec Murdered

By Matt O'Connor

America's thoroughbred industry is currently dealing with the fallout of the death of Aurelio Gomez, vice president of racing operations at Madison Park, last week the third murder victim among prominent racetrack employees in the past three months. Ogden Cripps, president of the National Association of Racing Commissioners, said today, "We are horrified. And baffled. What the heck is going on here?"

Ms. Gomez, 38, was attacked outside her Madison, IL condominium near midnight.. A resident of the building heard a woman's scream, looked out her window, and watched in horror as Ms. Gomez was grabbed from the back by a burly assailant, and thrown to the pavement. She was then strangled. This took less than a minute, according to the shaken observer, who called 911 to report the attack.

She told police the murderer fled toward a nearby parking lot. She was unable to see if he was heading for a vehicle.

Ms. Gomez began her life on the racetrack as a groom for her trainer-fatherm Eduardo Gomezm at thoroughbred tracks in New Mexico and Colorado.

An excellent student, she gained a scholarship to the University of Arizona's Racetrack Program and graduated with honors. She then began a progression of jobs at small tracks leading to large ones. Her appointment to the Madison Park position came seven years ago, where her work and work ethic were widely admired.

Said Madison Park owner Paul Nordine, "We are devastated. Aurelio was a brilliant, warm hearted, and tremendously efficient employee. She loved racing at all its levels. And she treated workers in all those levels equally—with respect and compassion. This loss is just unbelievable."

A memorial service for Ms. Gomez will be held at Mount Carmel Catholic Church on Saturday. Her father will attend. She is also survived by her husband, Garret, and their two daughters."

In the deaths of these three women—first, Marcy Darcy of Pleasant Prairie, followed by Nancy Roth of Cahokia Park—no suspect or suspects in the killings has ever been identified. The common thread is all three women, worked at tracks that had barred the horses of prominent owner, Ted Tilley.

Reached for comment early today, Tilley said he was, "horrified by these developments. I have no idea why this murderous campaign is being carried out. I have filed lawsuits against these tracks that have so unfairly and arbitrarily acted against me. That's all I've done. Again, my heartfelt condolences to the relatives of all these women."

INQUIRY

CHAPTER FORTY-THREE

Gary called Ted at his home that night. "Ted, I have to go out of town for a day or two. Chicago."

"What for, Gary? I thought you were going to chair our staff meeting on Friday?"

"Sorry, can't do it. There's some personal business I have to take care of."

Ted said, "Okay then. Travel well."

***

Gary had called Rudy early that morning. "Rudy, I'm flying in later today. We need to talk."

Rudy sat up in bed, cell phone in hand. As he got up, he gave Vicki Dupree's ass a sharp pat. She moaned and rolled away from him. In the kitchen, Rudy started the coffee maker.

"What time's your flight, Gary? Want me to pick you up?"

"No thanks. Let's have lunch at our favorite Chicago place. I'll cab there, meet you at noon. Okay?

Rudy said, "Sure. See you there." He turned off his cell phone and poured his first cup of coffee, frowning, thinking this must be some serious shit Gary's coming here for.

***

Morrie's Deli and Cafeteria on S. Jefferson St. in Chicago was a landmark gathering place for politicians, police officers, and various movers and shakers for some 80 years. Gary had introduced Rudy to it four years before. Since then, Rudy had become a twice-a-week customer, even driving in from construction projects in the western suburbs.

When asked why he would bother to make those trips, Rudy said, "Numerous good reasons. The pickled tongue. The babka. The smoked sable. The best pastrami outside of New York City. Top notch Jew food."

Neither Rudy nor Gary were Jewish, but that did not hinder their appreciation for the fare Morrie's provided.

They met at the crowded entrance, shook hands, and smiled at each other. Rudy said, "Looks like all the tables are taken in there and there's a long line of people waiting for them. How about we order takeout?"

Gary shrugged. "Okay. I'll wait here. Get me a regular pastrami on onion roll. Where are you parked?"

"Pastrami it shall be. You remember what that one comedian said years ago about that food?"

"No."

"He said pastrami killed more Jews than Hitler." Laughing, Rudy clapped Gary on the shoulder and pointed to his black pickup truck double parked on the south side of 22nd St. "Here's the key. Sit in and turn on the air conditioning. No, don't reach for your wallet. Lunch is on me." Gary watched as broad-shouldered Rudy made his way past the crowded outside line and entered Morrie's. Gary had begun to feel the effects of a typical 95-degree Chicago summer afternoon. Sweat starting to curl down his spine. He hustled across the street to the truck.

Minutes later Rudy yanked open his door, handed Gary a bulging brown bag of food, and said, "Get me a beer, will you? Cooler's behind my seat."

"You gonna drink and drive?"

Rudy, checking his text messages, didn't reply. Then he started the engine, made a U-Turn, and headed for the Kennedy Expressway.

"Rudy, where are you going?"

"Relax, Gary. I know you've only got a couple of hours before your flight back East. I'm going to get us a nice shady spot in that forest preserve just east of O'Hare, Schiller Woods. We can have our lunch and our talk there. Then I can bring you to the airport."

Gary nodded. He wiped his still-moist forehead as Rudy reached forward and turned on his radio that was set loud to a tape by the rocker Neil Young.

Gary poked Rudy's right arm. "You know, or do you remember, that I can't stand Neil Young?"

"So," Rudy grinned. "You want my Ted Nugent tape?"

Gary groaned and said "I'd rather listen to the sounds of root canals being performed." He looked out his window at the heavy traffic they were leaving in their wake. Jesus, he thought, my man Rudy ain't my man Rudy anymore. I think he's run off the rails.

***

There were only three well-spaced vehicles in the Schiller Woods forest preserve parking lot when Rudy sped into it before slamming on his brakes at the far south end. He got out, reached in for the red cooler that was now sloshing with ice water and the few remaining beer cans, and marched to a picnic table positioned under a towering weeping willow tree.

"Want a beer, Gary?"

"No thanks. I think I'm going to hold off on my food for awhile, too."

Rudy shrugged before taking a huge bite out of his sandwich. When he'd swallowed, he said, "Okay, Gary, lay it on the table. What are you here

INQUIRY

for? What do you want with me?"

"You must have a pretty good idea, Rudy. I'm here about the killings you've done." He reached across the worn wooden table and gripped his old friend's wrist. "When this all started, the whole idea was for you to scare these targets. Nudge them toward complying with my plan to get Ted Tilley back in the game. The idea never was for you to wipe them out."

Gary shook his head and paused, looking over the expanse of park land where they were sitting. None of the other picnic tables were occupied. Rudy's truck now was the only vehicle in the large parking lot.

"I just never figured you for anything like this, Rudy. You used to be a protector of the helpless when we first met in grade school. A stand-up guy. Now? Shit, I don't know who you are anymore."

Rudy shrugged. "Who I am anymore? Hell, I don't even know myself. Since I got conked in the cranium in that accident, I've started to see and feel things a lot differently. Way differently."

He got up and walked over to the trash can to deposit the beer can he'd just finished and crushed it in his hand like it was cellophane. "What can I tell you, Gary? You're dealing here with a much different Rudy than in the past." He winced visibly as another of the lighting pains shot through his head.

Gary waited for a further reply. Rudy took a huge bite of his pastrami sandwich while looking past his friend into the nearby forest. He burped loudly.

Gary said, "That's crass, man."

"Crass? Well kiss my ass if you think that, old buddy."

Gary leaned across the table. "I came here today for one reason, Rudy. To tell you to stop murdering these racetrack people. We've been friends for 30 years since the playground at St. James You were a hero of mine then. But, you've morphed into someone I can hardly recognize. Obviously troubled. Obviously dangerous. I just can't let you keep going."

He stood up. "Let me be clear on this, Rudy. Any other deaths of this kind and I will turn you into the authorities. Bet on it, old buddy."

Rudy concentrated on finishing his sandwich. Gary waited impatiently for a response, a way to start talking about this. He batted away a threatening wasp. Finally, Rudy said, "Look, Gary, I need to take a little time here. Get my thoughts in order for an answer to you. Okay?" He stood up and hitched up his jeans and said, "I also need to take a piss. I'm going over there behind those oak trees."

"Well, okay," Gary said. He rose. "I'm ready to take one, too."

When they were well off the walking path, a giant fluff of white cloud momentarily covered the sun. "I think it's cooling off a little," Gary said. Rudy did not answer. He opened his fly and let loose a strong stream of urine, burping again as he did so.

Gary smiled and shook his head. "This guy is something," he said to himself. He stepped behind another nearby tree, glanced at the path to assure himself that no joggers or dog walkers were coming, and unzipped his fly. He said, "Rudy, nobody's coming up the path, right?"

"Right you are old buddy," Rudy said, right before he came up behind Gary and drove him to the ground. Gary struggled but he was pinned down under Rudy's weight. He raised his head, trying to look back at Rudy. "What the fuck are you doing, man?" he started to say when he felt Rudy's powerful hands close around his head. "Sorry, Gary," he whispered, "but I can't take any chances with you."

Rudy grabbed Gary's head and quickly lowered it on an angle. He ignored Gary's choked sounds. With a powerful twist he broke Gary's neck. He waited briefly before feeling for a pulse in the body he was straddling. Nothing. He rose and wiped the sweat off his forehead and stood for a few moments before looking down on his dead friend. In the distance he heard a dog barking. That sound came closer as a woman on the leash of an active chocolate Labrador came around a bend in the walkway heading his way.

Rudy knelt down behind the large oak tree next to the corpse. He heard, "C'mon Stuart" she chirped. "Let's jog."

Afraid that she was accompanied, Rudy peered out. Just the woman and her dog. "Stuart," he muttered, "what the fuck kind of name is that for a mutt?"

When the dog and his walker disappeared around the next bend, Rudy picked up Gary's body and carried it some 50 yards deeper into the forest. The effort made him sweat heavily. So did what he found himself having to do.

He spotted a depression in the ground beneath a weeping willow tree. He quickly dumped Gary's body into it, then kicked leaves over it. As he did so, one of his lightening-strike headaches hit him again. He stumbled and almost fell into the depression atop Gary. Regaining his balance, he tore off an armful of willow branches and threw then atop Gary before hurrying to the walkway leading to the parking lot. He was careful to look both ways and found himself relieved that dog-walking lady and Stuart were not coming back his way. "Lucky for her as a possible witness," he said. He felt he'd done all the damage he could do in one day.

Rudy started his truck, bumped up the air conditioner to high, and called Carl Conforti, the assistant foreman on the construction crew Rudy was supervising in the current Arlington Heights project.

"Carlo, I'm just leaving the Loop where I had a business lunch. Everything okay out there?"

Carl said, "No worries, boss. I think we're ahead of schedule. The heat is hell but the guys are hustling."

"Great. I'll see you soon."

INQUIRY

Rudy reached back in the cooler for a Coors as he drove on to the expressway. He was satisfied that he had, with this call, established any alibi that might be required of him. He regretted that he hadn't had time to finish his Morrie's pastrami sandwich. That was his only flash of remorse.

"Gary, RIP" he muttered. "Always liked you, buddy, but a man's got to do what he has to do."

***

Ted Tilley placed the latest Thomas Perry thriller on his night table and turned off his reading light. Then the landline rang. His wife JoAnn, asleep for the past half-hour, stirred, her back to him, as he got out of bed and hurried to his den.

"Yes, this is Ted Tilley. Who's calling at nearly midnight?"

"Mr. Tilley, this is Sgt. William Popp of the Cook County Illinois Sheriffs Dept. Sorry to bother you this late. Also sorry to give you the bad news about an employee of yours. Mr. Gary Grunwald."

Tilley sat down heavily on his desk chair. "What kind of bad news?"

"Mr. Grunwald is dead. Murdered. Body found in a Cook County forest preserve earlier today. His neck apparently broken. No witnesses. No clues. We found his business card with your name and phone numbers."

JoAnn, rubbing sleep from her eyes, stood in the den doorway. "Ted, what's going on?"

Tilley sat, stunned, tan face drained of color. "Gary's dead," he croaked. "Near Chicago. Unbelievable! I'm talking to the police. Good God almighty."

Sgt. Popp said, "Mr. Tilley, can you give us Mr. Grunwald's next of kin? They have to be notified. Are you there?"

Ted hesitated before saying, "I will inform Gary's wife, Janet. They, or she, lives about a mile away from us. I'll go there as soon as I'm dressed. Please don't attempt to reach her before I do. Sergeant, give me your number. I'll call you at the Grunwalds and you can talk to Janet then. Okay?"

Sgt. Popp said, "Here's my cell phone number. Get back to me as soon as you can, Mr. Tilley."

Ted got up, reached to hug JoAnn, then hurriedly dressed, mentally rehearsing what he would have to say to Janet Grunwald. How to help her with the planning of whatever funeral or service she would want for Gary. How to break this awful news later this morning to the work force at his company where Gary had been an admired colleague for so many years.

Rudy looked up from the desk in his office to see assistant foreman Dan Dwyer. He gestured him in. As Dwyer sat down, he said, "I guess you heard about Gary Grunwald getting killed."

"Yeah. Terrible thing."

Dwyer was a Chicago south side Canaryville neighborhood product and resident. His accent Rudy sometimes found briefly daunting. "You knew Grunwald, right?"

"Sure did. We were at parochial school together in Kenosha."

Dwyer said, "You going to da service?"

"I haven't heard where it is. What do you know?"

Dwyer said, "Grunwald was a catolick, so…"

"He was a what?"

Frowning, Dwyer said, "You know. A roaming catolick."

There was a pause. Then Rudy said, "You mean Roman Catholic, right?"

Exasperated, Dwyer jumped up from his seat and started to the door. "Dat's what I said," he said. "You can read about da details in da paper."

Ozinga sat still in his chair. Not thinking about Dan Dwyer's impertinence. Thinking about the sound made when he broke Gary Grunwald's neck in the forest preserve. He shuddered. Then shook it off and reached into the office fridge for a Coors.

INQUIRY

CHAPTER FORTY-FOUR

Moe said, "Pass the cream and the butter." He and Jack had finished their workouts in the boxing room and were having breakfast. They had exercised for an hour, Jack on the speed bag, then the heavy bag, followed by 60 pushups and ten minutes of jumping rope. Moe went through his usual brisk routine of pushups, stomach crunches, and 20-pound free weights.

"Here's several calories' worth," Jack said, shaking his head. "You eat like every meal is your last supper but never gain an ounce even at your age."

Moe grinned as he slathered butter on his toasted onion bagel. "As a solid septuagenarian, Jack, I resent the suggestion that I should be getting fat as I further mature."

Jack laughed. He felt great this summer morning after the kind of strenuous workout he'd continued doing even after his time as an amateur boxer. But his mood changed rapidly as he saw on the television screen WGN-TV's ace anchorman, Mark Suppelsa, who had preempted an inane family squabble program with "Important breaking news."

"Bonnie," Jack said to the server handling the remote, "will you turn up the sound? Thanks."

He and Moe leaned forward to listen as Suppelsa led off by saying, "A tourist's body has been discovered in the Schiller Woods Forest Preserve. This report just in. A forest preserve ranger, less than an hour ago, discovered the body of a man identified as Gary Grunwald of upstate New York in a shallow depression several yards from the walking path. Preliminary reports say he died of a broken neck sometime within the last 12 hours.

"Mr. Grunwald's wallet was emptied of money, but his driver's license photo helped with the identification. Another possibly significant finding was receipts from a cab company coming out of O'Hare Airport. When more information becomes available, we will pass it on to you."

The screen momentarily went blank before programming resumed coverage of a violently-vocal confrontation involving a man, his former wife, his current mistress, and his ex-wife's new husband. The audience was hooting loudly as shouted charges and threats flew back and forth.

"Well, goddam," Jack said.

"What are you talking about?"

Jack said, "Moe, I knew this guy Grunwald. Talked to him not long ago. He works for, or used to work for, the horse owner and hardware chain king of upstate New York Ted Tilley. You know, the guy who was winning all those races all over the place before tracks started to ban him. I questioned Ted about the recent spate of murders of executives at tracks that had kicked him out. Did he have any idea as to who might be doing this? He was forcefully adamant in his denial. I believed him.

"On the other hand, I was closely watching this assistant, Gary. He wouldn't look me in the eye when he said he knew nothing about the murders. He expressed what I took to be real remorse over them happening. But, there was something else going on there. Gary seemed to be holding something back. I don't get it. What was he doing in a Chicago area forest preserve."

Moe shrugged. "Well, he's not holding back any more, is he? Whatever it was, it's gone now."

Jack finished his coffee before saying, "Maybe not."

"Maybe not what?"

Jack said, "You heard Suppelsa say the cops found a restaurant card in his wallet? From Morrie's in the south Loop? I know you go there. You know the owner?"

"Yes, I know Morrie Epstein from grade school on. Nice guy who took over his dad's little deli and turned it into a money machine. What about him?"

Jack said, "How about you asking Morrie if his place has video surveillance cameras? I would imagine that with the high powered customers there, it would be a requirement. Safety issues and all."

"Okay. I'll call him."

***

A half hour later, Morrie Epstein was waiting at the restaurant door for Jack. The place was jammed, every table taken, long lines at the deli service counters. Morrie smiled as he took Jack by the elbow and began to lead him away, saying, "Moesy described you, Jack."

"In his usual glowing terms?"

Morrie ignored that question and guided Jack to the rear of the building and a stairway leading down. "We'll go into my office," he said.

That was a spacious room with a desk, card table, two long leather couches, and an impressive collection of athletic trophies on shelves along two walls. Jack stopped to inspect them. There was Morrie's Marauders, a Little League team. Morrie's Marvels, a Youth League basketball squad. And Morrie's Minnows, a team of grade school girl swimmers. Champions all.

Jack said, "I see you've sponsored some real winners. Congrats."

"I've got three children, Jack, and they've come up with nine grand-

INQUIRY

children, all of whom play all kinds of sports. So, I backed them. Come over here and sit next to me and I'll roll whatever recorded video we have from that day."

They watched in silence at the late morning activity. Then Jack said, "How about moving it closer to noon?"

"Will do."

Jack suddenly leaned forward in his chair. "Wait. Pause it right there please."

There was Gary Grunwald at the end of the sandwich line talking to a muscular, broad shouldered man standing next to him. The big man was laughing as he put an arm around Gary's shoulders. Gary did not appear to be enjoying this. He shook off the man's arm, turned to face him, spoke to him with a frown on his face for some 30 seconds.

The big man shrugged. Suddenly, the line began to rapidly advance and Gary, with his companion, moved off the screen.

"Morrie," Jack said, "could you backtrack here? Get a close up of the guy with Gary?"

"Sure, Jack. I've seen that guy here many times. He's kind of a loud mouth. But, he's a loyal customer. Comes here at lunch time at least once a week, sometimes more. Always orders takeout."

Jack said, "Today we're looking at who paid for their lunches."

Morrie advanced the tape. "Looks like the big guy did. He brushed away this Grunwald's attempt to pay cash. Slid a credit card to the cashier."

"Do you keep copies of the credit card payments?"

Morrie said, "Sure. For at least a couple of weeks to make sure they clear and we get our money. Why do you ask?"

"I'm thinking there must be a name on that credit card. I'd sure as hell like to know what it is. Can you help?"

Morrie quickly obliged. He called his accountant on the intercom and told him, "I need the card names from around noon yesterday. Give them to me." He wrote on the memo pad in front of him.

"Right around the time we're interested in, we had credit card charges to a bailiff I know, a circuit court judge who is a cousin of my wife's, and our local alderman. Then," he smiled, "there was the one used by the big guy. That card belongs to something called Ozinga Construction."

"You ever hear of that company, Morrie?"

"Not much. They work the northwest suburbs. They got in a jam a couple of years ago when they got sued for shoddy work and late completion in some Arlington Heights development."

Jack got up and reached across the desk to shake Morrie Epstein's hand. "Thank much, Morrie. This gives me at least a start at where to look next."

155

Morrie said, "Give Moe my best." They walked up the stairs into the restaurant. "Jack, how about a sandwich to go? On the house."

"Naw, Morrie, but thanks for the offer. Maybe next time."

"As my beloved grandmother used to say to us, 'May there be a next time.' Take care."

INQUIRY

CHAPTER FORTY-FIVE

After a week of listening to Max Tyson's stream of braggadocio and bullshit, Treasure looked for Skip after the morning workouts were over.

"Tenuta says you're doing a good job hot walking," she smiled, patting his arm.

Skip blushed. "Glad to hear I'm doing something right. And Treasure, thanks for getting me this job."

"You're welcome. Now I've got a new assignment in mind for you."

Skip said, "You do? What is it?"

"I don't want to talk about it here Skip. Why don't you come to my place after the races? Have a couple of beers, then go out for dinner."

Skip said nothing would please him more. He watched admiringly as Treasure walked to the exit knowing full well his eyes were not the only ones on her.

***

Shortly after six p.m., Skip knocked on Treasure's door. She quickly opened it, took his hand, and pulled him in. Skip did a double take. Treasure was naked and hot eyed. She guided him to her bed, got up on it to straddle him, and began to unbutton his shirt, then his jeans, a lascivious smile on her face all the time.

Skip started to say something but she put her index finger to his lips. Shushing him. Then she slid down the bed a bit and put his pulsing penis in her mouth. Skip moaned with pleasure. She licked and sucked for several minutes, often looking up from her task, green eyes glowing. At last she moved up on the bed and straddled him and inserted his cock and began to ride, eyes now aimed at the ceiling. Skip's trembling hands cupped her breasts and then tweaked her extended nipples.

"Come to me baby," Treasure repeated in a sing song voice as the bed rocked. Skip could not hold on. He raised his hips and thrust himself deeper within her.

***

They lay side by side. Skip was breathing heavily as he turned to enwrap her torso. Skip couldn't see it, her lovely back was turned to him, but Treasure was smiling broadly. She finally turned to him, reaching over to stroke his flushed face. She sat up, right hand gripping his penis. "There's something I want you to do for me, Skipper. Let me tell you about it. First I want to go in and rinse off. You stay right here you lovely man."

Tossing her towel into the laundry basket, she peered from the bathroom door into the bedroom. She smiled at the sight of Skip lying in her rumpled bed with a satiated look on his face.

Treasure walked up to the bed, naked. Skip quickly sat up and held out his arms to her. "No, no, Skipper, not anymore right now. I need to talk to you."

She handed him her recently-purchased cell phone. "Go ahead. Turn it on and aim it at me with the sound on. No, don't aim it at my pussy, Skipper, just my face."

Dumke followed directions, fingers shaky on the small black device.

"Did you get my picture? Good. Play it back for me." Treasure nodded in approval when she saw herself on the screen and heard her voice. "Perfect! Good work. Now, this is what I want you to do for me with this device."

***

Next morning at the Tenuta barn, Treasure jumped off the third horse she'd worked. When she saw Skip hot walking a big bay toward her, she nodded toward Max Tyson. He was four stalls down the bustling shedrow, but they could hear his booming voice.

Max stopped upbraiding a trembling Mexican woman, a new groom at the Tenuta barn, when Treasure said, "Morning, Max. Hello Evita."

The groom sidled away. Out of the corner of her eye, Treasure saw Skip approaching. He was carrying a rake to be used smoothing out the dirt pathway. Their eyes met. She nodded and Skipper nodded back.

"So, Max, why were you laying into that little groom, Evita?"

Max shifted the tobacco chaw in his mouth before spitting toward the path Skip had started to rake. "That little brown broad. No English, no clue how to do what I tell her she's supposed to be doing."

Treasure's eyebrows lifted. Behind her back, she gave a hand signal to Skip to start recording. "Well, Max, why don't you learn a few simple Spanish phrases in order to set her right?"

Max laughed loudly. "I should learn her language? She came to my country, I didn't go to hers. Dumb broad should pick up some fucking English in order to work here. You done riding this morning?"

Treasure said, "Yes. I just had three to work."

"Okay," Tyson said, "follow me. I'll give you a look at the fucking challenges I'm facing here."

She followed behind Max as he walked to the end of the shed row. Dumke, rake in hand and cell phone in his jacket pocket at the ready, fell in behind them.

Max stopped midway down the aisle. Lifting up the netting at the front of the stall, he went in and grabbed the halter of the filly Goldielox, and yanked her forward.

"Treasure, take a look at this bitch. She's mean, lazy, an all around pain in the ass." Goldielox started to back away from this tirade. Max yanked her shank heavily, slapped her on the forehead, saying, "That's the only kind of treatment she understands."

"Yeah, I know Goldielox," Treasure said. I work her—when she feels like working."

Max stepped out of the stall and wiped sweat from his forehead. He paid no attention to Skip who was standing nearby. "This here Goldielox is just one of the pampered crows in Tenuta's barn. He's way too fucking lenient in his treatment of them. They need discipline. The lazy ones? Hell, he should start training them on batteries, like a trainer I used to work with did. That'd goose them forward."

Treasure said, "Wouldn't some kind of drug help them move up?"

"Sure," Tyson said. "Hit 'em with some of those new designer drugs floating around. Undetectable in post-race tests I've heard. At least so far. Worth a try."

"I don't think Ralph Tenuta would ever go that route," Treasure said.

Max said, "What Tenuta doesn't seem to understand is you can't treat these creatures like they're made of fucking porcelain! They are large dumb animals. Most of them need a hell of a lot of discipline."

Max led the way down the shedrow, talking loudly, obviously relishing the attention he was getting from this attractive young woman. "See that black mare sticking her head out of her stall on the right. Rhondo Dear, she's named. Hah! That sour bitch can't run worth a damn! She should be sold to the slaughter house. But one of Tenuta's granddaughters owns her. That's the only reason she's here wasting everybody's time." He moved his tobacco chaw from left to right and spat into the dirt.

Pretending to be interested at the callous comments from blowhard Max, she worked to entice more. She tapped him on the shoulder. "So, Max, you see all of racing as more a business than a sport, I take it?"

"You bet, honey."

"Then why did you go into it?"

Max adjusted his black ballcap with its crimson inscription of Trumpster Forever. "Hell, there wasn't much more I could hope to do. I was brought up on a farm in central Indiana. Hated school. Dropped out when I was 15. I had an uncle who trained a half-assed small string on the minor circuit. He gave me a job. I've been around racetracks ever since. I know what to do with horses when I'm given the chance. That's why people hire me like Ralph did.

"Now, come over here." He stopped at the last stall. They both peered in. The hulking chestnut gelding was deeply asleep. "That's what he does best," Max said bitterly. "Look at this lazy old package of crow bait. Must be 12 by now. The only other time I worked for Tenuta was maybe three, four years ago, and this thing could at least do a little running then. Won a few cheap claiming races. But that was long ago. He hasn't earned a check in a year. This pig is another I would sell to the horse slaughter people if he was mine. But Tenuta keeps him around."

They walked up the shedrow toward the entrance, Skip quietly trailing a few yards behind. Treasure said, "Max, do you like horses at all?

"Hah! I like it when they win me a bet. Otherwise, they're tools to be used. Polished, prepped, prepared, and if they don't produce I say fuck 'em."

CHAPTER FORTY-SIX

DES MOINES, IA—Penny Vandervoort, 43-year-old executive vice president of Oakbrook Downs here, was found murdered early this morning in the driveway of her south suburban home. She became the fourth thoroughbred racing executive to be killed in the last three months.

Des Moines police spokesman Morris Henley said Ms. Vandervoort was attacked, "probably as she was about to enter her car to head for Oakbrook Downs, a trip she took six days each week. "Probably just before dawn when she usually left home," Henley said.

"There were no witnesses. Her body was discovered by her son, Josh, her only survivor. Ms. Vandervoort's husband Jason preceded her in death four years earlier, a victim of lung cancer."

Henley said the cause of death was "apparently a broken neck. Ms. Vandervoort's body was found just a few feet from her auto. It's likely she was approached from behind, then violently assaulted. Her purse and brief case were found next to her body apparently undisturbed. So robbery does not seem to be a motive for this crime. No, at this point we have no suspects or leads in this disturbing case."

All four murdered women were employed by tracks that had barred the powerful stable of Ted Tilley. Reached for comment at his upstate New York breeding farm, Tilley said he was "horrified to hear of Ms. Vandervoort's death. I never met her or the other recent victims. On the face of it, this pattern looks beyond coincidence. But it's beyond me! My deepest sympathy to her son."

Because Ms. Vandervoort's death was a violent one, an autopsy is mandatory, according to spokesman Henley.

Josh Vandervoort said, "At some point we'll have a private service. This is hard for me to believe. My mother had no enemies I ever knew of."

The murders have shaken the racing world which is insular and replete with people who know each other either directly or through industry associations.

Chris Cerf, public relations director for the National Association of Race Tracks, said his organization was offering a $25,000 reward "for information leading to the apprehension of whoever is committing these horrendous crimes."

CHAPTER FORTY-SEVEN

Jack had finished his early morning run and was sitting on a park bench overlooking Lake Michigan's gently moving azure waters when his cell phone buzzed. He removed it from his back pack along with a small towel he used to wipe his face. He was surprised to see Ralph Tenuta's number on the screen. Ralph rarely called him. He had left a message: "Jack, please come see me as soon as you can. I need help."

Jack recognized the urgency in the voice of his ordinarily-calm friend, easily the least volatile among the several Italian Americans he knew. Jack stood up and headed for his condo, picking up his running pace as he went. Fifty minutes later, he parked his Accord in the lot behind the long white barn occupied by Ralph's trainees. It was a place he knew well from his season as a jockey's agent for young Mickey Sheehan, and the preceding summer spent as stable agent for Ralph.

Walking down the shedrow, Jack exchanged waves and holas with several of the stable workers he'd come to know. He tapped on the screen door and walked through into Ralph's Heartland Downs backstretch office. It was, as always, crowded with tack equipment, condition books, and piles of *Racing Dailys*. Ralph was on the phone. He nodded at Jack and help up his finger signaling just a minute.

Jack went to the battered brown leather couch and sat down next to the stable cat named Tuxedo for its black and white coloring. She was as ill-tempered an animal as Jack had ever known. She stood up, indignant at his intrusion, arched her back, then leaped to the floor and went under Ralph's desk. "Same old black and white Tuxedo," Jack said. "Lovable as ever."

Ralph finished his phone call and heard Jack say, "Ralph, good morning. What's up my friend?"

He got up from the chair behind his desk and extended his hand. "That was quick. Thanks for coming on such short notice, Jack." He returned to his chair before saying, "Did you hear about poor Peggy Vandervoort?"

"No."

Ralph said, "She was murdered yesterday morning in her own driveway. Apparently strangled. Can you believe this? Four racing women now dead in the last few months? This is beyond unusual."

Jack grimaced. "It's some kind of insane campaign against these women. And if I remember correctly, they all worked at racetracks that barred

INQUIRY

Ted Tilley. Hard to believe the authorities haven't made any progress looking at that aspect of the situation.

"Peggy Vandervoort," Jack continued. "I met her once at a press dinner at Monee Park. Very nice person. Goddam, Ralph…"

Ralph said, "I know how you feel, Jack. But that's not the only bad news today."

Ralph got up from behind his desk and closed the office door. "Jack, I've got a big problem of my own that I don't know how to handle. Came at me out of the blue. You might be able to help me deal with this potential disaster. I wouldn't be bothering you if this wasn't so damn serious."

Jack discerned the tension in the trainer's voice, the voice of a man he'd come to admire in his years in racing. "Of course I'll try to help you Ralph. What's this about?"

Ralph paused and Jack could hear the office door opening and then quickly closing, Ralph saying "Max, here's the morning work list. I'll see you later." He handed the sheet to the burly man who silently accepted it and left without a glance at Jack.

"Who was that?" Jack asked.

Ralph replied , "A guy I hired as a replacement for my main man, Paul Albano, in Mexico. Huge mistake on my part."

"What do you mean?"

"Jack, watch the video that was sent to me on this cell phone. You'll see what I mean."

Jack sat down in the chair in front of the trainer's desk. His eyebrows elevated as he watched and heard the voluble Max Tyson describe, in far from flattering terms, his association with the Tenuta stable and horse racing. Ten minutes later, he laid the phone on the desk. "I can see this is pretty embarrassing for the Sport of Kings. This asshole Tyson makes a fool of himself in what appears to be a carefully edited video. You can see the gaps between scenes. He's the star bad ass all the way through. But, Ralph, so what?"

"This video came on my phone last night. I was home, just about to go to bed when it appeared. I watched it three times. I didn't sleep all night. Early this morning, there was a text message on there saying this video was going to be sent to news organizations, the Racing Board, and that radical animal rights group ALWD."

Jack grunted, "Yeah, I'm familiar with that looney outfit. Animal Life With Dignity. They make PETA look laid back."

"That wasn't all on that phone text, Jack. It said the only way I could prevent the distribution of the video was to come up with 50 grand by the end of the week."

"And blackmail rears its hideous head," Jack said.

Ralph started to pace the small office."I haven't got $50,000 ready to make this blackmail payoff. I just don't. I just spent a huge chunk of our savings helping our oldest daughter and her husband buy their first house. I don't know what the heck to do."

Jack grabbed his arm as he was passing for the third time. "Ralph, for God's sake, sit down. Let's talk this over."

Ralph slumped into his chair. Jack said, "What the hell are you so worried about? There's nothing on that video that implicates you in any wrongdoing. No rules were broken. Nothing on there that could lead to a fine or suspension for you. Not even loudmouth Tyson, for that matter. He wasn't proving that any laws were broken. That video comes out, you could rip it apart. It's edited, deceptive, doesn't prove anything. I don't understand why it so concerns you, Ralph."

"That damned Tyson is shown suggesting that he knows about horses being drugged, jockeys using batteries. And for a lot of it he's posed under a sign in the barn that says Tenuta Stable."

Jack said, "Obviously, that's the intended implication. But that's all it is."

Ralph said, "Jack, it's serious for me. I should never let him get under radar of that hustling little exercise rider, Treasure Defee. You never see her face in the video. But I recognize her being filmed from behind. I'm sure she's the one Max Tyson is blathering to. I'm sure she set it up so this dumb braggart comes up with what she's threatening to sensationalize. She's the one trying to blackmail me. I can't afford to let her publicize this video. It could kill my stable, my reputation."

Jack said, "Somebody else was involved here. That girl isn't doing the recording. She's too busy stroking Tyson's raging ego and leading him on. Who the hell around here, working for you, would be recording the Tyson-Treasure show?"

Ralph thought for a minute. He sat up in his chair. "I've got a new hot walker here. Guy named Dumke. He follows Treasure Defee around like a stud horse after a mare in heat. Could be him."

"Dumke? " Jack said. "Skip Dumke?"

"Yeah. You know him, Jack?"

Jack shook his head and said "Hard to make this shit up. Yeah, I know Skip Dumke. He was running a touting scam that entrapped Moe Kellman's son-in-law, Scott Epstein, in it. At Moe's request, I had a serious talk with Dumke. I guess he got out of the touting business after that and moved on to attempted racetrack blackmail. Jesus!"

He started to pace in a path that drove Ralph back to behind his desk. "Ralph, I hope you're not considering paying this demand."

Ralph sat forward, placing his head in his hands. "Of course I'm thinking of that, Jack. What else can I do? I can't afford any damage like that." He looked up at Jack. "I'm not in good shape here. After 40 years of training."

INQUIRY

Tuxedo tried to rub against Jack's right ankle. He gave her a gentle boot across the room. "But, Ralph, you're the leading trainer here at Heartland. Like you've been for years."

"That doesn't mean as much as it used to, Jack. The game has changed. Business here at Heartland, as many tracks in this country, is way down. The competition from casinos and lotteries has crippled us. So, purses are down. But expenses—feed, veterinarian bills, insurance—keep going up. If I don't come up with a couple of good stakes horses every year, I'm in trouble. I'm like a guy teetering on the edge of a diving board. This crap, this video, could push me off it.

"Jack, you know this video is phony as hell. That doesn't make it any less damaging, less dangerous, if it gets distributed. Going viral on the Internet, all that." He shook his head. "This is some ballsy broad, Jack. After she says she's going to blackmail me if I don't pay up, she asked me how many head I wanted her to work that morning. My reply was not, well, very gentlemanly."

Jack leaned across the desk. "My friend, I'm not going to let that happen. Trust me. You tell this Treasure that you need a couple of days to get her money together. Have her meet you here two mornings from now."

Puzzled, Ralph said, "Well, what happens then, Jack?"

Jack got up and turned to leave. "I've got something in mind. I'll get back to you soon. Keep the faith, my friend." He hurried out of the office door.

CHAPTER FORTY-EIGHT

Cook County Sheriff's Police Detective, Sgt. William Popp, was approaching his car in the parking lot of the Skokie courthouse building on Old Orchard Road. It was a blisteringly hot morning. The brief walk from exit to auto had brought a sheen of sweat to Popp's broad forehead. Even when he'd left his Bridgeport home in Chicago two hours earlier, the thermometer was on the rise.

Popp was, as usual, wearing a rumpled sport coat and trousers along with a grim expression that was a constant on the middle-aged detective's face. Meeting him for the first time, people were reminded of the character actor Charlies Durning, but always in a grumpy mood.

He entered the car, cranked the engine and the air conditioning and was about to pull out of the lot when his cell phone buzzed. One glance told him it was a call from his headquarters supervisor, Marty Morrison. "Sgt. Popp, I've got a phone call request here for you. Guy named Jack Doyle wants to talk to you."

Popp groaned. Morrison said, "Doesn't sound like you're too enthusiastic about giving this Jack a call back. You know this guy?"

"Oh, yes, Marty. We helped each other out a couple of times. Always pretty challenging. Racetrack stuff. That's where Jack makes his living. He's a standup guy. But he gets himself into some of the damndest scrapes."

Morrison said, "Is this Jack an informant? A friend?"

Popp hesitated before saying, "Kind of a combination of the two."

"Do you want Jack's call back number?"

"No need, Marty. I have it."

***

Sgt. Popp met Jack in a dimly lit tavern/restaurant called Losers Lounge, located in the Old Orchard shopping center just a few miles from the Skokie Courthouse. They shook hands. Popp said, "Well, Jack, I suppose you're in another jam. Am I right?"

Jack sipped at his pint of Harp before answering. He had to restrain himself from smiling at Popp's well-worn wardrobe and grim facial expression, both central to the detective's identity.

"Yeah, you're right, Popp. It's a jackpot, but not mine. You want lunch while we talk? I'll buy."

INQUIRY

Popp shook his head. He summoned the waitress and ordered a double Jack on the rocks. He said, "Let me hear what I'm here for first. Then I'll decide what kind of appetite I'll have."

"It's not really complicated Popp. But it's a situation I could use your help with," Jack said.

Popp produced one of his very-few-per-day laughs. "Seems to me, Jack, that whatever concerns you is always complicated. Lay it on me."

Jack spent the next 20 minutes informing the detective about Ralph Tenuta's dilemma. "A hustling girl enticed one of Ralph's temporary employees to make a series of damaging statements that she had videoed by a guy she'd planted there. This loudmouth guy, named Tyson, bragged about horses he knew had been doped. None, by the way, trained by Ralph Tenuta. But the suggestion of Ralph's involvement is definitely there. Hurtful. So is this jerk's chest pounding statement about how, quote, 'these hothouse thoroughbreds, ' should really be treated—with an iron hand."

"What does this all add up to, Jack?"

Jack said, "Here's the deal. This girl, name of Treasure Defee, believe it or not, wants Ralph Tenuta to pay her $50,000 or she'll send copies of this video to racing authorities, media outlets, etc. fucking etc. She's got to be stopped."

Popp listened intently. When Jack finished, he summoned a waitress. "BLT heavy on the mayo. You want anything, Jack?"

"Just your thoughts on this situation."

"Well," Popp said, "this is nickel and dime stuff. I'm not about to spend the Sheriff Department's money and resources to thwart an amateur blackmailer."

Jack's face flushed. "This is not nickel and dime to my friend Ralph Tenuta. He believes exposure like this could ruin him."

"Calm down, Jack. What I suggest is this: get this woman into his office and have her repeat her blackmail plan. That should be easy enough to do without involving me."

Jack said, "Okay, so we get the devious Treasure to do that. Then what?"

Popp smiled at the arrival of his sandwich. He took a huge bite before saying, "Then you play back to her what she said about blackmailing Ralph. Show her you've got her on record."

"Play what back? How? This girl is no dummy. Don't you think she mightsuspect Ralph of wearing a wire? Or me, for that matter."

Popp, a man with a lifelong avoidance of laughter, permitted himself a chuckle. "Treasure could maybe give Ralph and you an exciting body search. Good looking broad, hands all over you both. "He took another chunk out of his rapidly-diminishing sandwich before saying, "But Treasure would not find a wire on either of you."

"Treasure is a cocky little broad. According to Ralph, we wouldn't have any trouble getting her to repeat her blackmail plan. But how do we get that on record, Sargeant?"

Popp smiled. He quickly polished off his BLT before reaching into his jacket pocket and extracting a chain containing keys and a small black device for opening auto doors. He put it on the table and pushed it across to Jack.

"What's the deal with this thing?"

Popp said, "These things were brought into our department last year. They are very, very effective in recording conversations without people knowing they're being recorded. Let me show you." He pushed a button on the car opener and laid it on the table. "How's the dessert here, Jack?"

"The dessert here? What the hell are you talking about ?"

The detective smiled as he reached to pick up the key chain. He pressed a button. Jack heard himself say, "What the hell…"before Popp stopped the recording. "Get the point, Jack? It's a wonderful little device. There's a tiny, but very effective, little bug built into the back of this car opener. I'm going to give this little gem to you. You can use it to get this Treasure Defee on record admitting to blackmail and coercion. Ralph can decide what to tell her after the recording is played back. Whether to turn it over to police, or just usher Treasure Defee out the door convinced she must drop her young career as a blackmailer."

"This is great. I'll call Ralph and set this in motion. Have him get Treasure into his office tomorrow morning. I'll be there to meet her." He picked up the key chain. "Wonderful little advance in technology, Sgt. Popp. I congratulate the Sheriff's Department."

"Thanks for lunch, Jack." He stood up, put on his battered porkpie hat, and said "Let me know how this works out."

***

When Jack got home that night, there was a message from Detective Popp on his answering machine.

"Jack, I know you're good with your fists. But sometimes things come up that demand more. Especially in your life." There was pause. Jack wondered if he heard Popp chuckling or coughing. Then he said, "So I'm sending you a little item that might come in handy for you some day. Or night."

The next morning Jack had just opened the condo lobby door when a hustling UPS man met him. "Excuse me," the man said as he started to sidestep Jack and enter the interior.

"Hold it a minute, will you?" Jack said.

"Why?"

Jack said "That package might be for me. My name is Jack Doyle."

The UPS man quickly looked down at the address label on the small

INQUIRY

rectangular box. When he looked up, Jack was smiling. "I can prove I'm Jack Doyle. Want some ID?"

"Naw, that's okay, I believe you. Here, take it. And have a nice day," he said over his shoulder as he exited and then trotted to his double-parked brown truck.

Jack looked at his watch. He still had an hour to spare before leaving for Heartland Downs for his next meeting with Ralph. He opened the lobby door and entered his condo with the box that felt as if it contained something of little weight. He carefully shook it. The return address contained only one word: Popp.

"Well, I can assume this isn't a bomb," he said to himself.

The item inside was wrapped in a Chicago Tribune sports section from the previous day. It was a collapsible metal baton, standard police issues in recent years. Jack picked it up and figured it didn't weight even a pound despite its reputation as a very effective weapon.

Also in the box was yellow Post It note. The message said, "You never know, Jack. Be prepared." There was no signature.

"Who knew Grumpy Old Popp had a sense of humor," he said. Then he put the box and baton on the top shelf of his hall closet.

CHAPTER FORTY-NINE

Jack got to Heartland Downs just after five the next morning. He popped into the bustling track kitchen and bought an extra large black coffee and two Krispy Kreme doughnuts. He walked into Ralph's office, said good morning, and offered the trainer one of the pastries. Ralph declined. "No thanks, Jack. I haven't had much of an appetite for the last two days thinking about Treasure and her damned video."

Jack pushed the resentful Tuxedo to the far end of the battered brown couch, then put his feet up on the scarred coffee table in front of it. He started on a doughnut, followed with a gulp of coffee, before saying, "Relax, Ralph. Relax. This is all going to work out fine. All I want you to do is watch for the horrified look on Treasure Defee's face when what I've got in mind for her becomes clear."

Ralph shifted in his seat. "I don't even know what you've got in mind, Jack."

"Just as well," Jack said. "Just sit back and enjoy the show."

Treasure Defee strode into the office at six on the button. "Morning, Ralph." She turned to Jack. "And who are you?"

"Name's Jack Doyle. An old friend of Ralph's. I just stopped by in order to listen to what you have to say to him."

Treasure sat in the chair in front of Ralph's desk. Jack watched her animated face and agreed that Ralph's earlier description of her as "ballsy" was right on. The girl exuded confidence. She reached forward to tap the cell phone on the desk. "I guess you've probably watched the video several times by now."

Ralph was silent. Treasure, a bit agitated, said, "So, Mr. Tenuta, do you have my money?"

"What if I don't, Treasure? What if I decide not to be shaken down by you for the $50,000?"

Treasure looked momentarily uncertain. She sat back in her chair before saying, "Well, that complicates matters. And not to any benefit for you. You know where I'm going with the video? To every media outlet involved in racing! I'll be the ruin of you if you don't pay up. People listen to Max Tyson's statements made while working for you. You'll be ruined. If you don't pay me." She sat back and exhaled, chin thrust at a confident angle. Ralph was silent.

INQUIRY

Jack leaned forward. "Ms. Defee, how did you decide to become a blackmailer? I'm just curious."

She smirked. "I saw an opportunity, Mr. Doyle. And I took it. All I'm waiting for now here this morning is word from Mr. Tenuta how he's going to pay me."

"Well, Treasure," Jack said, "it's not going to be a long wait, or a short wait, or any wait at all." He picked up Ralph's cell phone and pulled up the Max Tyson video. "What a crock this is, Treasure. Obviously edited in an amateurish way to present this blowhard in the worst way. It's phony stuff. And it's obvious. But you know all that."

Jack activated the recording device Popp had given him. He had placed it next the stapler on Ralph's desk. At first Treasure, surprised at the sound of her voice, leaned forward. But as she listened to her blackmail threats, she sat back, deflated.

"Interesting, eh, Treasure?" Jack said. "You are on record damning your own self. A Sheriff's Department friend of mine is going to go to town with this."

Treasure said, "Look, I'm sorry. I made a mistake, a stupid one. No police, please. I'll destroy the video. I promise."

Jack smiled. "A promise from you? Larcenous Treasure? What would that be worth? I'm going to let Detective Popp decide what to do with you."

He got up and stretched. "Nice meeting you, Ms. Defee. Now I'll be on my way with this recording of your attempted blackmail. I'll personally deliver it to the detective."

Treasure jumped up. "Wait, wait, please. Maybe I can help you with something if you don't turn that tape in to the cops." Tears began to stream down her tanned face. She sat down suddenly, head in her hands. Then she took a deep breath and sat up.

"There's a guy I know," she said, "that I think has something to do with the killings of those racetrack women. He's kind of bragged about it. He's a big, strong, brutal bastard. I made the mistake of going out with him a few times. Another mistake in going to bed with him. But that was weeks ago. I've stayed away from him. He calls my cell phone and I never pick up. Then he leaves messages that have started to scare the crap out of me. "

Jack said, "Would you be willing to tell Sgt. Popp about this guy?"

"Well, sure. Sure I would. You want to know his name?"

"Oh, I think I already do," Jack said. He turned to the door. "I'll talk to Popp, and he'll want to talk to you. Okay?"

Treasure, relieved, stood up and went to the door. She looked back over her shoulder and said, "Mr. Tenuta, I'm sorry I did this to you. A huge mistake. I guess you won't want me working any more horses for you."

Ralph shook his head. "Treasure, you screwed up big time. But I try to be a forgiving person. You cooperate with Jack and his cop friend, I'll keep you employed."

Treasure trembled and nearly sank to her knees. "God bless you Mr. Tenuta. I promise I'll never do anything like that again."

Jack lifted both his eyebrows as his gaze locked with Ralph's when Treasure had walked out. "I wonder what a promise from Treasure Defee is worth," he said.

INQUIRY

CHAPTER FIFTY

Friday morning Jack made a quick check of his email. Usual stuff: offers of financial bonanzas from African scam artists, then reports on politics and various perversions, often tied together in one entry. He clicked on the Paulick Report horse racing site as he always did and was about to get off the Internet when he spotted an email from Ted Tilley. That he opened.

"Jack," Tilley wrote, "in cleaning out poor Gary Grunwald's desk last night I found a copy of a letter he'd sent to a guy in Chicago. The letter listed five names of women racetrack personnel that Gary wanted the guy to scare into rescinding their orders barring my stable.

"I was astounded. Gary never said a word to me about this plan. Probably because he knew I never would have gone along with it. It's crazy. But in the letter he specifies payments to this guy to be taken from Gary's own private account--$3,000 per incident. I went on Google looking for the names of the women. Of the five listed by Gary, four are dead. All four murdered without a clue as to who did it. And now he's been killed, too.

"The Chicago guy Gary dealt with is Rudy Ozinga. I never had heard of him before this. But that's who the payments went to. The idea that he could somehow frighten the women into compliance was insane. Hard for me to come to grips with the fact that Gary started this. And what it led to.

"Jack, the reason I'm writing to you is to alert you the fact that the fifth woman on that awful list is still alive. Celia McCann. I believe you know her, that you worked as the publicity chief at her Monee Park.

"If you have any questions about this, call me day or night. You have my cell phone number," Ted concluded.

Minutes later Jack had Detective Popp on the phone, telling him what he'd just learned from Ted. Popp listened for some 90 seconds before saying, "So what?"

"What do you mean, 'so what?'" Doyle barked. "Aren't you going to do something about this Ozinga?"

Popp sighed. "Jack, calm down. What exactly do you expect me to do? Arrest this Ozinga on unproven charges from a guy in upstate New York? Get serious."

"That's all you have to say about this guy who has murdered four women in the past few months? That's the best law enforcement can do?

'Serve and protect,' my ass."

Popp said, "There has never been any vital physical evidence pointing toward a suspect in any of these incidents. I've read the files. Whether it was this Ozinga or the phantom of the opera, no clues were left. Sorry, Jack, but those are the facts. Now, if you come up with something substantial about this mess, get in touch." He hung up.

Jack, seething, clunked his cell phone down on his desk. He walked into the kitchen and got a glass of water. Then he dialed Calvin Douglas's number.

"Calvin. It's Jack Doyle."

"What's up Jack?"

Jack said, "We need to talk. About the safety of your wife. Soon."

After a pause, Calvin said, "Sure. But not here at Monee Park. I don't want Celia to know we are joining forces because we're concerned about her safety. Don't want to scare her."

Jack started to say, "Hard to scare that woman," but stopped. "Where do you want to meet, Calvin?"

"How about McGloon's? It's a sports bar in the South Loop. I meet a lot of my customers there. How about in an hour?"

"See you there," Jack said.

***

Though he'd never been there, Jacke knew McGloon's Saloon was a very popular gathering place for sports fans. When he walked in he saw that the long mahogany bar had been divided into two sections. Placards hung from the ceiling declared the closest to the door was for White Sox fans, the second for Cubs backers. At the far end was a small area labeled Neutrals.

Calvin Douglas turned and smiled when Jack tapped him on the shoulder. "Jack, my man, let's take a booth in the back." He picked up his glass of draft beer and said, "Something to drink?"

"Not just yet," Jack said. When they were seated in the booth, he said, "This is quite a joint. You come here often Calvin?"

Calvin smiled. "Sure do. I meet a lot of my customers here. It's a good place to get them in the mood to buy more of my company's products."

A pretty young black waitress approached the booth, smiling. "Good to see you, Calvin. Would you like to order now?"

"A bit later, Brianna," he said, reaching over to pat her hand. "I'll let you know."

Jack said, "Very cute kid. I guess you know her."

"I should. That's my brother Curtis's oldest daughter. She goes to the University of Chicago and works here part time. I got her the job. Talked to the owner, Danny McGloon, and convinced him he should add a little more color to the place. She's majoring in anthropology. "

INQUIRY

Jack laughed. "She should get several term papers out of observing the crowd in this place. But we need to get down to business, Calvin. Here's the situation. There's a guy named Rudy Ozinga who I believe is the attacker of the racetrack women."

"Well, what are the police doing about him?"

"Nothing," Jack said. "They're doing nothing because they have nothing to charge him with. We'll get no help from them. The help we need is going to have to come from us, Calvin. Your wife is the last woman on the list Ozinga was given. I guess the idea at the beginning was to frighten the women into reinstating Ted Tilley's horses at their tracks. Ozinga evidently banged into the first victim with his car door. Marcy Darcey at Prairie Meadows. She was battered in what was thought to be an accident. Died of her injuries that night. The next three just got dead in short order."

Calvin wrapped his large right hand around his beer stein and drained it. "It looks to you that my wife could be next?"

"I don't know for certain what this nutcase has in mind. But I sure as hell suspect Celia's his next target."

Calvin sat back in his chair. "Are you telling me that Ted Tilley is orchestrating these deaths?"

"No. What I'm saying is that this Ozinga, working on his behalf which I doubt Tilley is even aware of, is responsible for these murders. I think Tilley's pal Gary Grunwald started this ball rolling."

Calvin said, "Well, does Grunwald agree with this theory of yours?"

"He might. If he were alive."

"What?"

Jack said, "Grunwald's body was found in a Chicago area forest preserve. Neck broken. Cops have no suspects. But to my mind Rudy Ozinga qualifies as a person of interest."

Calvin said, "I've got to get Celia out of here. Maybe a vacation some place far away."

"You really believe that headstrong woman would leave her racetrack midway through the current meeting? No way."

Calvin said, "You're probably right, Jack. So what do you have in mind? How can we protect her?"

"Not by depending on the Monee Park security force headed up by the doddering Barry Shulman."

Calvin said, "Well, I'll agree with you on that. Okay. Then we should hire some outside security force without letting Celia know because she'd never go along with that."

"Naw," Jack said, "she'd find out damn quick and lay into us for acting without her. No, Calvin, we've got to handle this ourselves. Not just to protect Celia but to shut down this Rudy Ozinga. It's up to you and me."

Calvin said, "I've never been involved in anything like this in my life.

Closest I ever came to criminals when a couple of Indiana University basketball backers threatened to break my legs if I didn't sign on with the Hoosiers. God, how dumb were those sons a bitches."

"You were better off at Northwestern. I saw one of your games. In the last minute of the second half your Wildcats were tied with Michigan State. Then you took a three from the corner. Swisheroo, it went through."

Calvin said, "You have a great memory. But what does that basketball game have to do with protecting the life of my wife?"

"Just reminds me that you can come through under pressure. That we can get this done acting together to stop Ozinga before he kills again."

"But how?" Calvin said. "What have you got in mind, Jack?"

"I've got to do a little research. Then we'll talk."

CHAPTER FIFTY-ONE

Jack spent the rest of the afternoon in his condo rummaging through the Internet. He wound up calling the Ozinga Construction Company and asked, "Mr. Ozinga, please. I have a project in mind for him."

Receptionist Denise DiBlasio said, "Rudy, I mean Mr. Ozinga, is not available at this time."

"When will he be?"

"Hard to tell, sir. He's got a lot of balls in the fire. I mean irons. I mean balls in the air."

Jack thought of saying, "Mix me another metaphor, Denise," but restrained himself and said, "Can you give me his cell phone number?"

"No, sir. He's probably at his current McMansion project in Palatine. Give me your number and I'll have him reach you."

"Where in Palatine?"

***

Denise having reluctantly provided the address, Jack left Chicago early the next morning and headed west. He located the Ozinga project, parked across the street and down three houses, and had his Dunkin Donuts breakfast of extra large black coffee and a vanilla long john. He listened to his favorite jazzstation WDCB as he waited. Rolled his car windows up so the tattoo of nearby carpenters' hammers didn't impinge on the music.

Shortly after nine o'clock, a black SUV appeared in his rear view mirror and zoomed into the access driveway of the construction site. The driver emerged. While talking on his cell phone, he was simultaneously gesturing orders to a man Jack thought must be the foreman on this job.

Watching the person that must be Rudy Ozinga, Jack said to himself, "He's a big bastard all right. Got to figure out a way to handle him."

Rudy, having issued instructions, took the foreman by the elbow and walked him to the rear of the partially-built house. When they disappeared from view, Jack said to himself, "this McMansion is bad taste on steroids. Time to leave."

CHAPTER FIFTY-TWO

"You must be out of your minds. Both of you," Celia said glaring at Jack and Calvin who sat on her long office couch." She came out from behind her desk and began pacing over the carpet, stopping on each pivot to repeat her assessment of their plan.

Calvin just sat back, arms crossed, saying quietly to Jack, "I've never seen her so worked up."

Jack, bemused, watched this dynamic woman who was in full rant. Finally, he said, "Could we have a little conversation here, Celia? Without you walking up and down like an enraged drill sergeant."

She paused, standing in front of them, arms crossed, face flushed.

"This idea of yours is doomed. Can't you see that?" She suddenly covered her face with her hands and began to shake as she wept. Jack and Calvin both jumped up to reach for her. Jack stopped himself, letting Celia's husband do the comforting. Calvin took her hand and led her to the couch, sat her down, put his arm around her.

Hands still covering her face, Celia said, "I just can't live with the idea of you two confronting this Ozinga monster."

Jack said, "Celia, what else can we do? We can't, you and Calvin and me can't, go on living in fear of this Ozinga."

Celia sparked up at that statement. "What have you got to lose? How about your lives?"

"Ah, 'pish tush.' That's what my Grandpa Doyle used to say when confronted by a supposedly-unsolvable problem. It became a family motto. Furthermore, my dear, there's no getting around the fact that we have to try and stop Ozinga. I think we can lure him into an attack on me, which will be recorded on the new parking lot security cameras Calvin has ordered to be put into place. After he starts that, we'll take care of Rudy Ozinga.

"We've got to try this, Celia. There's no other legal way to stop this madman. If we can lure him into an attack on me, which will be recorded on those new cameras, he'll get arrested. Sgt. Popp says they can then get DNA sample from Ozinga. They have on file DNA that quite possibly could be Ozinga's." He shrugged. "Gotta be worth a try."

Celia shook her head, eyes glowing as she said, "What if this obviously dangerous man gets the jump on you?"

"Then, dear Celia, your able husband springs into action and comes to my rescue and then we take down Ozinga." Jack reached over and gave a fist bump to the smiling Calvin.

Celia sighed, sat down behind her desk, and said, "What do you want me to do?"

"As I told you, we want Ozinga to attack what he thinks is you as you walk to your car after the races. But he'll find himself dealing with me," Jack said. "So, I need a Monee Park ball cap like the one you wear. I need to get the same color windbreaker you wear. Also, some same-colored slacks. You're only a couple of inches shorter than me, so if I scrunch down a little bit after I walk out the door, I should make a convincing sight. Then, bring the bastard on!"

Celia said, "What about my pony tail? I haven't noticed any sign of one on you, Jack."

"No worries. My cousin Lara has her own beauty shop in Park Ridge. She told me she sells clip-on detachable pony tails. They're 22-inchs long. This caper will be taking place in dim light in the parking lot. One of those items should be enough to fool Ozinga and bring him into play."

Calvin frowned. "Jack, you've got short hair. What can you clip this pony tail on to?"

"Cousin Lara is a bright woman. She thought of that, too, and will loan me a wig that I can attach the pony tail to."

Celia said, "When are you going to carry out this entrapment plan?"

"Tomorrow night."

CHAPTER FIFTY-THREE

His SUV parked two blocks away on the street bordering the Monee Park parking lot, Rudy Ozinga spent two nights sitting in a camp chair on a hillock, night vision binoculars in hand.

He watched as, each night, races ended, Celia McCann exited the track's clubhouse building. As she waved goodbye to the security man at the door, her pony tail swung slightly. She walked rapidly to her white Lexus, a distance of some 20 yards. Rudy was confident he could grab her from behind as she started to open her car door. He smiled at the prospect as he began his drive home.

But euphoria evaporated as he neared the Willow Road exit off the expressway and, out of nowhere and unbidden as always, Show Tune Torment took over.

"Chicks and ducks and geese better scurry when I take out in my surrey…On a clear day, you can see forever…When you walk through a storm there's a golden light…"

He yanked the steering wheel right and skidded onto the shoulder of the road. Parked, panting, he pounded his forehead on the wheel, then banged both temples with the palms of his big hands, cursing loudly, crying out, "What the fuck has happened to me?"

Two minutes later, a State Trooper pulled up behind Rudy, flashing his lights. The Trooper walked up to Rudy's door gesturing for the window to be lowered. Rudy complied. The Trooper said, "What's your problem, sir? You can't sit here any longer. This is a very busy exit."

The medley of despised show tune lyrics suddenly ended in Rudy's damaged head. "Nothing serious, officer. I was almost sideswiped by some broad in a red convertible. Had to pull over to avoid being hit. You want to see my license?"

"No. That's okay. I just wanted to find out what you were doing. Go on your way. Drive carefully. And have a great night."

Rudy carefully drove up the ramp. "A great night? Not tonight, officer," he said to himself. "But tomorrow to be sure."

INQUIRY

CHAPTER FIFTY-FOUR

Celia, Calvin and Jack met for the third straight night in Celia's Monee Park office. She again had ordered a tray of soup and sandwiches from the track kitchen. Again, most of the food went untouched.

Celia nibbled at a chicken sandwich. Jack took two bites out of his BLT and pushed it aside. Calvin ignored the platter, looking moodily into space. "I'm surprised at you, Jack," Celia said. "You've always been a good 'doer,'" the racetrack term for a hearty eater, man or horse.

"Just not in the mood for food, Celia," Jack said. "Probably won't be until this is over with. If it ever is," he muttered.

Jack's masquerade as Celia had resulted in no Ozinga action the previous two nights. He was jumpy, irritable, and anxious as the Monee Park tote board went dark following the last race of the night.

On his feet, Doyle put on the windbreaker, his sunglasses that with the ball cap brim pulled down covered most of his face. "Calvin, let's hit it." He picked up the briefcase.

"Jack what's that you got in your hand?" Celia said.

"Just a little item for protection. It's a police baton. Gift from a cop I know. Very useful item for inflicting pain and producing compliance. I'm going to carry it in my left hand with it hidden behind the briefcase. Secret weapons are my signature Celia."

Celia put her hand to her mouth attempting to muffle a laugh.

"What's with you, Celia?" Jack barked.

"Nothing much. Just the sight of Jack Doyle in drag."

At the first floor employee parking lot exit, Jack said, "Same routine. I'll go out, pull the door almost shut, leaving enough room for you to see me."

"Fine," Calvin said. Grinning, he added, "Remember to swing that pony tail. Good luck, brother."

***

An hour earlier, Rudy Ozinga had entered his black SUV carrying his binoculars in one hand, a six-pack of Coors Lite in the other. He placed the beer beside him on the passenger seat, cracked open one can, drank deeply. It was just after nine p.m. He had plenty of time to drive to Monee Park before the races were over and his target, he hoped, emerged from the employee's entrance for the third straight night.

The previous midnight Rudy had once again stolen license plates from an SUV in the parking lot of the Arlington Heights main shopping mall. He had driven home to strip his current plates, also stolen, replaced them and walked to the street fronting his house and dropped them down the sewer grate.

Back at his SUV, he inspected the driver's side door. Looked just fine. Just a few small scratches from its impacts on unsuspecting women. "Lock and load, ready to rock and roll," he said to himself as he backed out of his driveway. His adrenaline was already surging as he envisioned the action to come. "Celia, baby, I'm on my way." He used his big right hand to crack open another Coors.

INQUIRY

CHAPTER FIFTY-FIVE

Jack, key in hand as he bent to open Celia's driver door, heard footsteps. Before he could turn around, he was grabbed from behind in a powerful grip pinning his arms to his sides. He thought his ribs might crack. He stomped down with his right foot but didn't hit his assailant's. "Damn," he croaked, breath almost out of him.

"Goddam," he heard from behind him, hot beer breath on his neck. "Where the fuck is Celia? Who the fuck are you?"

"Can't talk," Jack whispered. "You're squeezing the breath out of me."

Rudy Ozinga slightly loosened his hold on Jack. "Answer my questions, asshole, or I'll increase the pressure. Talk."

Jack nodded. "Okay," he murmured before suddenly raising his voice to shout level. "Calvin, c'mon. C'mon." Startled, Rudy tightened his grip on Jack. "Who the fuck is Calvin? Answer me, goddamit!" He lifted Jack up and shook him violently. Jack's teeth clicked together.

Feet back on the pavement, Jack braced himself, then thrust his head backwards into Rudy's face. He heard a satisfying crunch and a howl of pain. Rudy's grip loosened. He held his hands up to his broken nose. Jack pivoted and drove four of his best left hooks into Rudy's side. "Christ," he said, "this is like hitting a wet sand bag. Only thing I've hurt is my hand."

Rudy wiped the blood from his face and reached for Jack, who stepped left and dodged him. Calvin Douglas appeared behind the enraged Rudy. Jack shoveled the baton toward him. Calvin snatched it out of the air like one of many rebounds he'd corralled at Northwestern. He quickly extended the expandable baton and thrust it square between Rudy's bushy eyebrows. He crumpled to the pavement.

"Nice work, Calvin. Now, let's turn this bastard over before he starts to get up." They placed Rudy face down. He was cursing and struggling to get to his feet when Calvin sat down on his back close to his neck. Jack, laughing, dropped himself on Rudy's legs, immobilizing him. "Give me your phone, Calvin."

Jack dialed 911 to report an, "unsuccessful mugging in the west lot of Monee Park Racetrack. The assailant has been subdued. No, I didn't say some dude! I said subdued. He's on the ground. Get some squads here quick. This s.o.b. is a handful."

"Hold him down, Calvin." Jack dashed to his nearby Accord, opened the trunk, and took out a roll of duct tape. He hurried back and taped the moaning Rudy's ankles together, then his hands. "Okay, Calvin, you can get off the bastard. Sucker ain't gonna move now."

Jack picked up the phone again. The 911 dispatcher was still on. "Put me through to Sgt. Popp."

***

The Sheriff Dept. deputies examined Rudy, who was now uttering a stream of curses, and yanked him to his feet. When Sgt. Popp arrived, nine minutes later, he ordered, "Keep the tapes on that sorry asshole and move him to the station. Book him for assault. We'll start with that. Tomorrow, we'll compare his DNA to those from the two murder victims we have."

Popp turned to Jack and Calvin. "Nice work, fellas." He produced one of his rare smiles when he said, "Aren't you glad you got that package I sent you, Jack?"

Jack leaned over, trying to quell the pain in his rib cage from being put in Rudy Ozinga's human blender machine. He took a deep breath, stood up, and said, "You're a great man Sgt. Popp. I've always said that."

INQUIRY

CHAPTER FIFTY-SIX

The cars and pick-up trucks lined the driveway in front of Ted Tilley's house this late Saturday afternoon. Thunder had rumbled across the sky earlier and many of the vehicles were rain spattered. But as four o'clock approached the sun made a break through, pouring through the wide windows of the large living room that was stocked with chairs, a long buffet table, and an active bartender.

Tilley walked to the front of the packed room. "Let's get started. We are here to honor the memory of our great friend Gary Grunwald. Many of you knew him from his work at my hardware company, others from the racing and breeding aspects of my business. You knew him as being a hardworking standup guy. He was…" Tilley paused to compose himself. "He was all of that. How he—without my knowledge—chose to go to Chicago and get himself involved with this guy Ozinga, the murderer exposed by Jack Doyle, is beyond me. I am sure Gary thought he had my best interests in mind." Another pause. He looked around the room. Gary's widow was in the front row, face frozen with grief. Buck Norman and his wife surrounded her with comforting noises and gentle hugs.

"Let's not blow this out of proportion," Tilley resumed. "Gary could, at times, be an overbearing pain the ass." He waited for the laughter to subside before adding, "Like most of us who try hard at life. But we never disrespected him for that. Because we always knew he was trying his very best—even when he linked up with this Ozinga, who killed four innocent women and our Gary.

"This whole thing started when five tracks unilaterally without state sanction barred my horses. It was a shock of major proportions. I fought it in court, but couldn't win. Gary eventually undertook another tactic that proved disastrous." He paused to take a drink of water.

"Last week, in a piece of choice and bitter irony, I was informed all five of those tracks were now ready to welcome my horses back. To that I say no bleeping way! The damage that has been done as a result of their original action against me can never be undone. Or forgotten. Or forgiven.

"So, I am announcing here today that I am disbanding my racing stable." The crowd buzzed. Tilley said, "But I am NOT leaving the horse business. I love it too much to do that. I will continue in it on the breeding side. I plan to purchase promising fillies and mares, breed them to good stallions, and sell their foals at the yearling sales in Kentucky and New York. All of my great staff of farm workers here will be retained. And I will be adding new workers from the now defunct racetrack side if they so wish. No worker of mine will be left behind."

Tilley glanced at his notes on the podium. "I think Gary would be pleased by that. And I guarantee you that the first most promising youngster from those mares will, even before he's sold, be named Gary Grunwald!"

The crowd applauded and hollered out approval.

Tilley smiled and said, laughingly, "Yes, I think Gary would approve that plan. Now, let's have something to eat and drink and start telling a few stories about that good man. I know many of you have many of them."

INQUIRY

CHAPTER FIFTY-SEVEN

Jack, still feeling the adrenaline flow from the capture of Rudy Ozinga, got no rest in his slumber, tossing and turning until the light of dawn seeped into his bedroom window. He got up, started the coffee maker, shaved and dressed. Twenty minutes later he was in the Accord heading for Heartland Downs. Watching hundreds of horses go through their workouts in the early morning had always pleased him. His ribs still hurt, but the thought of Rudy Ozinga in custody helped ease that pain.

He parked behind Ralph Tenuta's barn. Approaching the office door, he saw Ralph starting to pull away in his golf cart. Jack sprinted forward and jumped into the passenger seat. Ralph, at first startled, smiled. "Morning, Jack. I guess you're ready to watch the six horses I'll have out there this morning."

Driving up the cart path to the track, Ralph said, "I understand you masterminded the capture of that Ozinga, the murderer."

Jack grimaced. "I wouldn't quite put it in the masterminded category. My ribs are still hurting like hell, thanks to that criminal."

"Well," Ralph said, "I've got some news for you. Remember Treasure Defee?"

"Who could forget that little hustler?"

Ralph said, "She got married a couple of days ago. She's still exercising horses for me, though."

"Who's the chosen victim?"

Ralph said, "None other than that loud-mouth Max Tyson, who is also still working for me."

"God help Max," Jack said. "What about your hot walker, Skip Dumke? Treasure's dupe in her blackmail scheme?"

Ralph said, "I don't know about dupe, but Dumke is no dope. I've got him in my office now working as stable agent. The guy's a whiz with the computer and he's already straightened out most of my files. I'm gonna keep him on."

"You are turning into the Father Teresa of the backstretch. Just don't let him start betting, or touting, horses."

Ralph parked the golf cart and they walked up to the rail on the Heartland Downs Clubhouse turn. Ralph said, "Here comes my first set. See the dark bay filly galloping next to the inner rail? Gonna be a good one I think. That's Treasure on her." He held his binoculars to his eyes with his left hand while keeping his stop watch in his right.

"Hope springs," Jack smiled. Then he sat back and raised his face toward the brightening sun. The sounds of pounding hooves and exercise riders' voices mingled in the morning air.

"There's hardly any place I'd rather be than at the racetrack this time of day," Jack said.

"Me, too," Ralph said. "For nearly 40 years now." He lowered his binoculars and checked his stop watch. "Treasure got that filly to work five furlongs just like I asked. Fifty-nine and change."

He put his binoculars down and turned to Jack. "What's next for you, Jack? If you've got nothing else in mind, you could come back andact as my stable agent again. What do you think?"

Jack patted Ralph on his shoulder. "Thanks for the offer, Ralph. But I've got something else in mind. A trip."

Ralph frowned. "What, you leaving Chicago?"

Jack stepped out of the golf cart, then reached back to shake Ralph's hand. "That's my plan, Ralph."

Surprised, he said, "You said a trip. To where, Jack?"

He reached back to shake the trainer's hand before saying, "Another visit to Ireland, Ralph. Nora Sheehan says she is waiting there for me."

Inquiry" is the seventh horse racing mystery featuring intrepid amateur sleuth Jack Doyle from John McEvoy,, former editor and executive columnist for *Daily Racing Form*, thoroughbred racing's "bible." Two of his books won Ben Franklin Awards from the Independent Publishers' Association. He has been a horse owner and is a widely published poet. He and his wife Judy live in Evanston, IL